Women in Policing around the World

Women in Policing around the World is a historical, legal, political, and social examination of women in policing. The book opens with a comparison of cultural definitions of gender and how this affects women's work in general and policing specifically. The book then takes the reader through women in policing in the Eastern and Western Hemispheres, featuring several countries within the major regions of the world. Major commonalities and differences are identified in the areas of recruitment, training, deployment, promotion, and violence against women.

Among the key features of this book is a balanced coverage of historical and timely events that led to the current status of women police in their respective countries. The book identifies the commonalities that women police experience throughout the world, relying on the most current research. The book also dedicates coverage to policing violence against women in society as well as within the police organization itself. The author includes tables to allow for national comparisons throughout the book, as well as current and historical photos.

This book is intended for researchers and students of police culture and women in policing. It does not rely heavily on one country or region, thus allowing for an enlightening international comparison.

Venessa Garcia received her Ph.D. in sociology from SUNY University at Buffalo. She is Associate Professor of Criminal Justice at New Jersey City University. Dr. Garcia's research focuses on oppressed groups but mainly on women as officials, criminals, and victims, paying attention to intersectionality. Dr. Garcia has authored, coauthored, and edited books in the areas of policing, intimate partner violence, female victims of crime, and crime in the media. Titles include *Women Police Across the Globe: Shared Challenges and Successes in the Integration of Women Police Worldwide*; *Crime, Media, and Reality: Examining Mixed Messages about Crime and Justice in Popular Media*; *Gendered Justice: Intimate Partner Violence and the Criminal Justice System*; and *Female Victims Of Crime: Reality Reconsidered.* Dr. Garcia has also published research articles in these areas in refereed journals, including in *Children and Youth Services Review*; *Deviant Behavior*; *Journal of Addictions and Offender Counseling*; *Journal of Criminal Justice*; *Police Practice and Research: An International Journal*; and *Journal of Contemporary Criminal Justice*. She has been a member of the American Society of Criminology (ASC) since 1994 and has served in many capacities. She has served as Deputy Editor and Editorial Board Member of *Feminist Criminology* since 2005. Dr. Garcia has also worked with the newsletter staff of Division of Women and Crime of the ASC since 2002. Dr. Garcia is dedicated to higher education. She was recently awarded the 2019 Excellence in Teaching Award from the New Jersey City University Chapter of the National Society of Leadership and Success.

Advances in Police Theory and Practice Series
Series Editor: Dilip K. Das

Police Investigative Interviews and Interpreting
Context, Challenges, and Strategies
Sedat Mulayim, Miranda Lai, and Caroline Norma

Policing White-Collar Crime
Characteristics of White-Collar Criminals
Petter Gottschalk

Honor-Based Violence
Policing and Prevention
Karl Anton Roberts, Gerry Campbell, and Glen Lloyd

Policing and the Mentally Ill
International Perspectives
Duncan Chappell

Security Governance, Policing, and Local Capacity
Jan Froestad and Clifford Shearing

Police Performance Appraisals
A Comparative Perspective
Serdar Kenan Gul and Paul O'Connell

Policing in France
Jacques de Maillard and Wesley G. Skogan

Women in Policing around the World
Doing Gender and Policing in a Gendered Organization
Venessa Garcia

Women in Policing around the World

Doing Gender and Policing in a Gendered Organization

Venessa Garcia

Routledge
Taylor & Francis Group
NEW YORK AND LONDON

First published 2021
by Routledge
52 Vanderbilt Avenue, New York, NY 10017

and by Routledge
2 Park Square, Milton Park, Abingdon, Oxon, OX14 4RN

Routledge is an imprint of the Taylor & Francis Group, an informa business

Library of Congress Cataloging-in-Publication Data
Names: Garcia, Venessa, author.
Title: Women in policing around the world : doing gender and policing in a gendered organization / Venessa Garcia.
Description: New York, NY : Routledge, 2021. | Series: Advances in police theory and practice | Includes bibliographical references and index.
Identifiers: LCCN 2020044278 | ISBN 9781466566392 (hardback) | ISBN 9780367568528 (paperback) | ISBN 9781315117607 (ebook)
Subjects: LCSH: Policewomen. | Sexual harassment in law enforcement.
Classification: LCC HV8023 .G37 2021 | DDC 363.2082—dc23
LC record available at https://lccn.loc.gov/2020044278

ISBN: 978-1-4665-6639-2 (hbk)
ISBN: 978-0-367-56852-8 (pbk)
ISBN: 978-1-315-11760-7 (ebk)

Typeset in Bembo
by Apex CoVantage, LLC

"This book is a long-overdue global account of how policing is gendered wherever it occurs as known through myriad studies about women and policing since the 1970s. Garcia takes a bird's eye view of the facts on the ground, in addition to conducting original research, and shows that gender difference and gender stratification within police forces form the dominant themes in policing and gender across societies. By exploring the police subculture of institutionalized masculinity and its emanation across time and space, she provides a compelling explanation for why women are almost universally underrepresented in police forces, marginalized and rejected by other officers, and often relegated to gender-restricted duties. This is an important work that calls attention to a profession that exhibits more barriers to gender balance than most. Garcia asks police reformers to take seriously comprehensive policies that would achieve gender equity and provide pathways for women in policing through deliberate programs of recruitment, training, mentorship, and protection from sexual harassment. With less than one in ten police officers in the world being non-male on average, this book is a timely clarion call and a significant contribution to police studies."

Staci Strobl, *Professor, Criminal Justice, UW-Platteville*

"Venessa Garcia has produced a remarkable book filling a vacuum in the current literature on women in policing by providing a panoramic account across five continents combining historic, cultural, geo-political and sociological analyses. With meticulous research unearthing previously uncharted details of the origins of women's entry into policing in Africa, Asia, Eastern Europe and Latin America combined with supporting contemporary statistics and enriched by personal interviews with former officers, this is a model of comparative analysis. The framing of the position of women in a wider context, enables a deeper understanding of the police occupational culture not only to explain the subordination of female officers but also providing the template for radical police reform."

Jennifer Brown, *Visiting Professor at Mannheim Centre for Criminology at the London School of Economics and Political Science*

"*Women in Policing around the World* is a much needed and timely addition to police literature. The police profession is currently under severe assault, based on claims of racism and brutality; however, police organizations across the globe also have a long history of discrimination and sexual harassment against its female employees. This book sheds a very bright light on the decades' long institutional injustices from the historical as well as sociological perspective up to 2020, where policewomen are still treated as inferior to their male counterparts.

The way the author approaches the problem, from a global and comparative perspective, addressing issues of prescribed roles that, frequently, drive decisions about recruitment, training and promotions, is extremely compelling and creates a picture of a sisterhood in misery. It is a must read for scholars who focus on gender roles and discrimination, police culture and police ethics but, first and foremost, for all the law enforcement practitioners who aspire to change, in a transformational manner, police organizational cultures regardless of the size or geographic location of their departments."

Maria (Maki) Haberfeld, *Professor of Police Science, John Jay College of Criminal Justice*

For Michael. For your encouragement, your love, and your patience.

In memory of my mother, Norma Vazquez.

Contents

List of Illustrations xi
Acknowledgments xiii

1 **The Sociology of Gender** 1
The Sociology of Gender 3
Gender and Difference 5
Gender Stratification 8
Women's Rights and Women's Work 9
Gendered Organizations 17
Gender, Leadership, and Policing 21
Conclusion 24

2 **Ideology and Images of Women and Policing** 26
The Nature of Policing 26
Traditional Gender Role Ideologies 29
From Ideology to Practice: Police Culture and Institutionalized Masculinity 34
The Ottoman Empire and Colonial Influence on Policing 37
Early History of Women in Police Work 39
Conclusion 45

3 **Past and Current Status of Women Police in the Eastern Hemisphere** 47
Asia and Oceania 49
Sub-Saharan Africa 56
Middle East and North Africa 62
Eastern Europe 68
Conclusion 73

4 **Past and Current Status of Women Police in the Western Hemisphere** 75
Latin America and the Caribbean 75
North America 81
Western Europe 85
Conclusion 91

5 **Recruitment, Training, and Promotion of Women in the Gendered Police Organization** 93
Recruitment/Inroads Into Policing 95
Gendered Training 106
Barriers to Promotion 108
Conclusion 113

6 **Gendered Policing: Working Conditions and Gender-Based Violence** 115
Doing Policing/Doing Gender: Resistance to Women Police 115
Sexual Harassment and Assault in the Police Force 121
Policing Gender-Based Violence 131
Police Attitudes Toward Intimate Partner Violence 133
Generalized Policing Strategies for Combating Intimate Partner Violence 138
Specialist Policing Strategies for Combating Intimate Partner Violence 140
Conclusion 142

7 **Revisiting the Police Organization: Future Directions** 144
Gendered Stress 145
Social Capital, Mentorship, and Women's Networks 147
Future Directions 151

References 156
Index 175

Illustrations

Figures

1.1	Women at Work in an Unidentified Laundry, Possibly in Boston, Massachusetts, ca. 1905	7
1.2	Three Suffragists Casting Votes in New York City? New York, ca. 1917	10
2.1	Suffragist Posed in Police Uniform to Illustrate Woman Police Concept, Cincinnati, Ohio	27
2.2	Training a Policewoman—Chief among the Policewoman's Duties Is the Prevention of Delinquency among Young Girls	40
2.3	Israeli Policewoman, 1968	44
3.1	Israeli Police Women in Tel Aviv, 1948	64
5.1	Israel Border Police, 2020	96
5.2	Israeli YASAM (SWAT) Operative, 2005	105
5.3	Colonel Sigal Bar Tzvi, Commander of Ayalon Sub-Division	111
6.1	Dr. Maki Haberfeld, Former Israeli Officer, Being pinned with Second Lieutenant Rank by Her Commanding Officer	117
6.2	Dr. Maki Haberfeld, Former Israeli Officer, Being Congratulated on Promotion to Second Lieutenant by the General in charge of the INP Human Resources	118
6.3	Dr. Maki Haberfeld, Former Israeli Officer	127
7.1	Israeli Police Officers, 2019	147
7.2	Israeli YASAM (SWAT) Operative, 2019	148
7.3	Israeli Patrol Officer, 2019	151

Tables

1.1	First and Last Nations to Grant Women's Suffrage	11
1.2	Percentage of Women in the Labor Force, 2018	19
3.1	Democracy Regimes in Asia and Oceania	49
3.2	Women Police in Asia and Oceania, 2015 (UNODC)	50
3.3	Democracy Regimes in Sub-Saharan Africa	56

3.4 Women Police in Sub-Saharan Africa, 2015 (UNODC) 57
3.5 Democracy Regimes in the Middle East and North Africa 63
3.6 Democracy Regimes in Eastern Europe 68
3.7 Women Police in Eastern Europe, 2015 (UNODC) 69
4.1 Democracy Regimes in Latin America and the Caribbean 76
4.2 Women Police in Latin America, the Caribbean, and North America, 2015 (UNODC) 77
4.3 Democracy Regimes in Western Europe 85
4.4 Women Police in Western Europe, 2015 (UNODC) 86
5.1 Labor Laws Constraining Women's Movement in the Workplace, 2020 97
5.2 Labor Laws Hindering Women's Movement into Policing in the Western Hemisphere, 2020 99
5.3 Labor Laws Hindering Women's Movement into Policing in the Eastern Hemisphere, 2020 100
6.1 Labor Laws on Discrimination and Sexual Harassment in the Workforce by Region, 2020 122
6.2 Labor Laws Prohibiting Gender Discrimination and Sexual Harassment in Employment in the Western Hemisphere, 2020 124
6.3 Labor Laws Prohibiting Gender Discrimination and Sexual Harassment in Employment in the Eastern Hemisphere, 2020 125
6.4 Percent IPV Prevalence among Ever-Partnered Females (15–69) by Sub-Region, 2010 133

Boxes

1.1 The United Nations' Indian Female Police Unit 5
1.2 Saudi Arabian Women Win Suffrage 13
1.3 Women Police in Gulf Cooperation Council National Police Forces 25
2.1 Policewomen in the Early 1900s 28
2.2 The Influence of Victorian Ideologies around the Globe 30
5.1 Women Police in China: Recruitment, Training, and Promotion 109
6.1 Dr. Maria (Maki) Haberfeld, The Life of a Military Trained Israeli Policewoman: Sexual Harassment and Sexual Discrimination on the Job 117
7.1 Women in the UNPOL: Training, Mentoring, and Leadership 150

Acknowledgments

I would like to thank Dr. Maria (Maki) Haberfeld for her contributions to this book. Her story, her photos, and her help in connecting me to researchers in Israel was invaluable. I would also like to thank Sergeant Ruhan Ding for providing her story. She provided an insight into Chinese policing not found in the literature. I would also like to thank my writing group and friends for their inspiration and encouragement. Thank you Esther Nir and Siyu Liu. To Michael, my best friend and my heart, for your patience and encouragement during the long and late hours writing this book. Finally, thank you Ellen Boyne for your patience and understanding during this writing process.

Chapter 1

The Sociology of Gender

The police organization has always been what social scientists call a gendered organization. A gendered organization is one in which organizational policies, practices, and ideologies are patterned according to gender differences (Acker 1992). Within policing, the gender of focus is the male. The police organization has always been male dominated, valuing aggression and male gender roles. However, women in both the Eastern and Western Hemispheres started joining police organizations around the world in the early 1900s, leading researchers and reformers to label this time the international policewoman's movement. Initially, women joined under the campaign that they brought qualities that only women possess. As a result, they started as matrons working only with women and children and did not have arrest power (Garcia 2003). This campaign allowed women to find a place in policing, but for many decades around the world, they were not fully accepted. Today, policing remains a male-dominated gendered organization. We find many more men holding official police positions of authority. We also find that men are much more likely to hold higher-ranking positions.

Research on policing abounds; however, we find a lack of focus on the gendered nature of policing, the central concept within this book. In this book, I examine the historical, legal, political, and social context of women in policing. Furthermore, I take a global look at women's experiences within this gendered occupation. Most research focuses on policing within one nation. This book examines women in policing around the globe. An examination of various nations reinforces the fact that gender stratification is a major part of every culture. It is my intention to take the reader around the globe by focusing on various nations and examining how their police systems treat female police. This chapter introduces the reader to the sociology of gender as we examine gender in society. After defining major concepts within the sociology of gender, I guide the reader through understanding gender difference and gender stratification. I then describe women's rights and their movement into the workforce and ultimately into the police workforce.

Chapter 2 situates our understanding of gender in policing by examining gender ideologies, religious edicts, and the politics of gender as they play out in policing. In Chapter 3, I examine the historical and current images of women in policing in the various regions of the Eastern Hemisphere: Asia and Oceania (Australasia), Sub-Saharan Africa, the Middle East and North Africa (MENA), and Central and Eastern Europe. In Chapter 4, I examine women in policing in the Western Hemisphere: Latin America and the Caribbean, North America, and Western Europe. This examination will provide the evidence that policing as a gendered organization is a worldwide phenomenon.

Bringing women's work to the present day and focusing on structural forms of gendered policing, Chapter 5 examines women's inroads into policing via the police structure. Chapter 5 takes a closer look at gendered substructure and subtext within the police organization. Women on the job often find themselves in a no-win situation within a male-dominated organization. They are expected to behave like women but are evaluated on a male standard of policing. However, since gender ideologies dictate that women are not capable of doing man's work, their evaluations often indicate that they fall short of being worthy of wearing the badge. Specifically, I examine recruitment, training, promotion, and social and legal resistance to women in policing, as well as legal reform. Chapter 6 moves further into this conversation by examining gendered policing in relation to resistance, sexual harassment, and policing gender-based violence. One can often gain insight into the gender ideologies of a society by examining how the justice system responds to crimes involving special victims.

I end the book with Chapter 7 and an assessment of the progress that women have made within policing. I start the chapter with an examination of the gendered stress that results from the rejection, gender discrimination, and sexual harassment discussed in earlier chapters. Women's rights groups have always aided the progression of women into the police organization. Here, I look at women police associations, networking, and mentoring. I also briefly examine women in global policing, specifically women in the UN Police. I end the book with strategies for the equality and equity of women in policing. Because this book's author is from the United States, this is the frame of reference. However, this does not presume that the United States policing system is the measuring rod against which we should hold other nations. Additionally, it must be noted that throughout the book I use the terms "women police" and "policewomen." The term "women police" refers to the status of women police in countries where they are integrated or given the title. The term "policewomen" is used to refer to early women police who typically were not integrated and were not given equal police power. It is also used when examining countries that refer to women police as "policewomen."

The Sociology of Gender

In this book, the sociology of gender is applied to examine women in policing. The sociology of gender is the study of the conditions of men and women in society. To understand these conditions, we must first define major concepts within the sociology of gender. Sex and gender are master statuses within our society. This means that they are primary to our understanding of human identity within society. Just as gender is a master status, we find that race, age, income, sexual orientation, physical ability, religion, and nationality are also master statuses that bring complexity to understanding gender. Gender is defined as the social construction of masculinity and femininity, which includes nonbinary genders in many countries. Sex, on the other hand, is defined as the biological distinctions of male and female based on reproductive organs. When examining sex and gender as they are constructed by society (see Garcia 2003), sociologists find that society tends to define these concepts as one and the same. That is, society claims that sex determines gender, and to know one's gender is to know one's sex. However, we must recognize that while society claims that sex is a biological distinction, it denies anything other than male and female. Here, transgender people are included in the binary sex and gender categories.

It has long been discovered that there also exists the sex category intersex, previously identified as hermaphrodite. Yet, society has never identified intersex as a sex category. Instead, it is considered a condition. This sex category is a mesh of male and female in which the individual is born with both female and male reproductive organs to varying degrees (Rosenblum and Travis 1996). Individuals who are intersex do not fit into the neat two-category construct of male and female. Denying the intersex status thus tells us that sex itself is a socially constructed status.

Gender, on the other hand, is identified as the socially acceptable behaviors, appearances, and ways of being that are linked to one's specific sex. We will say that people embody gender. While social scientists have identified gender as socially constructed, members of society tend to define and practice gender as an *essential* part of one's sex. Accordingly, one must practice gender roles congruent with one's sex. Thus, males must be masculine (a concept of gender), do men's work, such as policing, firefighting, doctoring, and look like males, such as wearing pants or suits, masculine shoes, and men's hairstyles. We identify males as boys and men. They are expected to embody maleness or masculinity. Females, on the other hand, must be feminine (also a concept of gender), do women's work, such as nursing and teaching, and look like females, such as wearing dresses and skirts, dainty shoes, and women's hairstyles. We identify females as girls and women. They are expected to embody femaleness, womanhood, or femininity.

Gender differences tend to be identified as sex differences. Thus, embodying gender is defined as natural to one's sex (Garcia and McManimon 2011). This is a stance taken by *essentialism*, which claims that the conditions in social life are innate to people. It is a fundamental ideology of culture (Loseke 1999). Hence, it is believed that acting like a boy or a girl is part of the biological makeup of boys and girls. When society considers the play activities that girls desire it assumes that girls want to play ballerina, house, Barbie©, and so on. When society considers the career aspirations of girls and women, it assumes that girls want to be mothers (aka domestic engineers), schoolteachers (K–12), and health care providers (nurses and social workers). These play and work activities fundamentally separate girls from boys and ultimately men from women. Considering the play activities of boys, it is assumed that boys want to play sports (but more specifically contact and team sports), cars, Power Rangers™, and cops and robbers. Considering boys' and men's career aspirations, society assumes that they want to be soldiers, firefighters, and policemen. These assumptions are linked to the ideology that requires people to "do gender" as a natural way of being and is fundamentally linked to every culture's gender ideology.

Society dictates that we must constantly engage in gender roles. This is known as *doing gender. Doing gender* is the consistent engagement in day-to-day activities associated with one's sex (Acker 1992; West and Zimmerman 1987). Hence, for essentialists, girls and women naturally want to be mothers and do women's work that is directly related with childcare and the emotional well-being of the family; while boys and males naturally want to focus their time on the workforce and be the protectors of and providers for their families. The unfortunate fact is that doing gender is a social rule that when violated is assumed to be abnormal. Thus, people who do not do gender are assumed to be biologically deficient. These people are often ostracized within society and in some cases criminalized. Considering the focus of this book, women who become police officers are stepping out of their gender role expectations. They are not doing gender and so become ostracized both within the police organization and within the communities they police. However, as Box 1.1 reveals, while women in law enforcement are stepping out of gender role expectations, they still manage to do gender in policing.

Unlike essentialists, social constructionists define sex and gender as social constructs placed on members of society that invariably result in simplistic categorizations and social worth (Garcia and Schweikert 2010). The argument is that sex is socially constructed. One point of evidence is that society denies the scientifically proven sex category intersex. When intersex individuals are born, society rejects them as biological aberrations that must be corrected via medical procedures. As a result, gender must to be understood within the context of *difference* and the value given to the two genders.

Box 1.1 The United Nations' Indian Female Police Unit

Under the October 31, 2000, United Nations Resolution 1325, the United Nations sends female peace officers to various nations in conflict in order to aid in the prevention and resolution of conflicts (United Nations n.d.a). The Interagency Taskforce on Women, Peace and Security was established in February 2001 in order to ensure the implementation of Resolution 1325 (United Nations n.d.b). Between 2007 and 2016, the Indian Female Police Unit (FPU) worked to help keep the peace in Liberia (UN News Centre 2016). The officers of the Indian FPU completed one-year rotations in Liberia providing 24-hour guard duty and public order management. The FPU is an all-female Indian police unit that has served as a role model for other females in the nation. Resolution 1325 stresses the importance of women not only in conflict resolution but also with helping to protect women and girls from gender-based violence. To this end, the FPU also taught women self-defense, conducted classes on sexual violence and HIV/AIDS, provided medical services, and helped the Congo Town orphanage and school. The women of the FPU define themselves as officers who are women. The FPU's commander claimed that FPU officers can perform peacekeeping duties just like their male counterparts. However, as seen from their many roles in Liberia, they are still doing gender.

Sources: UN News Centre. 2016. *Hailed as 'role models,' all-female Indian police unit departs UN mission in Liberia.* https://www.un.org/africarenewal/news/hailed-%E2%80%98role-models%E2%80%99-all-female-indian-police-unit-departs-un-mission-liberia (accessed May 4, 2020); United Nations. n.d.a. *Landmark resolution on Women, Peace, and Security.* http://www.un.org/womenwatch/osagi/wps/ (accessed May 4, 2020); United Nations. n.d.b. *Taskforce on Women, Peace, and Security.* https://www.un.org/womenwatch/ianwge/activities/tfwpsecurity.htm (accessed May 4, 2020).

Gender and Difference

Understanding women's inroads and experiences as police officers requires that we understand the concept of difference. Difference is fundamental to every society. The concept of difference, from a sociological perspective, refers to the value system used to situate social groups within a society. Hence, societies tend to focus mostly on differences that exist within social groupings of gender, sexual orientation, race and ethnicity, age, income, religion, and nationality. In order to understand difference, one must understand how society categorizes, typifies, and values or devalues categories within a social group, such as gender. This value system can only be understood within the historical, legal, and social contexts of various ideologies, including gender ideologies, family ideologies, work ideologies, and religious ideologies, within a given society.

One must look at a particular society, or country, in order to understand gender difference. Society only accepts male and female sex categories. However, this does not mean that intersex is the difference. Difference must be understood within the context of the norm. Norms are the social rules of any society and are determined based on what is considered normal and what is considered abnormal. The abnormal is considered a violation of the norms. Norms are also directly linked to what a society values. Examining social statuses, these statuses are categorized into the norm and the *other*. The normative group is the group whose behaviors and beliefs define the hegemonic ideologies of society (Morash 2006). Hegemonic ideology refers to the dominant ideology of a society and drives what the society values and how it is structured. It is the *other* that is considered to be different (Rosenblum and Travis 1996). In most known societies, male is the norm while female (and hence intersex) is the *other* or different. Within policing, male officers are the norm. Additionally, their style of policing, which is directly connected to doing gender, is defined as the appropriate style of policing, i.e., the norm. Women, as *other*, often bring their own gendered socialization to the job that can be distinguished from male styles of policing and are thus considered inappropriate and incompetent (Martin and Jurik 2007).

When examining the master status of gender, we see that society defines manhood as the norm and womanhood as different, while any other is ignored. Since the norm determines hegemonic ideology, it is through a male lens that we come to understand femaleness and women's work. Furthermore, as with all hegemonic ideologies, it is not just the normative group that adopts these ideologies but all members of society. These ideologies are socially constructed within a society over time and are supported, even forced upon people, by the dominant culture. Through this process of social construction, we determine the rules of doing gender and define women's work and men's work. Through this same process, we learn the value (and devalue) of women's work.

I would be remiss if I did not examine the social system of *patriarchy* in our assessment of difference and gender. Patriarchy is the organization of a society in which power, wealth, and higher status are relegated to males. A patriarchal society is one in which men are the political, economic, familial, and religious leaders of a society. In a patriarchal society, men are relegated to the economic sphere of society. In any society, people with the most wealth have the most power. As a result, men accrue the most wealth and amass power. The cultural norms in a patriarchal society are structured so that males are socialized to desire to join the workforce to be able to financially support their families. Their work is viewed as very important for the functioning of society as a whole and is given higher status and more money. Any male who does not desire to engage in this activity is ostracized for not doing gender. On the other side of this socially constructed dichotomy, women are socialized to support the working male by keeping the home and family intact. She is expected to work in the home. Work that she engages in tends to be defined as support work and is given lower status and less money (see Figure 1.1). Any female who does not desire to keep the home and the children is ostracized for not doing gender.

Patriarchy is found within every ideology of society, including work, family, gender, sexual orientation, religion, education, sports, and so on. However, we must keep in mind that societies differ in the degree of patriarchy that is practiced. Traditional societies, such as Kenya and Saudi Arabia, have stronger patterns of patriarchy and tend to place very strict limitations on women. Less traditional societies, such as the United Kingdom (U.K.) and the United States (U.S.), have weaker patterns of patriarchy. While women face lower wages for equal work and face pressure to remain in the home, this is not required by law and is not as

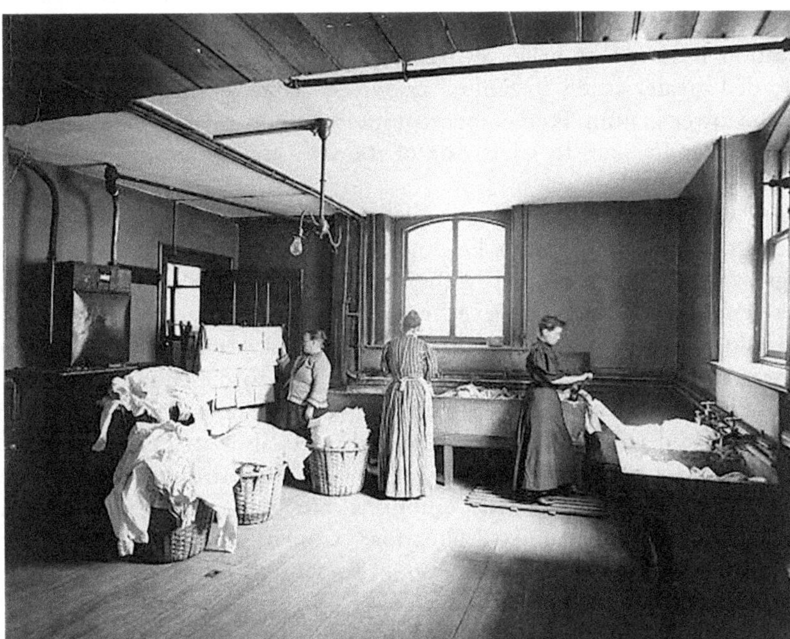

Figure 1.1 Women at Work in an Unidentified Laundry, Possibly in Boston, Massachusetts, ca. 1905.

Source: Photograph. www.loc.gov/item/2004673394/. Photo in the public domain. (www.loc.gov/resource/ppmsca.05917/).

strictly enforced by social norms. However, we must also acknowledge that within all patriarchal societies is the ideology that men are the protectors of women and children. It does not fit that women would become the protectors and join the ranks of law enforcement. As a result, women encounter a lot of resistance as officers.

Gender Stratification

Emphasizing difference within society leads to social stratification. Within any given society, the social structure represents the patterns of organizational and social relationships. These relationships are determined by hegemonic ideologies, which in turn determine the meanings of the different groups within society. As these meanings are put into action, dominant groups become the normative and power groups within society, while groups that represent difference (i.e., the *other*) are marginalized and placed on a lower rung within the opportunity structures. This process of constructing meaning becomes the stratification system within a society.

Gender categories, as with other master statuses such as race, age, and wealth, are given social meaning that allows gender stratification. This stratification is such that males are represented on the higher stratum being afforded greater access to limited resources, while females are represented on the lower stratum. Remember that intersex individuals are ignored, forcing these individuals to select one of the two socially constructed gender categories.

So what are these meanings and how do they influence the type of access that men and women have in society? When we talk about meanings, we link these meanings to the process of giving value and devalue to the gender categories. However, this is not as simple as stating that men are valued in society while women are devalued, leaving men with more power and wealth. The meanings that we give to masculinity and femininity are understood within the daily activity of doing gender. Masculinity is equated with physical strength, which is also equated with mental strength. As a group, men tend to grow taller and stronger than women do. Femininity is equated with emotional nurturance, and emotions tend to be defined as a weakness. Therefore, women are seen as weak, both physically and mentally. In the eyes of society, this does not make for a capable police officer.

Since men are defined as stronger, they are relegated to the public sphere of society where they must work in order to financially provide for their family. Work results in income and income may result in wealth and power. People with employment and with higher levels of income have more access to resources within society as well as to civil rights. As Laura Kramer (2005) describes, links to the economy influence one's political power, material well-being, educational opportunities, length of one's life, and economic opportunities of one's children.

In many societies, women are relegated to the home but must work in order to enable familial financial stability. In 2019, females 15 years and older represented 52.5 percent of the world's labor force (World Bank Group 2019). This female population represented 55 percent of the labor force in the U.K. In Nepal in that same year, where traditional gender roles are held to more strictly, 86 percent of females of the same age bracket worked in the labor force. In 2012 within the U.K., women's wages in manufacturing were 81 percent of men's wages; while in Nepal they were 45 percent (United Nations 2012). On the other hand, in Iran, where women have very few rights, 18 percent of women work but earn 90 percent of men's wages within manufacturing. Today, the world's average gender pay gap is 21.4 percent, with Brazil's gender pay gap at 25.7 percent and Sweden's at 5.7 percent (International Labour Organization 2019). The U.S. and the U.K. are not far below Brazil. Within nations such as Iran, the laws are used to deny women access to equality; while in nations such as the U.K. and the U.S., the laws are gender neutral but the gender wage gap helps to maintain the society's stratification system.

Women's Rights and Women's Work

Paxton and Hughes (2007) describe that the limitations in women's leadership and power in the workforce can be explained by culture and social structure. I will examine societal as well as police culture in Chapter 2. Here, I will examine the social structure guiding women's right to vote and work and how that affects where women work. Throughout history, women have been excluded from citizenship in every nation. As we see with stratification systems and women's exclusion from the economy, exclusion from citizenship negatively affects one's political power (the obvious effect), but it also affects one's economic opportunities, which in turn affects material well-being, educational opportunities, and so on. Gender and religious ideologies as well as cultural traditions have defined women as lacking the intellectual or moral capacity necessary for equal citizenship and laws have followed suit.

Women's Suffrage

Women the world over have mobilized in order to fight for equality. The Feminist Movement, also referred to as the Women's Movement, has occurred in waves in some nations and has helped to move women into positions of equality and power. The first wave of the Feminist Movement in the U.K. and the U.S. started in 1848 and focused primarily on the right to vote and stand for election (see Figure 1.2). International efforts

Figure 1.2 Three Suffragists Casting Votes in New York City? New York, ca. 1917.
Source: Photograph. www.loc.gov/item/97510725/. Photo in the public domain.

resulted in the founding of such organizations as the International Council of Women in 1888, the International Woman Suffrage Alliance in 1904 and the Women's International League for Peace and Freedom in 1915 (Offen 2000).

Most of Europe has been a relatively progressive continent. Within most European nations, women won the right to vote in the late nineteen teens through the 1920s; although Finnish women gained the right to vote in 1906 (Women Suffrage and Beyond 2015). However, nations such as Bulgaria, Croatia, France, and Italy did not give women the right to vote until the 1940s. Greek women could not vote until 1952, and women in Andorra, Moldova, and Switzerland could not vote until after the 1970s. Liechtenstein was the last European nation to grant women suffrage in 1984. Table 1.1 provides a snapshot of the first and last nations to grant women's suffrage. Today, Freedom House (2015) ranks Andorra as free and very high in political rights and civil liberties. Norway, Iceland, Sweden, New Zealand, and Finland are ranked on the Top 5 on the Democracy Index 2019 (The Economist 2020). Chad, Syria, Central African Republic, Democratic Republic of Congo, and North Korea are ranked in the Bottom 5 of the Democracy Index 2019.

Comparing Western European nations to Central and Eastern European nations, there is not much to distinguish these regions when considering the time that women won suffrage. However, when we examine Western Europe today, we find that most of these nations are identified as free with high civil liberties scores and as full democracies with high rankings on the democracy index. Central and Eastern Europe, however, is heavy with flawed democracies and have a comparable number of hybrid and authoritarian regimes. Furthermore, Freedom House has determined that these nations have slightly weaker civil liberties scores. Freedom House (2019) revealed that the world consisted of 86 countries that were free, 59 that were partly free, and 50 that were not free. Table 1.1 reveals that most of the first nations to grant women suffrage around the globe were European.

In North America, Canada was the first nation to grant non-Aboriginal women the right to vote in 1917. The U.S. followed in 1920; however,

Table 1.1 First and Last Nations to Grant Women's Suffrage

First Nations to Grant Women's Suffrage		*Last Nations to Grant Women's Suffrage*	
Year	*Nation*	*Year*	*Nation*
1893	New Zealand	1986	Central African Republic
1902	Australia[1]	1989	Namibia
1906	Finland	1990	Samoa
1913	Norway	1994	South Africa[6]
1915	Denmark, Iceland	1997	Oman
1917	Canada[1]	1999	Qatar
1918	Austria, Estonia, Georgia, Germany, Ireland[2], Kyrgyzstan, Latvia, Poland, Russia, United Kingdom	2002	Bahrain
1919	Belgium[3], Belarus, Kenya[4], Luxembourg, Netherlands, Sweden, Ukraine	2005	Kuwait
1920	Albania, Czech Republic, Slovakia, United States[5]	2015	Saudi Arabia[7]

Source: Paxton, P. and M. Hughes. 2007. *Women, politics, and power: A global perspective.* Los Angeles: Pine Forge Press; Women Suffrage and Beyond. 2015. *Women suffrage and beyond: Confronting the democratic deficit.* http://womensuffrage.org (accessed June 1, 2015).

[1] Non-Aboriginal women.
[2] Women over 30 years of age, national elections.
[3] Mothers and widows of WWI fallen servicemen, of citizens shot or killed by the enemy, and to female political prisoners held by the enemy.
[4] European women in Kenya.
[5] Did not include black women.
[6] Black women.
[7] Municipal elections.

African American women did not gain the right to vote until 1965. Nonetheless, the U.S. has come a long way and is ranked 25 on the democracy index; while Canada (along with Denmark) is ranked seven (The Economist 2020). In 1924, Saint Lucia granted women suffrage. Following this progress, most nations granted suffrage in the 1950s (Antigua and Barbuda, Barbados, Canada-Aboriginal vote, Dominica, Grenada, Haiti, Saint Kitts and Nevis, Saint Vincent and the Grenadines), with Cuba giving women the right to vote in 1934 and the Bahamas ending the fight for North American women in 1961. The Economist identifies all nations outside of Canada and the U.S. as Latin American and Caribbean. It reports that while most of these nations have been able to shed their dictatorships and have gained respect for civil liberties since the 1970s, most of these nations remain flawed democracies or hybrid regimes with no current move toward improving. According to Freedom House (2019), Cuba, Nicaragua, and Venezuela are the only nations in the Americas that are not free.

Central and South American nations were late to join the Women's Suffrage Movement. Ecuador was the first South American nation to grant women suffrage in 1929. Other nations joined in the 1930s (Bolivia: limited, Brazil, Chile: limited, El Salvador, Suriname, and Uruguay). The last nation to grant women suffrage was Paraguay in 1961. The Economist (2020) has determined that this region of the globe has three full democracies, 14 flawed democracies, four hybrid democracies, and three authoritarian regimes.

Asia and Australasia/Oceania saw most of women's suffrage occurring in the 1960s. However, New Zealand, a nation ranked fourth on the democratic index, granted women's suffrage in 1893. While Australia granted non-Aboriginal women the vote in 1902, Aboriginal women did not gain suffrage until 1962. Mongolia granted women's rights in the 1920s. The next move toward women's rights was in 1947 when Tuvalu granted women suffrage. After that time, it was not until 1960 that Tonga granted women the right to vote. The majority of the Asian and Australasian/Oceanian nations granted women suffrage in the 1970s. The last nation to grant women suffrage was Samoa in 1990. This region of the world is currently more likely to have flawed democracies and hybrid regimes.

In Eastern Europe, Georgia (often placed in Asia) and Kyrgyzstan granted women suffrage in 1918, while some nations granted women the right to vote in the 1920s (Armenia, Azerbaijan, Kazakhstan, Tajikistan, Turkmenistan). The majority of the nations in the Middle East and North Africa (MENA) did not grant suffrage until after the 1930s, but several nations were very late in gaining suffrage: Bangladesh (1972), Jordan (1974), Oman (1997), Qatar (1999), Bahrain (2002), United Arab Emirates (2006), and Saudi Arabia (2015, municipal elections, see Box 1.2) (Women Suffrage and Beyond 2015).

Box 1.2 Saudi Arabian Women Win Suffrage

On December 12, 2015, Saudi Arabian women voted and stood as candidates, in municipal elections only, for the first time. In a nation where women gained the right to drive in 2017, women's suffrage is monumental. Saudi Arabia did not allow elections for any of its citizens between 1965 and 2005, and the December election was the third election in the nation's history. On December 12, 2015, there were 978 female candidates and 130,000 female registered voters. This is compared to the 5,938 male candidates and 1.35 million male registered voters. While election polls are segregated by gender, as is common everywhere within the very conservative Saudi Arabia, women stated that they were very happy to be living through the monumental change, even if women were not elected. Twenty women were elected into office.

Source: BBC. 2015. *Saudi Arabia's women vote in election for first time.* https://www.bbc.com/news/world-middle-east-35075702 (accessed May 20, 2016).

African nations started to grant suffrage much later than Europe and North America. A few nations started in the 1930s and 1940s, such as Cameroon (1946), Djibouti and Liberia (1946), Niger (1948), Senegal (1945), Seychelles (1948), South Africa (1930, "whites" only), and Togo (1945). In 1989, Namibia was the last nation to legislate any law that allowed women to vote; however, South Africa completed women's suffrage when it granted black women the right to vote in 1994 (Women Suffrage and Beyond 2015).

Table 1.1 reveals that the last nations to grant women suffrage were in MENA and Sub-Saharan Africa. Furthermore, a survey of the Sub-Saharan region of Africa revealed that among the countries surveyed in 2019, there was one full democracy, six flawed democracies, 15 hybrid regimes, and 22 authoritarian governments, and little improvement toward functioning governments (The Economist 2020). MENA has been identified as the most oppressive region in the world. Within this region, 15 out of 20 nations are authoritarian, and there are no full democracies. Similarly, Freedom House (2015) found declines in democratic characteristics within MENA, such as civil liberties and an increase in violence.

Women's suffrage was the first move toward recognizing women as equal within a nation's system of gender stratification. However, the right to vote is complicated by oppression within the government, the workforce, education, religion, and the family. The right to vote is a great start to equality but does not overcome the lack of the right to work or to go to school. In fact, the first wave of the Feminist Movement was directly correlated with education and wealth (Paxton and Hughes 2007). Most women's rights movements around the globe began by fighting for the right to education. These women, who were predominantly middle- and upper-class with international ties, realized that the right to vote would secure other rights within society. Paxton and Hughes described various instances in which this was the case. For example, within the U.S., Brazil, Egypt, and Sri Lanka, wealthy female leaders with international ties strongly influenced the movements' successes. While the first wave of the Feminist Movement in the U.S. ended around 1919 and was followed by passage of the 19th Amendment granting non-African American women suffrage, African American women and women within many other nations around the world were still fighting for suffrage.

Feminism and the Right to Work

Women's equality is further complicated by the actual implementation of the law. However, we must also consider other systems of inequality. When considering the rights of women in the Oceanic region, for example, we must consider the fact that Aboriginal people are still struggling with political, racial, and economic inequality. In the U.S., African Americans and immigrants suffer systemic discrimination. Within MENA as well as Sub-Saharan Africa, traditional culture and religion are at the forefront of the oppression experienced by women, where going to school or obtaining a driver's license is very difficult. Here, many females still experience honor killings and genital mutilation.

Within Central and Eastern Europe as well as Asia, government systems remain oppressive, denying women equality. Many more nations within Africa, Asia, Central and Eastern Europe, and MENA rate low on the electoral process, political pluralism, and political participation (The Economist 2020). Examining civil liberties, these regions are plagued with a lack of freedom of expression and belief, associational and organizational rights, the rule of law, and personal autonomy and individual rights (Freedom House 2015). Nations with fewer civil rights in these areas tend to be more oppressive toward women and other minority groups. Furthermore, in all regions, violence against women is still a major social problem that works to undermine women's equality.

In the 1960s within many nations, women renewed their efforts to gain equality by mobilizing a second Feminist Movement. The second wave of the Feminist Movement focused on equality in the workplace, the value of women's work, and control over one's own body (Morash 2006). Focusing on the workplace, these activists fought to eliminate sex discrimination. A major focus was on the hiring, retention, and promotion of women in the workplace, as well as securing equal pay. Within the U.S., women gained legal recognition in the workforce in 1972 with the passage of Title VII of the Civil Rights Act of 1964. Among the provisions of Title VII, it became unlawful for any employer:

1. to fail or refuse to hire or to discharge any individual, or otherwise to discriminate against any individual with respect to his compensation, terms, conditions, or privileges of employment, because of such individual's race, color, religion, sex, or national origin; or
2. to limit, segregate, or classify his employees or applicants for employment in any way which would deprive or tend to deprive any individual of employment opportunities or otherwise adversely affect his status as an employee, because of such individual's race, color, religion, sex, or national origin (Pub. L. 88–352, Title VII in US EEOA 2000).

The Equal Employment Opportunity Act of 1972 (EEOA) expanded Title VII to include most private and public employers. As we will see with women's experiences in the U.S. and other nations' police organizations, enforcement of these laws has been slow.

Not all nations underwent a clear second wave of feminism as did the U.S. and the U.K. Yet, we can find many instances of continued and renewed feminism that also focused on employment opportunities for women. Arab feminism, for instance, while not the same in all Arab nations, has among its focus employment and education opportunities for women (Badran 2001). Palestine saw feminism in the 1940s become organized and institutionalized. In the 1970s, Palestinian feminism was revived and focused on health education, home, and office skills development. In the 1970s, Afghani women started fighting for the rights of women. In 1930s Egypt, women saw the same laws passed as in the Western nations that restricted the work that women were legally allowed to engage in. Nevertheless, as feminism and nationalism progressed in Egypt and other Arab nations, women began to gain access to the workforce (El-Mahdi 2010). While many claim that Egypt did not have an actual feminist movement, the political activities of many women gained some rights for women. The barriers that Arab women face in gaining equality stem from state (structural) and religious (cultural) institutions that see women with power as a threat. In Egypt, women started to enter high-level government positions, and in the 1970s, their entry into these positions increased dramatically. In recent decades, however, the institutionalization of Islamic law (*shari'a* law) resulted in a decrease in women's rights in many Islamic nations.

Similar to Western feminism, early Arab feminism was led by middle- and upper-class women and ignored the conditions of the poor. As feminism progressed through time, however, Western and Arab feminism began to focus on marginalized groups. Within the Western region of the globe, this was identified as the third wave of feminism (around the 1980s) and the concept of intersectionality was introduced. Intersectionality considers the complexity of one's social position as it is influenced by gender, race, income, age, sexual orientation, and so on. In Arab feminism, activists began to give lower income groups more attention. However, much of women's activism within Arab nations stemmed from the fight for nationalism and independence.

Eastern and Central European nations faced a unique phenomenon not experienced in other parts of the world. The fall of the Iron Curtain beginning in 1989 changed the political and economic systems of the nations behind the curtain: Albania, Bulgaria, Czechoslovakia, Eastern Germany, Hungary, Poland, Romania, the Soviet Union, and Yugoslavia. Within communist nations, mothers were typically cared for within the labor force. However, in these post-communist nations, women's socialist circumstances experienced a backlash (Fabian 2006). As the democratic government became stronger, backlash to socialist policies and practices became stronger. Hungarian women were forced to mobilize in order to fight for welfare-related needs, including equality in the workplace. Today, they are still struggling for equality. In Bulgaria, single mothers were excluded from the workforce. As the U.S. saw in the 1980s, Eastern and Central Europe experienced a feminization of poverty as women's participation in the workforce worsened (Duffy 2000).

Women's emancipation under communist-ruled nations required that they care for the household, hold down a full-time job, and engage in political participation. Under this organization, women were awarded the same education, given social support as mothers, and required to work, although they did not earn the same wages as men. With the implementation of a male-dominated democracy and free labor markets in post-communist nations, women lost these benefits as they faced discrimination in the workforce and the privatization of childcare. For many women in these nations, feminism was equated with Western feminism, which was equated with forcing women to work as part of their emancipation (Galligan, Clavero, and Calloni 2007). This has also resulted in women's rights advocacy being done via traditional women's roles (Duffy 2000). Furthermore, nations such as Estonia, Latvia, Lithuania, and Poland had many women's organizations but only a few were feminist. We see that there has not been any great protest on the working conditions of women in this region. Many researchers claim that post-communist Europe did not experience a women's movement (Duffy 2000; Galligan, Clavero, and Calloni 2007; Fabian 2006).

Within the Asian and Australasian/Oceanian regions of the globe, we see women's movements focused on women and work occurring around the 1970s and 1980s. Chiang and Liu (2011) describe that the first women's movement in Hong Kong occurred between the 1940s and then again in the 1970s and focused on polygamy, equal pay, improvement of maternity benefits, and court procedures for rape cases. Feminism of the 1980s resulted in the passage of laws regarding sex discrimination, women's inheritance rights, and equal opportunities. In Taiwan, the contemporary Women's Movement began in the early 1970s and fought for child prostitutes and equal rights in women's education and participation in the workforce. Feminist advocacy in the 1990s resulted in the 2000 Gender Equality in Employment Act in Taiwan.

Japan experienced a women's movement in the 1970s. Traditional Japanese culture values the idea of the good wife and wise mother, known as *ryousai kenbo* (Geraghty 2008). As late as the 1970s, the Japanese housewife resembled the 1950s U.S. housewife. Although Japan's Article 14 to the Constitution provides for the equality of women, this has been loosely interpreted. When Japan's Labour Standards Law was passed in 1947, women found that while wage equality was mandated and maternity leave was protected, they were also faced with other "protections" common in other nations. Overtime and night work exemptions, physical labor restrictions, and maternity leave were written into the law. However, the law ignored issues of hiring, promotion, firing, and job assignment. Still, by the end of the 1970s, there were more working women in Japan than there were housewives (Matsui 1990).

Feminists in Japan questioned the rapid industrialization occurring in Japan and claimed that women were the most oppressed group in Japan because their reproductive role was devalued in the workforce. By 1985, Japan passed the Equal Employment Opportunity Law (EEOL). Geraghty (2008) described claims that the law would not have passed if not for the pressure of the United Nation's Convention on the Elimination of All Forms of Discrimination Against Women. The EEOL expanded the Labour Standards Law to *discourage* discrimination in recruitment, hiring, job assignment, promotion, training, benefits, retirement, and dismissal. With the lack of penalties within the law, women's equality became stagnant in the 1990s. In 1997, the EEOL was revised and added the *prohibition* of discrimination of women in the workforce. The EEOL was further revised in 2006 to include prohibitions of indirect discrimination. However, by 2005, Japanese women still made 67 percent of men's wages and represented only 10 percent of managers in the workforce. In 2005, 63 percent of Japanese firms reported that they did not plan to hire women.

Gendered Organizations

Gender and Work

The preceding discussion outlined the legal barriers found within the social structure that slowed women's progress into the workforce and into policing. Here, I examine the workforce as part of this social structure. A clear division of labor by sex has always organized work the world over. This brings us back to the theory of the gendered organization. Within a patriarchal ideology, work dominated by women is devalued as less important and receives lower status and lower wages. When today's industrialized nations moved away from an agricultural economy, the family's financial stability became less dependent on women's work in the fields and in the home. Women became more dependent on men and their employment rights became more limited. As discussed in gender and work, during the Victorian Era, many nations limited women's right to work under equal conditions by enacting protective laws. In nations not influenced by British culture, racial, ethnic, and religious minorities also had fewer rights, and the working conditions of women were harsher than those of men. As industrialized nations moved through their Feminist Movements, women gained more humane conditions of work. However, in Third World nations today, the working conditions of women resemble the oppressive conditions of industrialized nations of the early 1900s (Momsen 1991).

While women's groups from Third World nations have been active in the United Nations Development Decades and the United Nations Decade for Women, their nations have not fulfilled the promise of equality (Momsen 1991; Freedom House 2015; The Economist 2015, 2020). The working conditions of women have a level of similarity across the Third World. As Momsen pointed out, women in the Third World comprise 70 percent of agricultural workers, with their representation higher in Sub-Saharan Africa, Asia, and the Caribbean regions. Examining the division of labor, women are more likely to engage in weeding and planting, while men do the heavy physical labor and application of pesticides. Women also take care of the household, the meals, and the children. They often put in twice the work hours that men work. In urban areas of Third World nations, women are increasingly joining the workforce. However, as was done in Victorian Era nations, Third World nations tend to limit women's access to certain jobs on the grounds of protection (World Bank Group 2020a). Women are often excluded from industrial jobs that require physical labor, jobs that are defined as morally dangerous, or jobs that do not have facilities for women. As Momsen (1991) described, these circumstances push women into marginalized jobs that are linked to low status, low wages, and poor working conditions.

As we saw from the discussion on feminist movements, work organizations tend to be gendered in their recruitment, promotion, job assignments, and firing. Today, we still find reluctance or refusal to hire women. Women tend to be given job assignments that are deemed suitable to the weaker sex and are more likely to be fired, especially after childbirth. Additionally, governments tend to support these practices either by legally restricting women's work or by not enforcing anti-discriminatory laws. In a study by the International Labour Organization of the United Nations, we see that Burundi, Nepal, Rwanda, Mozambique, and Lithuania are among the nations with the most females in the labor force, while Oman, Qatar, and Yemen are among the nations with the fewest females in the labor force (World Bank Group 2020a) (see Table 1.2).

The institutionalization of gender within the labor force also results in women being overrepresented in the agriculture and service sectors and underrepresented in the industry sector. Agriculture and service have been more strongly linked to women's work, while the industry sector is more strongly linked to men's work. In 2020, Botswanan women, for example, represented 44 percent of the adult labor force (World Bank Group 2020a). However, 17.39 percent of employed women worked in the agriculture sector and 73 percent worked in the service sector, while only 9.58 percent of employed women worked in industry. On the other hand, 25 percent of employed men in Botswana worked in industry.

Within Third World nations, women are more likely to be required to work in order to support their families. As a result, we found that 49 percent of women in Madagascar and Tanzania participated in the paid labor force, while 52 percent of the women in Rwanda participated in the paid labor force (World Bank Group 2020a). In Timor-Leste, ranked the most

Table 1.2 Percentage of Women in the Labor Force, 2018

Top 20 Nations with the Most Women in the Labor Force		*Bottom 20 Nations with the Least Women in Labor Force*	
Burundi	52%	Yemen	8%
Nepal	52%	Oman	13%
Rwanda	52%	Qatar	14%
Mozambique	52%	Iraq	15%
Lithuania	51%	Syrian Arab Republic	15%
Sierra Leone	51%	United Arab Emirates	15%
Angola	50%	Saudi Arabia	17%
Barbados	50%	Jordan	18%
Latvia	50%	Algeria	18%
Belarus	50%	Iran, Islamic Republic	19%
Lao People's Democratic Republic	50%	Bahrain	21%
Guinea	50%	Somalia	21%
Togo	49%	West Bank and Gaza	21%
Benin	49%	Pakistan	22%
Hong Kong SAR, China	49%	India	22%
Zimbabwe	49%	Egypt, Arab Republic	24%
Virgin Islands (U.S.)	49%	Morocco	24%
Tanzania	49%	Libya	25%
Portugal	49%	Lebanon	25%
Madagascar	49%	Sudan	26%

Source: World Bank Group. 2020a. *Gender Statistics: Labor force, female (% of total labor force)*. https://databank.worldbank.org/source/gender-statistics# (accessed May 5, 2020).

impoverished Third World nation, 24 percent of females participated in the paid labor force. However, Yemen, ranked fifth most impoverished Third World nation, reported that only 8 percent of females participated in the paid labor force.

This brings us back to our discussion of gendered organizations. Nations that place greater restrictions on women will have fewer women in the workforce. Freedom House (2015) ranks Yemen as "not free" and low in political rights and civil liberties. In Second and First World nations, women may work by necessity or by choice with fewer restrictions. Norway was ranked as a First World nation with the highest human development index and the most equality (United Nations 2014). Within Norway, 59.9 percent of females participated in the paid labor force. However, following gender roles only 6.5 percent of employed women worked in the industry sector, compared to 30 percent of employed males, while 95 percent of employed women worked in the service sector, compared to 67 percent of employed men (World Bank Group 2020a). Further examining traditional gender roles, women in Norway on average spent half the time in the paid labor force as did men and twice as much time in unpaid work.

Overall, in more developed nations, the service sector predominates. In fact, the service sector is growing faster than agriculture and industry in most parts of the world (United Nations 2015). Within more developed nations in Latin America and the Caribbean, about 80 percent of women's employment is located within the service sector (United Nations 2015). In Southern Europe, the service sector accounts for about 80 percent of women's employment. However, in Oceania, Sub-Saharan Africa, and Southern Asia, the agriculture sector employs more than half of all working women. In the last two decades, industry sector jobs have decreased for women the world over and for men in East Asia, Europe, North America, and the more developed region of Oceania.

Gender and the Pay Gap

Paid labor engaged in by women tends to be devalued. We see evidence of this in the gender pay gap (United Nations 2012, 2015). African and Asian nations have the largest gender pay gaps in the world. In Africa, between 2006 and 2008, the pay of Botswanan women employed in manufacturing was 55 percent that of men's pay. In Asia, the pay of the women of Nepal who worked in manufacturing was 45 percent that of men's pay. Within Occupied Palestine, the gender pay gap was 50 percent in 2008. However, these continents also boasted the smallest gender pay gaps. In Madagascar, women's pay in manufacturing was 85 percent of men's pay. Australia, Bahrain, Iran, and the Philippines all had manufacturing gender pay gaps of 90 percent or higher. The European nations of Belgium, Denmark, Finland,

France, Ireland, Latvia, Malta, Norway, Sweden, and the U.K. all reported that the pay of women working in manufacturing was over 80 percent of men's pay. Within the nations of the Americas, we also find smaller gender pay gaps. El Salvador's gender pay gap was 84 percent. Paraguay's gender pay gap was 108 percent. Saint Lucia and Costa Rica's gender pay gaps were 81 percent, while Bermuda's gender pay gap was 91 percent.

The manufacturing gender pay gap is important to examine because the differentiation in pay helps to stress the work ideologies in relation to gender within male-dominated occupations. The U.S. Bureau of Labor Statistics (2019) reported that in 2018, women's earnings as a percentage of men's for full-time wage and salary workers was 81 percent. In the U.S., women who worked in predominantly female occupations earned approximately 26 percent less than women working in predominantly male occupations, while men who worked in predominantly female occupations earned approximately 13 percent less than men who worked in predominantly male occupations (Boraas and Rodgers 2003). While paid work has come to be defined as men's work, manufacturing tends to be reserved for men. The working conditions, including pay, are harsher for women when they engage in men's work. The more masculine the job is believed to be the more resistance women experience.

Gender, Leadership, and Policing

No occupation is more likely to be viewed as man's work than are government occupations. As discussed in the section on gender stratification, men are delegated to the public sphere of society. There is no more public a job than that of the public servant. The public sphere is the sphere in which people work, gain income, and participate in the political arena of society. In every society, men have always been delegated the intelligent, rational, political body of the family. Further, the family is the primary unit in which the male practices his power. While women have served in official government positions throughout history, it was not until after a nation granted suffrage to women and after rights in the workforce started to be granted that women started to enter into government leadership positions in real numbers.

If we examine the percentage of women working as legislators, senior officials, and managers with the time women were granted suffrage in that nation, we find that nations with the largest percentage of women working in these occupations granted women suffrage after 1935. For instance, Bermuda and the Philippines have the largest percentage of women working as legislators, senior officials, and managers. In 2008, Philippine women represented 55 percent of legislators, senior officials, and managers (International Labour Organization 2013). However, women were not granted suffrage until 1937. In 2000, women in Bermuda also represented 55 percent of these positions, and suffrage was not granted until 1944. However, these numbers are heavily weighted toward managerial positions.

Women Heads of State

According to a report released by the United Nations (2015), heads of state or government positions in which power and decision-making is great are not widely available to women. While all regions of the globe have made progress in increasing women's representation, this progress has been slow. In 2015, women were 10 out of 152 elected Heads of State and 14 out of 194 heads of government. Most of these countries were in Latin America and the Caribbean. There were only 28 out of 191 countries (15 percent) in which women presided over lower or single houses of parliament and 15 out of 76 countries (20 percent) in which women presided over the upper house or senate. Women represented 22 percent of seats in lower or single houses of parliament. These countries are in Western Europe and Sub-Saharan Africa, including Rwanda (64 percent). The Caribbean boasted the largest representation of women in lower or single chamber houses with over 30 percent followed by Latin America with over 25 percent representation. In 2009, Belize, Micronesia, Oman, Qatar, Saudi Arabia, Solomon Islands, and Yemen still had no women in lower or single chamber houses. Within the United States, in 2020, women represented 23.4 percent of members of the lower house (House of Representatives) and 25 percent of members of the upper house (Congress) (Congressional Research Service 2020). By 2017, in 17 nations the percentage of women in parliament was 30 percent or higher, with Iceland having 47.6 percent female representation (Organisation for Economic Co-Operation and Development 2019).

Women in Local Government

Representation of women in government is very important in empowering women. This also extends to local government in which power is more decentralized and has the potential to touch lives more closely. Research has found that the more women in power in local government, the more women are hired as police officers (Belknap 2015). Official data shows that within Northern African and Western Asian nations, women represented as little as 8 percent of elected councilors in 2015, while in nations in Sub-Saharan Africa, women represented as much as 30 percent (United Nations 2015). Women represented over 20 percent of elected councilors in nations of the Americas, Europe, and other more developed nations. Similar to national governments, some local governments have enacted constitutional or legislative gender quotas in order to approach a gender balance in government, including South Africa, Bosnia and Herzegovina, Iraq, Kyrgyzstan, Libya, Serbia, Macedonia, and Timor-Leste. In more developed nations in Europe, approximately 14 percent of mayors were women in 2013. However, in Iceland and Sweden, women made up 30 percent of mayoral positions. Cyprus and Liechtenstein had the lowest representation with no women mayors, while Greece, Romania, and Serbia all had less than 5 percent.

Women in the Judiciary

Data are not as readily available on gender balance in the judiciary and civil service. The United Nations uncovered data for 76 nations in 2015. Male judges in over half of the countries outnumbered female judges. Additionally, the higher the judicial position the less women's representation. In 2015, Armenia, Azerbaijan, Japan, Nigeria, Russia, Tajikistan, Togo, and the U.K. all had less than 25 percent women judges, while Jamaica, Latvia, Saint Kitts and Nevis, and Slovenia had more than 75 percent women judges. Latvia carried the largest representation of women in the judiciary with 77 percent. However, women represented a much smaller proportion of Supreme Court judges in this region, 41 percent. In South America, one of two Supreme Court judges was a woman in Honduras, while women made up one third of the Supreme Court in the Philippines. In 2016, women made up 33.3 percent of the United States Supreme Court, 36.8 percent of the Circuit Court of Appeals, and 34 percent of overall federal court judges (American Bar Association 2019). White women represented 22 percent of all state court judges in the U.S., while women of color only represented 8 percent. Again, Latvia had the highest percentage of female Supreme Court judges (68 percent) followed by Slovak Republic (59 percent) (Organisation for Economic Co-Operation and Development 2019). Spain had 12 percent female Supreme Court judges and Luxembourg had none.

Women Prosecutors

Prosecutors play a dual role within any criminal justice system. On one end, they are officers of the court and must abide by strict rules of the court when prosecuting a criminal case. On the other hand, prosecutors are first and foremost law enforcement. They have the power to determine who will go before a judge and under what charges. The prosecutor's decisions constrain the sentencing options of the judge and, thus, represent a powerful decision maker in government.

The United Nations Office of Drugs and Crime (2015) released statistics on prosecution personnel for 42 nations around the globe. Of the data available, between 2011 and 2013, Guyana had the most female prosecution personnel (100 percent) and Armenia had the fewest (9.7 percent). Asian nations within the sample had the smallest proportion of women prosecutors with Japan having 14.5 percent and Kyrgyzstan 11.9 percent, in addition to Armenia's 9.7 percent. However, Hong Kong boasted 60 percent female representation during this time. The three Central American nations in the sample (Costa Rica, Mexico, and Panama) had over 47 percent female representation. European nations also had a high representation of female prosecutors. In 14 out of 21 European nations, women represented over 50 percent of prosecution personnel. The United Nations Office of Drugs and Crime's (2017) more recent statistics on prosecution personnel for 60 nations around the globe showed that of the data available, in 2015, Iceland had the fewest female prosecutors (8) and the Russian Federation had the most (15,869).

Women in Policing

Police represent the gateway to the criminal justice system. They also embody all that is masculine. Police officials have the power to apprehend, question, and arrest suspects. They often carry guns and have the authority to inflict bodily injury. Those powers are given to the police because they are the protectors of society. Men have always been given the task of protecting society. As a result, policing has always been a male-dominated occupation.

The United Nations Office of Drugs and Crime (2015) gathered statistics on gender in policing for 55 nations in 2013. The data revealed that women made up 3 to 34 percent of police forces around the globe. In Africa, women represented 3 to 12 percent of the police in most nations. The exception was Rwanda where women made up 30 percent of Rwandan police personnel. As has been found with other government jobs in Rwanda, women have achieved such a large representation of employees because they were the majority of the survivors in the post-conflict reconstruction starting in 1994.

In the Americas, women made up 9 to 25 percent of the police forces. Guyana's police force consisted of one quarter women. Canada, Guyana, Trinidad and Tobago, and Uruguay all had police forces in which women represented over 20 percent. While the United States claims equality, women only comprised 12 percent of police personnel. Among Asian nations within the 55-nation dataset, women comprised 4 to 25 percent of police personnel, with Cyprus having the largest female representation (25 percent). Women made up 19 percent of police in Macao, a Special Administrative Region of China (also see Box 1.3).

Conclusion

As with other government positions, we find throughout the globe that social structure, both historically and currently, has hindered women's entry and progression into policing. Women's delayed movement into government

Box 1.3 Women Police in Gulf Cooperation Council National Police Forces

Staci Strobl (2010) examined the entrance of women in the police force within the Gulf Cooperation Council (GCC) countries. Strobl found that in the six GCC countries, women can represent 5 to 10 percent of a country's national police force. The representation of female sworn personnel was 10 percent of the police force in Bahrain and 10 percent in Dubai, United Arab Emirates (UAE). Their exact representation is unknown in Kuwait, but women police have reached close to 5 percent in Qatar and Oman and 10 percent in UAE. In 2018, Saudi Arabia announced that women would be allowed to apply for traffic police; however, their numbers are not yet known (Alhashmi 2018). The level of integration in GCC countries is not too dissimilar to some countries in that women officers in the GCC focus on women and juveniles. Strobl found that these nations are either hailed as unique for having women in policing or criticized as oppressive for segregating female officers. However, many fail to examine the entrance of women into GCC police forces in light of the nation's cultural context. Strobl suggested that women police in the GCC are "both progressive and neo-traditional, a position that is not merely hedging, but instead reflects a deeper understanding of the nature of gender and policing in these countries" (2010, p. 71).

Source: Alhashmi, T. 2018. Cracking the glass ceiling: Gulf women in the police. *Cracking the glass ceiling*. https://agsiw.org/cracking-glass-ceiling-gulf-women-police/ (accessed May 13, 2020); Strobl, S. 2010. Progressive or neo-traditional? Policewomen in Gulf Cooperation Council (GCC) Countries. *Feminist Formations* 22:51–74.

positions of power were hindered first by the lack of the vote and then by discrimination in the workforce. However, as we witness nations increasing civil liberties, we also witness a move toward gender balance in government. Unfortunately, quota and anti-discriminatory laws are only one part of the solution. Culture also hinders women's equality. Paxton and Hughes (2007) describe two areas of culture that have stalled women's entry into positions of power: beliefs about women's inherent nature and beliefs about women's proper place. In the next chapter, I will address these two sets of beliefs and how they have stalled women's entry into and influence within policing.

Chapter 2

Ideology and Images of Women and Policing

In Chapter 1, I examined how social structure excludes women from the economy, limiting their political power and economic opportunities. I ended Chapter 1 by describing two cultural reasons why women have delayed entry into policing. The first reason focuses on the social beliefs that women's inherent nature is to nurture the family. The second belief is that women's proper place is in the home. In this chapter, I will examine how these cultural beliefs work to exclude women from politics and work.

The Nature of Policing

Policing the world over is the personification of masculinity. Police officers have the power to carry a gun, to detain and arrest people, and to use deadly force if the situation calls for it. Police officers are the protectors of society. Steve Herbert (2001) describes policing as a masculinist organization that supports patriarchy and, by its very existence, suppresses any non-masculine reforms. Policemen do gender on a daily basis with their very existence. This creates a hegemonic ideology of masculinity that is celebrated. Police officers are crime fighters who display courage and aggression. Herbert goes on to describe two types of officers, the *hard charger* who places himself in danger in order to handle the most dangerous calls and the *station queen* who is happy to sit at a desk safely doing paperwork. The hard charger in this scenario is the masculine officer and the station queen is effeminate and lacks masculinity.

As we examine traditional gender roles, we find that the job of policing was created in the image of masculinity. Men have always taken the role of protectors of society. The more aggression a police officer can display the more he is likely to be successful at protecting the women, children, and elderly of society. This is expected of men. Women, on the other hand, are expected to need protection. For this reason, women's entry into policing has been resisted. In more traditional times and societies, women tend to sway toward these same ideals. Even as women initially attempted to join the police force, they did not envision

Figure 2.1 Suffragist Posed in Police Uniform to Illustrate Woman Police Concept, Cincinnati, Ohio.

Source: Photograph. www.loc.gov/pictures/item/90712219/. Photo in the public domain.

that they should take on masculine traits. They joined in order to add a woman's touch. However, any attempts to work within this masculine occupation were ridiculed and forestalled (see Figure 2.1). Consider Box 2.1 as an example of women's desire to join the police force in 1900s United States.

In order to understand the resistance to women in policing, we must not only examine the culture of the police organization, but we must also examine traditional gender role ideologies. Gender role ideologies are embedded in all cultures and must be examined through a historical, legal, and religious context. Religion and government reinforce culture. Hence, an analysis of traditional gender roles must examine these roles within the context of the major religions of the world. Such religions include, but are not limited to, Christianity, Confucianism, Hinduism, Islamism, Judaism, and Buddhism. Major forms of government also reinforce gender roles and women's place in society through its laws, policies, and practices. Major forms of government today include communism, democracy (whether parliamentary or presidential), republic, monarchy (constitutional

Box 2.1 Policewomen in the Early 1900s

In the United States, female pioneers entered the police occupation in the early 1900s. Policing has always been a male-dominated occupation whose culture epitomizes masculinity. However, the first women entering the field of policing did not want to be considered one of the boys (Garcia 2003). Contrary to U.S. women police today, the policewomen of the early 1900s claimed a niche that was believed to be women's work, one that society believed men were incapable of filling. Policewomen joined policing by bringing with them their "inherent" higher morality. In the early 1900s, the U.S. was deeply embedded in Victorian Era traditions in which women were believed to be delicate and in need of protection. However, Victorian Era ideals also defined women as the moral guides of the family and, by extension, society as a whole. Who better than women to guide wayward women and children toward a more righteous way of living?

In a March 7, 1906, *New York Times* article, Mrs. Julie Goldzier wrote a letter to Mayor Pierre Garven of Bayonne, New Jersey imploring that he hire policewomen to deal with mischievous boys. She wrote, "We employ women to teach our children, and it would be no startling innovation to employ women as guardians over our children." Mrs. Goldzier argued that policewomen would be better suited to protecting boys on the streets while policemen protected property. She claimed, "Better citizens would result . . . , and the much needed feminine influence would be exercised upon the minds of the young." Unfortunately, 1906 was not the golden year for New Jersey to hire policewomen. Mrs. Goldzier's proposal was buried in committee and Mayor Garven announced that he would quit if he were required to run a female police force. Supporting ideologies of doing gender and gendered work, the newspaper article ends by stating, "Bayonne's ninety-five policemen, who would have to stay at home and do the washing and cooking if their wives landed their jobs, are standing solidly with the Mayor."

Sources: Garcia, V. 2003. 'Difference' in the police department: Women, policing and 'doing gender.' *Journal of Contemporary Criminal Justice*, 19:330–344; *New York Times* (1857–1922). (1906, March 7). Call for policewomen to protect the boys. *New York Times*.

or parliamentary), aristocracy, and dictatorship. Authoritarian is typically used to describe governments with unelected officials, such as dictatorships and monarchies (Freedom House 2015; The Economist 2020). Typically, the belief is that the more oppressive the government, the less likely are women to be employed in policing and military positions. However, some authoritarian regimes have female representation in policing that is comparable to or surpasses some full democracies: 10 percent in Bahrain,

5 percent in Qatar, 17 percent in Hong Kong, China, 19 percent in Macao Special, China, and 20 percent in Russia (Strobl 2010; United Nations Office of Drugs and Crime 2015).

Traditional Gender Role Ideologies

By the late 1800s, many societies held women to the traditional gender roles of the Victorian Era (see Box 2.2). The Victorian ideal of true womanhood was dubbed the "cult of domesticity" and required women to be pious, pure, domestic, and submissive. Victorian ideals taught that women should embrace religion for they were the new Eve, working with God to provide moral leadership. However, they could only do this from their rightful place, i.e., the home.

Victorian ideals touched on all ideologies of life. In the early 1900s, women in most nations were relegated to the private sphere, i.e., the home. Even within those nations not ruled by Victorian ideals, women were subordinate to men. Traditional political ideologies defined women as the property of men with no right to vote, own property, and no right to retain their own wages. For example, the ideal of womanhood was institutionalized in South Africa with the concept of *volksmoeder*, or "mother of the nation" (Blignaut 2013). *Volksmoeder* was an Afrikaner ideology developed in the early part of the twentieth century that was highly influenced by Victorian British rule. Briefly, *volksmoeder* strictly defined womanhood and its primary role in the home. Under the ideal of true womanhood, women's opportunities and rights were very limited. Today, most nations are still structured through patriarchal patterns of organization and ideologies. As we examine the consequences of Victorian ideals of womanhood, we can see their reinforcement within family, political, religious, and work ideologies.

Family Ideologies

Traditional family ideologies defined women as the property of men. First, she was required to marry a man (sexual ideologies) and have children. She was then required to care for her husband, her children, and her home. She was required to cook, clean, and take care of any other duties related to the household. She was also required to be obedient; otherwise, she would face legally sanctioned corporal punishment from her spouse. Legally, she gave up her rights, transferring them from her father to her husband. In his *Commentaries on the Laws of England*, Sir William Blackstone wrote that the "legal existence of a woman is [sus]pended during marriage" (Blackstone 1765, p. 442).

Box 2.2 The Influence of Victorian Ideologies around the Globe

Queen Victoria (1837–1901) was determined to expand British rule. The extent of British imperialism meant that the Victorian true womanhood ideology spread across the globe. Women were socialized to value family and religion above all else. The nature of work for women was redefined and women increasingly moved out of the workforce and into the home. During her 64 years on the throne, Queen Victoria colonized cities, regions within countries, islands, and whole countries on every continent. Great Britain had over 130 colonies around the world during the Victorian Era (Luscombe 2012). The list below, which excludes most colonized islands, demonstrates the reach of Victorian colonization and thus Victorian ideologies.

- **Africa:** British Kaffraria/Cape Colony, Egypt, Gambia, Ghana, Goree, Namibia, Nigeria, Rhodesia (now Zimbabwe), Senegal, Seychelles, Sierra Leone, South Africa, Sudan, Zambia
- **Asia-Pacific:** Afghanistan, Australia, British Indian Ocean Territory, Burma, China, Indonesia, Fiji, Hawaii, Hong Kong, India, Iran, Malaysia, New Guinea, New Zealand, Pakistan, Philippines, Singapore, Sri Lanka, Yemen
- **Americas:** Bahamas, Belize, Berbice, Bermuda, British Columbia, British Guiana, Canada, most of the Caribbean Islands, Guyana, Panama, Saint Pierre and Miquelon, Suriname, U.S. Colonies
- **Europe:** Gibraltar, Greece, Heligoland, Ireland, Malta, Portugal

Source: Luscombe, S. 2012. *Entering and exiting the Empire*. www.britishempire.co.uk/timeline/colonies.htm (accessed August 17, 2015).

Women within Western nations who entered policing in the late 1800s and early 1900s typically subscribed to the ideology that women's primary role was to care for the family. They claimed the niche of the protectors of women and children within society. Within other nations in the mid- to late 1900s and 2000s, women entering into policing still tended to subscribe to these ideologies as we see in India and Bahrain (Natarajan 2014; Strobl 2010, 2020). In her 2008 research, Staci Strobl found that policewomen in the Women's Police Directorate of Bahrain valued their traditional family role and engaged in family-oriented work such as child protection and working in juvenile detention centers. Among the reasons that many policewomen supported gender-segregated units was that integrating women into policing (equal to men) created "dishonorable situations on the basis of Arab and Muslim culture" (Strobl 2008, p. 47). They also believed that women working with other women is a more efficient way of handling women and children.

Political Ideologies

British culture and law were thrust upon many nations through British colonialism and often became common law within the U.S. Socially, women were required to silently take their lot in life and to socialize their children into these gender roles. While the U.S. colonial rights of unmarried women resembled those of men, their rights later resembled the lack of rights of married women. In Europe, unmarried women did not have many rights and faced harsh stigma for being unmarried (Ching and Ching 2001). Furthermore, not only were women kept out of the workforce, police were the strong arm of the law that kept women out of power. One example is the failure of the justice system to protect women who are victims of violence at the hands of their husbands. As the property of men, as defined by William Blackstone, the "rule of thumb" was imposed by the U.K. and U.S. courts and enforced by the police. This allowed a woman to be beaten by her husbands with a stick no thicker than his thumb (Garcia and McManimon 2011). This policy was practiced in Western industrialized nations until the 1970s and 1980s. However, research still shows a lack of enforcement of laws that protect women against intimate partner violence (see Chapter 6).

Afrikaner society held strongly to the "essential nature of gender" and influenced women to become politically active, insofar as their gender allowed. Hence, we find similar instances of doing gender within this part of the world. However, not all nations were colonized by Great Britain. Within Kenya, for example, we find that women's inequality today resembles that of the Colonial U.S. The Kenyan Bill of Rights includes nondiscrimination provisions. However, it exempts members from races and tribes that use customary law (Ellis et al. 2007). With at least 40 such groups, most Kenyan women have no legal recourse outside of local customary law. As a result, married women have few inheritance and property rights.

It is difficult to eliminate the political side of law enforcement. Feminists have long argued that the right to work provides a political voice for women. Added to this is the fact that law enforcement gives officials a level of political power, so that women who enter law enforcement are deemed to have political power. However, as we examine women's movement into policing, we see that women often did not have arrest powers or the authority to carry a firearm. Where women are often trained in similar tactics as men, they are often not afforded the power to use them (Garcia 2003; Martin 1980; Schulz 1995; Sherman 1977). In fact, Seikaly argues that Islamic revivalism in Bahrain has politicized gender by giving women the responsibility of transmitting traditions, morality, social values, and family values through the generations (1998, as cited in Strobl 2008). Hence, political ideologies of power are defined by culture.

Work Ideologies

Work ideologies of the early 1900s dictated that women did not work outside of the home, or at least wealthy women did not. Women who worked outside of the home were stigmatized as somehow defective. When women worked, they were required to engage in women's work. This relegated women to domestic work, such as nannies, schoolteachers working with young children, nurses, cooks, seamstresses, house cleaners, or boarding-house keepers or staff. Victorian Era ideologies of womanhood defined women as fragile and in need of protection, which resulted in many "protective laws" that oppressed women. These laws restricted the types of positions that women could take and the amount of money that they could earn. Laws in the U.S. prohibited women from working in men's jobs, such as in mining and bartending (Lehrer 1987). In 1873, the U.S. Supreme Court ruled that women could not practice law (*Bradwell v. Illinois* 1873). Laws also prohibited women from working more than eight hours a day and from working at night. Also prohibited was the lifting of objects weighing sometimes as little as 15 pounds. We find similar protective restrictions for women around the world, as discussed in Chapter 1.

The work of women police is still predominantly limited to women's work. In many full democracies, where it is assumed that women have gained equality and women have been integrated into the police force, there is still a lot of pressure for women to work with child and female victims of violence (Garcia 2017). The Indian Female Police Unit (FPU) and Bahrain's Women's Police Directorate work predominantly with women and child victims, offenders, and prisoners. The FPU also works with family disputes, especially in dealing with dowry disputes and domestic violence (Mallicoat and Ireland 2014).

Religious Ideologies

Early religious ideologies developed separate spheres for men and women that are intact today. Men were defined as leaders and financial providers for their families. They often painted women as temptresses who needed strict control lest they seduce males toward evil. In early Christian doctrine, women embodied Eve and, therefore, had an innate ability to tempt men. As a result, women were required to be obedient to their husband's authority (Ephesians 5:22–23). Early Buddhism also defined women as temptresses.

Buddhism defined women as evil incarnate with sexual drives not possessed by men (Paul 1985).

The impurity of women, including sexual impurity, has been a focus of many religions (Young 1987). As such, women needed to be guided in the way they dressed and with whom they associated. Women were also required to be obedient to their fathers and husbands. Judaism places great importance on the family but places the husband as central. In early Judaism, women were considered impure because of their menstruation. As a result, they could not hold religious positions. Under Confucianism, men dominated the family, and women were required to be subordinate. In early Hinduism, the subordination of women required that they walk behind their husbands and could not own property. In most religions today, male children are valued over female children to varying degrees.

In Muslim societies, laws are often based on Islamic law, also called *shari'a* law. Islamic law dictates that the public sphere is reserved for men and the private sphere of the family is reserved for women. The honor and reputation of the family is based on the honor and chastity of the women. Within many Islamic nations in the MENA today, women face oppressive laws. Many conservative religious leaders argue that gender equality is "un-Islamic" (Weaver 2007). Until the 2010s, the only nation in that region to give women rights in work and politics was Tunisia (Paxton and Hughes 2007). Examining other major religions of the world, we can find similar depictions of the subordination of women.

Whether or not a nation's government claims separation from religion, we know that religious ideologies are deeply embedded within every culture and government. This is largely unexamined within most Christian dominant nations. The research does not acknowledge religious influence on the work of women in most Western industrialized nations. Much of what is studied today involves nations with strong Islamic influence. As noted, Islamic revival has given women the political role of preserving tradition and the family (Strobl 2008). However, in an effort to increase gender equity, some Islamic nations have recently started giving some labor rights to women (Chu 2020). Yet, we see that many nations still require women police to do women's work. Typically, police forces within Islamic nations stress the importance of religion in molding their role. Within non-Islamic nations, women's "inherent" nurturing skill is the reason used to require women police to do women's work.

Men and Gender Ideologies

These same ideologies delegate various roles to men. Men in society are relegated to the public sphere. Men are required to work to financially support the family. In early 1900s U.S., the male was required to control his family since he was legally responsible for the actions of his wife and children. For example, if a wife was found violating alcohol laws, he could ultimately be held responsible. Any violation of the law or social rules by his children was also his responsibility. As a result, the courts allowed, even expected, the husband/father to keep strict control of his wife and children, even if through physical chastisement (*Bradley v. State* 1824; *State v. Oliver* 1879).

Men and women who did not follow these gender roles, who did not do gender, faced rejection and sometimes criminal charges (Keitner 2002; West and Fenstermaker 1993). In the U.S. and Europe, a woman was socially ostracized if she did not marry at a socially acceptable age. She was labeled a spinster and was considered unmarriageable. This then limited her economic opportunities. Additionally, women were not hired for jobs that were considered men's work and if they were hired within a male-dominated field, they worked as subordinates or support staff to men. As discussed, protective laws were often put in place to ensure that women were safe from the harms of the public sphere. Later, women who did the same work were given lower wages and were often denied promotions. Today, the U.S. Bureau of Labor Statistics (2020) reported that in the first quarter of 2020, women earned 80.4 percent of men's earning for the same work. This earnings gap is different for different racial groups. Women are substantially underrepresented in highly prestigious jobs that are often relegated to men. In Nepal, women working in manufacturing (man's work) earn 45 percent of men's wages (United Nations 2012). However, in Australia, Bahrain, Iran, the Philippines, and Bermuda, women working in manufacturing earn 90 percent or more of men's wages, while in Paraguay this differential is 108 percent. In what follows, I discuss the masculinity of policing and how this affected women's entry.

From Ideology to Practice: Police Culture and Institutionalized Masculinity

Many studies begin with an examination of police culture without placing this occupational subculture within the larger context of the societal culture. I have spent a lot of time up to this point focusing on gender ideologies in general and women in work in particular. I opened the chapter by briefly examining the nature of policing. However, to understand the conditions of women in this occupation, we must first examine how masculinity is institutionalized within policing.

Steve Herbert (2001) described the police organization as a place where men can express their masculinity. Among the expressions of masculinity within the police subculture we find danger, violence, including the possession and use of guns, bravery, athleticism, controlling spaces, tactical skills, and power. The danger and violence in policing is both real and perceived, and officers who subscribe to these ideals are identified as masculinists. As we think about violence in the world, we find this behavior equated with masculinity the world over. Furthermore, men need to be aggressive in order to engage in violence. The perception of violence may become a reality when an officer is confronted with a hostile or resisting suspect. Therefore, officers need the aggressiveness that enables them to apprehend suspects in situations that require violence. This violence can be expressed via brute force. Since men are the protectors and the physically stronger sex, they are perceived as most capable of using violence. Officers must possess the athleticism and physical agility needed to take down a strong suspect. It is not uncommon to find that officers, especially younger officers, are skilled in boxing or martial arts. Furthermore, the screening process searches for candidates who possess these skills of physical agility, which often includes military experience. The recruitment process further trains police in the tactical skills necessary to physically apprehend resistant and violent suspects.

Violence is also expressed with the use of guns. Using a gun has always been equated with masculinity. We see that in most early cultures, men were the hunters, initially using primitive tools, then knifes, and finally guns. Gender ideologies declare that carrying a gun and firing a gun is man's work. Therefore, policing is defined as man's work. Police academies train officers how to properly and effectively handle a gun. While police go through their careers, they must also requalify for firearms proficiency on a regular basis. Additionally, as police move through the ranks to more specialized crime fighting units, they may be required to learn to use automatic weapons more in line with military-style fighting. Regardless of how often police use their firearms, it is not uncommon to find them practicing their gun skills at government or private firing ranges.

Violence within policing is reiterated at roll call, in training, around the station house, and during off-duty gatherings. Expressing masculinity within policing is accomplished via the telling of "war stories" that convey to new recruits the dangers of policing involving violence and guns. However, the telling of war stories is not limited to on-the-clock interaction. It is common for police to continue their masculine expressions during off-duty shooting practice and at various points of convergence, such as bars and BBQs. The off-duty interactions typically include fellow officers and work to reinforce value systems within the police subculture. Ultimately, officers who wield these skills are able to demonstrate their power.

Controlling spaces involves defining and coding neighborhoods as dangerous or safe. The more dangerous a location is or is perceived to be, the more anti-police attitudes and violence an officer will find among its inhabitants and the more aggression and bravery the officer is required to display. Herbert (2001) found that masculinist officers tend to see dangerous spaces as more attractive to "real" policing because it allows them to demonstrate their prowess as crime fighters. In order to do this, however, the officer must control the space and the people within it. The more dangerous the space the more opportunity the officer has to test his masculinity and the more his status is elevated. Officers who seek to patrol safer neighborhoods are placed lower on the status hierarchy.

Herbert argues, "policing is mythologized as a test of agility, strength and tenacity" (2001, p. 59). This mythology can be found in two ironies within policing, as stressed by Herbert and supported by other researchers. First, aggression and violence is rarely needed in most police work (Herbert 2001). Research has long discovered that approximately 1 percent of police work may be too physically demanding for women (Bell 1982; Lehtinen 1976; Sherman 1973). If one examines policing closely, an 80–20 rule is uncovered (Garcia 2003). The majority of police work, approximately 80 percent or more, involves social work type jobs that Herbert describes as peacekeeping, while the rest of police work involves crime fighting. Maher (1984) claimed that crime fighting only represented 2 percent of police activity. Crime fighting is even less likely to occur in jurisdictions that are rural. In fact, Wilmore and Davis (1979) found that the sedentary nature of policing decreases one's physical fitness.

The second irony revealed by Herbert is that female officers are as effective as males. Although women initially entered policing under the flag of doing gender, research has revealed that they are as effective as male officers are. The National Center for Women and Policing (2002) found that male officers are more than eight times more likely to be accused of excessive force. Lonsway, Wood, and Spillar (2002) found that women were less likely to have citizen complaints filed against them, less likely to have sustained allegations, and less likely to have civil suits for excessive use of force. Women are more likely to use negotiation skills to defuse conflict, whereas men are more likely to escalate situations in a show of authority resulting in a greater use of force (Brown 1984; Morin et al. 2017; National Center for Women and Policing 2002). Foster (2009) found that while male and female officers used the same amount of verbal aggression, female officers were more likely to consider alternatives to violence.

Regardless of the research findings, masculinist officers reject the very presence of female officers because the reduced use of force to accomplish the job most likely threatens their masculinity (Herbert 2001). Messerschmidt's (2016) structured action theory on masculinities can be used to argue that the presence of women in policing makes it harder for men to construct a hegemonic masculinity. Hunt (1984) argues that in rejecting women in policing, male police are able to preserve the myth of police work and masculinity. She writes:

> Symbolically, then, she reminds him that he can only achieve illusory manhood by denying and repressing the essential feminine dimension of police work which involves social relations, paper work, and housekeeping in the public domain.
>
> (Hunt 1984, p. 294)

Returning to the discussion on social constructionism, constructs of gender within policing are reflections of gender constructions within the larger society. Following Ellwanger's (2015) argument, the very people recruited into the occupation are predisposed to holding these police values but also learn them on the job through occupational socialization. However, these ideologies have their foundations in history. Historical facts that have influenced policing as a gendered organization are the European colonization and Ottoman conquering of much of the world.

The Ottoman Empire and Colonial Influence on Policing

Police forces in most nations have their foundations in colonialism of the nineteenth century (Cole 1998). However, before European colonization, the Ottoman Empire (1299–1922) ruled a large part of the eastern world. The Ottoman Empire was an Islamic power founded around 1299 by Anatolian Turkish tribe leader Osman I (Finkel 2005). For over 600 years, the Ottoman Empire controlled nations in the Middle East, Eastern Europe, and North Africa. The Ottoman Empire conquered the Byzantine Empire and took control of its capital, Istanbul, in 1453. Nations under Ottoman control included Bulgaria, Egypt, Greece, Hungary, Jordan, Lebanon, Macedonia, Palestine, Romania, Syria, parts of Arabia, Turkey, and much of the coastal strip of North Africa. Scholars claim that the Ottoman Turk rulers were tolerant of non-Islamic religions. However, between the 1300s and 1600s, the *devshirme* system took 20 percent of Christian males, converted them, and enslaved them. These slaves served in the Ottoman military and government and many became powerful and wealthy.

Early Ottoman police had its foundation on *shari'a* law (Swanson 1972). The Ottoman police force was nationalized under the control of the Sultan. Security was made up of civil and military officers (Janissaries) who had police powers. Religious leaders also had police obligations over the public's morality. In many Ottoman-ruled countries, Janissaries maintained a strict military presence. However, they were eliminated, in part, in the 1826 European invasion and colonization of Ottoman territories. By 1870, the police became a separate ministry, and police stations were formed in 1880. Ottoman territories organized the police in two ways. Police such as in Istanbul became civil, while other nations such as Palestine and Syria maintained a military control of police (i.e., gendarmerie). However, some like Macedonia found that police were more effective in larger jurisdictions. The Ottoman Empire did not colonialize the way European nations did. Instead, they maintained strict rule through military and government presence. With the invasion and colonization by the European powers, the Ottoman Empire lost most of its power by the mid-1800s. Many of the Ottoman-controlled countries adapted to the European forms of policing.

However, we see a strong influence of *shari'a* law within the government and police structure within some Arab nations.

The British, French, Portuguese, and Spanish colonized most of the world by the 1800s and created police forces in order to protect their economic interests. Colonies annexed for the purpose of settlement typically created civilian police forces. Colonies annexed for the purpose of trade typically created paramilitary police forces in order to pacify the Indigenous peoples. Civilian police forces were established in German European settlements of Windhoek and Swakopmund in Namibia (Bley 1971); in French settlements of Algeria, Cochin-China (South Vietnam), Senegal, French Equatorial Africa, New Caledonia and New Hebrides; in the Spanish settlement of Santiago, Chile; in the Portuguese settlement of Rio de Janeiro, Brazil; and in the British settlements of East and West Africa (see Cole for a detailed discussion of colonial and postcolonial policing throughout the world). The civilian police forces, however, were more dominant in North America, Canada, and Australia.

Police forces in colonies annexed for trade purposes worked to pacify the colonies and resembled a paramilitary model (Cole 1998; Zollmann 2020). Here, we see the transnational transmission of Victorian ideals of womanhood most strongly. Police forces in trade colonies recruited officers from the imperial armies, mostly in Africa and Latin America. These police forces protected the European colonies and financial interests from African control. In many colonies, the distinction between the police and the military was blurred. For example, French West African police performed military functions in lieu of the military. Police worked to pacify the people of the Sahara region and Northeastern Chad. In African and Caribbean British colonies, the paramilitary police replaced the imperial armies. The police force in German colonies in Southwest Africa were required to undergo military training and were under the control of the army. In fact, police forces not under military control often worked in collaboration with the military within these trade colonies in order to suppress dissent and control warring tribes. Additionally, the Berlin Conference of 1884–1885 required that European powers no longer tolerate dissent from Africans.

During the end of colonization, however, civilian models of policing increased. This occurred after colonists were pacified and the colonies were well established. In one model of civilian policing, traditional authorities controlled the police under the supervision of colonial administrators. Some examples include French Indo-China and British Northern Nigeria. In the second more popular civilian police model, colonial loyalists were given the power to appoint police. Some examples include most of the British Empire, German East Africa, Fascist Ethiopia, and some of Spanish Latin America. However, as Cole (1998) points out, controlling insurrection was not the only duty of the police as there was a lot of crime in places like Santiago, Chile, Rio de Janeiro, and French Equatorial Africa.

The economic considerations linked with colonialism were the predominant causes of the crime problems in the colonies around the world. Concessionaires and chartered companies often played a large role in the development of police forces. Cole (1998) provides examples of many companies involved with policing, including the Royal Niger Company, the East India Company, and the British South Africa Company. These companies had exclusive rights over agricultural, forest, and industrial exploitation in exchange for building roads and maintaining law and order. These companies would develop police forces that were often paramilitary in nature. Thus, much of policing worked to control the laboring classes. Illegal raids, pillaging and extortion, corruption and brutality were common in the colonies (see Banda 1971 for a discussion).

During decolonization of the 1940s and 1950s, police mostly engaged in riot control. Postcolonialsim, many of the nations maintained the paramilitary structure of policing. Former French, Portuguese, and Spanish colonies often developed decentralized police structures. In West and North Africa, Brazil, and Mexico, paramilitary units exist. Former British colonies, however, followed the centralized model, such as in Africa and India. Countries formerly under British rule often have local police forces that are under the control of a national police force. Bringing this discussion back to our focus on women in policing, the over reliance on the military and the transmission of Victorian Era ideals of womanhood provide evidence of a history of male-dominated police organizations. So, how do some of these nations incorporate women into policing today? A review of the limited research on early history of women in policing around the world provides some answers.

Early History of Women in Police Work

Women throughout the world joined police forces in similar fashions. They often joined in order to provide moral guidance and protection to women and children, as was demonstrated in Boxes 1.1–3, Box 2.1, and Figure 2.2. This was believed to be something that policemen, because of their gender, could not accomplish. In Germany, the U.S., and the U.K., women joined police organizations in the early 1900s. In 1903, Germany was the first nation to hire women in the capacity of policewomen. In the U.S., the Portland, Oregon police department hired the first female "safety worker" in 1905. However, in 1910, Los Angeles, California was the first to hire a policewoman. The U.K. hired the first policewoman in 1919. As we will see, policewomen did not have the same powers and responsibilities as policemen. In fact, this was a common pattern in most countries upon women's first entry into the police force. Many countries still reflect this gendered structure.

Researchers have identified similar phases or eras of women's roles within policing in the U.S. and the U.K. (Martin 1980; Schulz 1995; Heidensohn

Figure 2.2 Training a Policewoman—Chief among the Policewoman's Duties Is the Prevention of Delinquency among Young Girls.

Source: Photograph. www.loc.gov/pictures/item/96514628/. Photo in the public domain.

1992). The period between 1840 and 1910 was a time in which women entered policing under moral reform. During this time, policewomen worked as matrons, often in jails, and rescued women, children, and the homeless from the dreads of society as well as from themselves. In the next phase, from around 1910/15 until around 1930, policewomen worked as specialists and pioneers (Martin 1980). At this time, women were being hired with the title of policewoman and worked with special populations—again women, children, and the homeless. It was not uncommon for special women's police units to be established. In the U.S. by the 1920s, there were 417 policewomen employed within 210 cities. However, 355 remained employed as matrons. During the Great Depression, employment was harder to come by and was more likely to be reserved for men. Researchers have labeled this period in policing (1930–1945) the latent era (Schulz 1995). During this era, the hiring of policewomen did not occur in large numbers. Schulz claims that the stagnation was greatly influenced by the Great Depression. However, Martin (1980) extended the latent era until 1970 since women did not make much progress within policing.

Between 1945 and 1970, the U.S. and the U.K. saw what is termed an informal expansion. Hiring policewomen was not a result of any organized push or the crusade of moral entrepreneurs. In the U.S., by 1950, there were 2,610 policewomen (Belknap 2015). By the 1970s, however, we start to see an awakening of the Women's Movement into policing as well as a change in their roles. Schulz (1995) labeled this the integration phase (1970–present). Within the U.S., passage of Title VII in 1972 opened the gates of opportunity for women in the workforce. This also reflected the second wave of the Women's Movement (1960s–1980s). The result was that women moved into policing in the U.K., the U.S., and West Germany with the full powers of an officer and wore uniforms, carried firearms, had arrest powers, and worked all crime types. During this era of women in policing, the *policewoman* became the *woman police* (Barlow and Barlow 2000). However, not all nations' police forces experienced the integration phase in the 1970s or at any point (Natarajan 2008; Strobl 2010, 2020). In 1977, Lewis Sherman published a survey of police departments in 46 nations. He found that within most of the nations surveyed, by the 1970s, policewomen still served a subservient and gendered role within policing. In the following sections, I outline women's role in policing through the 1970s.

Policewomen in Europe

The subservient gendered role was found in many European nations in the 1970s (Sherman 1977). Within Denmark's National Police Department, policewomen made up 3 percent of the police force. They did not wear uniforms and were assigned special duties that did not require physical strength. They worked with women and children charged with sex or drug offenses and handled family matters such as visitation rights and child abuse and neglect. Finnish policewomen in the 1970s held the lowest ranks and were rarely promoted. They worked minor crimes as well as sex crimes against women and children. Eighty seven percent of French policewomen in the 1970s were equivalent to the U.S. "meter maid." The other 13 percent only worked with women and children. In 1970s Italy, women had not yet made the ranks of policewoman. They were hired as police assistants and engaged in traditional women's work.

Ireland was one nation in Europe that had a more progressive stance on policewomen in the 1970s. Ireland's police force, known as *An Garda Siochana*, first hired policewomen (*bangharda*) in 1959 to guard the streets of Dublin. *Bangharda* wore uniforms and engaged in the same work as policemen but were often called to engage in specialized work involving women and children (i.e., women's work). Although they were considered equals, *bangharda* were paid less than policemen were. Similar to Ireland, Poland hired policewomen to engage in all of the same duties as policemen. However, like all other nations, they also specialized in crimes involving women and children. In the Netherlands, policewomen were first hired in 1930 as equals to their male counterparts. However, they experienced discrimination in hiring and promotion since they were held to a higher educational requirement and were restricted from the police college. Sweden, a nation known for gender equality today, did not distinguish the duties of men and women giving policewomen a wide array of duties. However, following gender role ideologies, Sweden's National Police Board believed that only policewomen could properly execute the searching and examination of women and children. As a result, every district was required to have policewomen available.

Switzerland, due to the fragmentation of its cultures and governments, had regional differences in how policewomen were utilized. In French-speaking Geneva, Lausanne, and Canton of Vaud, policewomen in the 1970s worked primarily as social assistants, dealing with children and moral crimes. In Canton of Vaud, policewomen also served as judicial clerks and secretaries. In German-speaking Zurich, women were known as police hostesses (*polzeihostess*) and were used primarily to control and manage traffic. This also applied to policewomen in Bern, Switzerland. In Italian-speaking Tessin, policewomen served as clerical assistants to the police department and to male officers.

Policewomen in Austria, Czechoslovakia, and the German Democratic Republic (East Germany) were employed mainly as clerical staff in the 1970s. However, Austrian policewomen as well as those in Spain were also employed to work in detention centers. Spanish and Icelandic policewomen also worked traffic control. Policewomen in Malta had expanded duties that involved price enforcement and they worked with female prisoners.

Turkey first hired policewomen in 1933. In 1934, Turkish women were emancipated. Policewomen, who were initially hired as secretaries, were given equal status to policemen. Yet again, as with many nations by the 1970s, whether by formal policy or informal practice, Turkish policewomen tended to specialize with juvenile and female offenders and educational and crime prevention programs. Additionally, as is still common in many Third World nations, policewomen in 1970s Turkey were restricted from physically hard work.

Policewomen in Asia and Oceania

Australia hired the first policewoman in 1915 (Wilkinson and Froyland 1996). At that time, they were not sworn officers and did not wear uniforms. They also worked as specialists dealing with women and children. By the 1970s, conditions for the policewoman had not changed much. For example, in South Wales, slightly more than half of the 105 policewomen in 1977 wore uniforms but did not carry firearms or handcuffs. The majority of their duties included traffic near schools and lecturing children and adults on safety.

In New Zealand, policewomen first joined the force in 1941. Their duties primarily entailed clerical work. However, in 1952, they were given uniforms and weapons. Moreover, by 1958, women were qualified to work as detectives. While New Zealand's police force was legislated as an equal and progressive organization, an internal investigation in 1973 revealed a quota system for policewomen and practices of "male protectionism" which limited policewomen's ability to obtain equal work and equal pay.

Iran was considered to have one of the most progressive police forces in the 1970s in relation to policewomen. Policewomen were hired using the same criteria as were used for policemen. They also experienced promotion and retirement on the same basis as policemen and were given most of the same responsibilities as policemen. However, as was common in the 1970s, they were restricted from general patrol.

Women started to join the Israeli police force in numbers in 1960. By 1972, Israel stood as the nation with the most policewomen (12.5 percent). It was reported that policewomen were given the same duties as policemen. Policewomen were also assigned to the special paramilitary unit. Moreover, policewomen made up 90 percent of the force's traffic police (see Figure 2.3).

Japanese women first joined the police occupation in 1946 and engaged in traffic and juvenile work. By the late 1970s, Japanese policewomen were still predominantly working in traffic and as guardians of schoolchildren. They also worked as emergency dispatchers and patrolled department stores and other crowded locations in order to curtail theft. Policewomen assisted policemen during riots in order to search and question female suspects. In the 1970s, it was still commonly believed that policewomen could not handle strenuous and dangerous jobs. However, they were presented as a very attractive face of the police in public areas.

Policewomen in Sri Lanka, China, the Republic of Korea (South Korea), and the Philippines worked predominantly in traffic. However, Philippine policewomen carried firearms in the 1970s. Sri Lankan policewomen were tasked with stationhouse duty working with female and juvenile offenders. South Korean policewomen also investigated crimes committed by women and engaged in childcare. Policewomen in India and Indonesia specialized in juvenile delinquency and moral crimes. Thai policewomen similarly worked with cases involving women. Jordanian policewomen in the 1970s had an extended duty working in customs. Jordanian policewomen, as well as Malaysian policewomen, also worked as prison matrons similar to the 1840s U.S. matrons. Finally, Pakistani policewomen worked traffic, vice, and social services. They were able to obtain command positions. However, Pakistani policewomen worked mostly with women and children.

Policewomen in Africa

There is not much research on policewomen in Africa. Policewomen were not employed in South Africa until 1972. Unlike many nations, policewomen were given the same duties as were policemen, including general

Figure 2.3 Israeli Policewoman, 1968.

Source: Photo used with permission from the Israel Police Heritage Center.

patrol. While policewomen on patrol were always partnered with policemen, patrol duty was not common for most policewomen in the 1970s. They also carried firearms and served in uniform and plainclothes capacities. The research also shows that there was no distinction in the hiring, promotion, or assignment of policewomen in Kenya in the 1970s. However, in Ghana, policewomen in the 1970s worked predominantly with females and juveniles as well as traffic duty. Finally, Zambian police created a women's unit in order to handle cases involving females and juveniles, including assisting with probation evaluations. Zambian policewomen also engaged in traffic duty.

Policewomen in the Americas

Canada's police system is complicated because of its British and French influences. In the 1970s, French-speaking Montreal still had very few policewomen. In British-influenced Toronto, policewomen were employed since the early 1900s. Hiring criteria were the same for men and women in Toronto, and they received the same training. However, while policewomen were given firearms training, they did not carry guns in the 1970s. Most policewomen worked in special women's bureaus where they handled crimes committed by and against children. Toronto policewomen in the 1970s were also tasked with community relations concerns and complaints and information services. However, quotas kept the numbers to 60 constables and 10 cadets. Policewomen in British Columbia Vancouver were hired to engage in the same tasks as were policemen. They engaged in investigations and apprehension but were tasked with handling women and children. They also engaged in general patrol and escorting all prisoners.

In Uruguay, policewomen served in their womanly capacity in the 1920s. They investigated crimes and complaints in which women were believed to be most qualified. In 1966, Montevideo developed a women's police corps. During tourist season, policewomen assisted tourists. During the rest of the year, they engaged in general police duties. In Caracas, Venezuela, by the 1970s a special unit called the Female Metropolitan Police was in operation. Within this unit, policewomen engaged in traffic and parking control, worked as school police and guarded all areas of mass transportation. Coracan policewomen also investigated crimes of vice and drugs involving women and children. However, because of their feminine vulnerability, their work hours were restricted. In Argentina, policewomen were tasked with the operation of orphanages. Colombian policewomen in the 1970s were social workers in that they engaged in childcare and monitored children's books. Jamaica had a progressive police force in the 1970s in which policewomen were integrated with policemen and were given the same duties as were policemen.

Conclusion

Women entered policing with the expectation that they should do gender and that meant working assignments congruent to women's role in the family. As such, early policewomen helped to preserve political ideologies that also maintained the culture's patriarchal structure. However, the question remains, have women truly integrated into policing? That is, are policewomen today viewed and treated as women police, as equals to male police? As Strobl (2020) and Natarajan (2008) argue, within many societies, integration does not fit with the dominant culture, and this must be recognized. As we move forward to the present day, one must wonder of nations that do not have integrated systems: is integration too out of line with those cultures or is it a matter that these nations have not yet reached integration similar to pre-1970s policing of the U.S. and the U.K.? Integration can be defined as encompassing one's role and the duties assigned to women police or it can be seen as the acceptance of women police as equals regardless of their work duties. While I give some focus to the integration versus specialist/segregation models, my primary focus is the equality and equity of women police throughout the world. In the following chapters, I examine current police practices and structures around the globe.

Chapter 3

Past and Current Status of Women Police in the Eastern Hemisphere

As a gendered organization, police forces worldwide have historically opposed the recruitment and integration of women. Chapter 2 ended by asking if women have truly integrated into policing. Integration into policing through a Western lens refers to women joining policing and experiencing gender equality in access and power while engaging in the same police activities as men. Jennifer Brown (1997) developed a model of integration for England and Wales that extended Heidensohn (1992), Martin (1980), and Schulz's (1995) analyses of the eras of women in policing in the U.S. and the U.K.

In Brown's early integration model, she argued that women entered in stages that included entry into the field, "separation"/restricted development, integration mandated more by law, "take-off," true organizational reform, and finally "tip-over" from minority status to gender balance (1997). Separation involved women joining policing as specialists in women's work, such as working with women and children. In her model, after a time of separation, women win recognition as capable officers and earn a level of equality and rank through legal mechanisms but only with token status. After a time of integration, the profession moves into the take-off stage in which the courts reject gender discrimination. This leads to the reform stage in which organizations undergo true reform when they are willing to allow outsiders into the ranks. Finally, women are truly integrated when they achieve a gender balance in the tip-over stage.

Brown refers to Ott's argument that women gain critical mass when they represent 20–25 percent of the police force (Ott 1989, as cited in Brown 1997). However, Brown later recognizes that the tip-over stage has not yet been achieved (Brown and Silvestri 2020). Additionally, in response to criticisms of the idea of integration, Brown and Silvestri stress that Brown's model was developed to examine women police in England and Wales. This model can be applied to many Western countries like the U.S. However, it does not apply to many countries with different political systems and cultural gender role definitions.

As we learn from research in Bahrain (Strobl 2020), India (Natarajan 2008), or China (Shen 2020), integration is not as simplistic as one might think. Cultural, religious, social, and political edicts in some nations do not lend to thinking that women *should* be integrated. Strobl (2020) argues that any model of integration must be country specific and circular instead of linear. Any integration model must take into account resistance and backslide. Strobl's circular model of gender integration of policewomen focused on the Arabian Golf, stressing that the movement of women flows theoretically from "no policewomen, entry of policewomen into the field, the implementation of gender-segregated units, and then, if conservative lawmakers were to prevail at a future date, back to no policewomen again" (2020, p. 60).

Studying women police in India, Natarajan (2008) found that many Indian women police have internalized negative perceptions of women in policing, resulting in a preference to remain in separate specialized women's police roles. Natarajan concluded that the police department should reconsider policies and attempts to integrate women and focus on gender-specific duties. Shen (2020) also argues for caution in assuming that integration is desirable in every country. Particularly, she found that China does not embrace gender equality. Her research found that many women were happy with their gender-specific duties with no eye to full integration. More importantly, however, as an authoritarian nation, women are legally restricted from integration, and there are no demands for reform, as the government tends to crush activism. Similarly, Chu (2020) found that Strobl's circular model of gender integration is more applicable to Arab nations such as the UAE.

Given the complexity of integration and separation, we must look more closely at the various nations' form of policing and how they came to include women in policing. This requires an examination of the political climate, the culture, and, in some instances, the religion of the nation. Because there is little research on women in policing around the world, nonexistent in many nations, this examination will be selective of the nations included. I will focus on countries where research is available in English but also examine countries that fall into each category of the democracy index on each continent as defined by The Economist (2020): full democracies, flawed democracies, hybrid regimes, and authoritarian regimes. Chapter 2 described the barriers that women police encountered within each continent through the 1970s. This chapter examines the historical progression of women into policing throughout the world, giving focus to the structure of policing in the nation and the historical events that led to women entering into the field. The current conditions of women police will then be discussed.

There are about 54 counties on the African continent, 44 in Asia, 47 in Europe, 23 countries in North and Central America, 12 in South America, and 14 in Oceania. Note that The Economist refers to the latter region as

Australasia. Unlike Chapter 2, nations in this chapter will be discussed by region. It has long been argued that the quality of democracy brings fuller political rights, especially for women (UN Women 2011a; Walsh 2012). Using The Economist's (2020) research on democracy in the world, I examine women in policing using the following seven world regions: Asia and Oceania, MENA, Sub-Saharan Africa, Eastern Europe, Western Europe, Latin America and the Caribbean, and North America. In order to give enough focus to each region, I divide the examination to the Eastern and Western Hemispheres. This chapter will examine women in policing in the Eastern Hemisphere. I begin the discussion with Asia and Oceania.

Asia and Oceania

In 2019, The Economist (2020) was able to gather data for 167 nations; 28 of the nations were in the Asia and Oceania regions (see Table 3.1). Only Oceania had democracies (Australia and New Zealand). Most of the nations were found to be flawed democracies (14), with five hybrid regimes, and eight authoritarian regimes. Since 2018, Thailand made the biggest change in democracy moving from a hybrid regime to a flawed democracy, while India's democracy rank dropped ten places. The major democratic problem for this region was in the erosion of civil liberties. China's score also fell substantially and is close to the bottom of the democracy index (153 out of 167). Political instability alongside violent protests in Hong Kong has also had a dramatic impact on the region's democracy index.

Table 3.2 shows 2017 statistics for women police gathered by the United Nations Office of Drugs and Crime (UNODC) (2020). Among the nations with available data within this region, only Australia (32 percent) has reached the tip-over stage. It is also the only full democracy. Communist Macao, China with over half a million people employs more women police (19 percent) than most nations around the world.

Table 3.1 Democracy Regimes in Asia and Oceania

Regime type	*Country*
Full democracy	Australia, New Zealand
Flawed democracy	Hong Kong, India, Indonesia, Japan, Malaysia, Mongolia, Papua New Guinea, Philippines, Singapore, South Korea, Sri Lanka, Taiwan, Thailand, Timor-Leste
Hybrid regimes	Bangladesh, Bhutan, Fiji, Pakistan, Nepal
Authoritarian regimes	Afghanistan, Cambodia, China, Laos, Myanmar, North Korea, Vietnam

Source: The Economist. 2020. Democracy Index 2019. *A Year of Democratic Setbacks and Popular Protest*. New York: The Economist Intelligence Unit Limited.

Table 3.2 Women Police in Asia and Oceania, 2015 (UNODC)

Country	*Regime*	*Number*	*Percent*
Australia	Full	20,301	32%
Macao (China)	Authoritarian	1,212	19%
Singapore	Flawed	1,671	18%
Timor-Leste	Flawed	589	16%
Republic of Korea	Flawed	11,047	10%
Myanmar	Authoritarian	4,432	6%

Source: United Nations Office of Drugs and Crime. 2020. *Administration of justice*. www.unodc.org/unodc/en/data-and-analysis/statistics/crime.html (accessed May 11, 2020).

Full Democracy: Tip Over Is Not Equality in Australia

Australia is a predominantly Christian nation with an ethnic makeup of 25.9 percent English and 25.4 percent Australian people (Pew Research Center 2020; Central Intelligence Agency 2020). Australia is a federal parliamentary democracy under a constitutional monarchy. The British took possession of the east coast of the continent in 1770 and colonized Western Australia in 1829. Australia was initially a penal colony. British troops guarded Australia not only from external attack but also from convict uprisings and Aboriginal resistance (Pierson and Chaudhuri 1998; Grey 2008). In 1825, the British established the Mounted Police to control the frontier (Woollacott 2015). This police force was paramilitary and very violent in keeping down uprisings. From 1839 to 1847, the Border Police controlled remote lands and was even more brutal. While the Mounted Police were usually military, the Border Police were often unpaid convicts who wore no uniform. In the 1840s, the British also established the Native Police, who were predominantly Aboriginal men with excellent tracking skills. Australia finally gained independence in 1901. Today, Australia has the Australian Federal Police (a.k.a., Commonwealth Police Force) and seven state/territory controlled police forces (Kurian 2006).

The first women were appointed to the police force in 1915 in the New South Wales Police Force and the South Australia Police Force. The Victoria, Western Australia, and Tasmania Police Forces quickly followed this move in 1917 (Fleming 2020). Queensland did not hire its first female officer until 1931, and the Australian Federal Police (AFP) hired women in 1947. It was not until 1961 that the Northern Territory Police Force hired the first five women (Archer 1965). By 1964, there were 206 women police in Australia with the largest number in the Victoria (60) and South Australia Police Forces (45). Women were hired, as with most countries, in response to the shortage of men during World War I and to protect and handle women and children. Although women police of the 1920s were involved in serious crimes such as rape and murder, most of their cases involved abandonment of children, bigamy, and larceny involving women and children (Higgs and Bettess 1987). The 1965 Commonwealth Year Book reported that women performed "special duties at places where young women and girls are subject to moral danger, control traffic at school crossings, and lecture school children on road safety" (Archer 1965, p. 643). Women also served in support roles to male police. The Year Book also lists female searchers, wardresses, and interpreters among women police.

Today, women in Australian law enforcement are integrated into mainstream policing roles. However, statistics reveal that women are still viewed as moral officers better at administrative, non-dangerous work. The UNODC found that women represented 32 percent of Australian police forces in 2017 (United Nations Office of Drugs and Crime 2020). By 2019, the AFP employed 773 (32.7 percent) female police officers. This represented 15.6 percent of the entire AFP (Australian Federal Police 2019). In total, women represented 13.3 percent of protective services within the federal arm but 37 percent of the total non-police staff. In Queensland, women represented 30 percent of all constables in 2017 but 68.8 percent of all public service officers and general employees (Queensland Police Service 2017). These data include 73 percent of all public service officers. Women represented 40 percent of the Tasmania Police Force, the highest percentage in the nation; however, there were only five police personnel within this organization (Australian Federal Police 2019). The data from the other states and territories revealed that women still filled gendered roles. A review of the police websites throughout the nation describes the attributes that women bring to policing, among them good communication skills, good decision-making and analytic skills, ability to diffuse situations, and compassion. Although their numbers have surpassed the tip-over point, their duties reveal that women are not integrated on an equal footing with men. Additionally, research has found that women in general still face discriminatory barriers that keep women in lower ranks, and Indigenous women experience "double tokenism" as women and as racial minorities (Fleming 2020).

Flawed Democracy: Gender-Restricted Roles of Women Police in India

India is the second most populated nation in the world with 1.3 billion people (Central Intelligence Agency 2020). The dominant ethnic groups are Indo-Aryan (72 percent) and Dravidian (25 percent). Hindi is the most common language spoken (43.6 percent) and Hinduism (78.9 percent) and Islamism (15.4 percent) are the most common religions (Pew Research Center 2020; Central Intelligence Agency 2020). India is a federal parliamentary republic that gained independence from the U.K. in 1947. The legal system is based on English common law with judicial review of legislative acts and separate personal laws that apply to Muslims, Christians, and Hindus. During British colonization, India's policing changed from a military organization to a civil model of policing (Hakeem 2008). In 1843, the British borrowed the newly developed Royal Irish Constabulary model for Sindh, so that the police organization would maintain a separate existence from the military and deal with maintaining law and order in the colonies. The police force was also centralized under one officer, the Superintendent. Today's Indian police force is centralized with an armed and unarmed branch in each state. The unarmed police engage in stationhouse and traffic duties, respond to routine complaints, and prevent and investigate crimes. The armed branch engages in crime fighting and civil disobedience activities.

Women entered into policing in 1938 in Kanpur, Uttar Pradesh in order to handle women workers on strike (Aleem 1991). Travancore and Greater Bombay first hired women in 1939 and Kerala in 1943. For the most part, women were hired to handle the growing crimes against women, including kidnappings and safety during riots, as well as to deal with the large numbers of female Pakistani refugees who entered India following the 1947 Partition. Similar to the U.S. and the U.K., the number of women police did not start to increase until the 1960s, though this was negligible. All-Women Police Stations were opened first in Kerala (1973) and then in Madhya Pradesh (1987) and Rajasthan (1979) (Amaral, Bhalotra, and Prakash 2019). By 2013, there were 479 Women Police Stations in India. In the late 1980s, women were still only less than 1 percent of the total police force (Aleem 1991). Furthermore, there were very few who reached higher positions in the hierarchy of the organization.

Women's movement into policing was one of need and legislative requirement. In 1986, India established the Women's Battalion of the Central Reserve Police Force, which is a paramilitary arm that deals with law and order. Requirements to join were the same for men and women, except for the physical requirements. The functions of the Women's Battalion consisted of civil administration in law and order maintenance, controlling female agitators, patrolling riot-hit areas, assisting the armed and unarmed branches in searches, and performing night duties involving guarding, patrolling, and picketing. Women were more likely to serve in the unarmed branches, however. In many cases, women served in the separate women's stations and cells working cases involving women in their jurisdictions, such as dowry deaths, harassment, and sexual assault. Aleem (1991) reported that these stations or cells helped to protect women's rights. However, police, both men and women, commonly believe that some women take advantage of these services by filing false complaints (Aleem 1991; Common Cause 2019).

In 1997, India passed a law requiring women to represent 33 percent of new government hires (Natarajan 2014; Common Cause 2019). Male officers in Tamil Nadu threatened to strike unless women were held to the same conditions and duties as men. As a result, all new recruits were required to complete six years of training in the armed reserve, referred to as the battalion, before they could be assigned full police duties. Tamil Nadu currently employees the largest number of women police in the country. By 2016, women police represented 7.3 percent of the Indian police force nationwide. In the Tamil Nadu Police, they represented 12.9 percent (Common Cause 2019).

The *Status of Policing in India Report 2019* released by Common Cause (2019) found that women police today are more likely to work in-house, while men engage in crime fighting and prevention work in the field. More than half of women and men police reported that women were not treated equally and both sexes were more likely to report that women were not able to perform the job effectively. In her study of Tamil Nadu Police, Natarajan (2014) found that men and women reported no real differences in their actual duties. Both groups were equally interested in the full range of duties but they believed that men were more effective at all police duties except when dealing with cases involving domestic disputes, women and children, and clerical and station duties, i.e., women's work. Natarajan found that as she studied the Tamil Nadu Police over the years, women were increasingly likely to prefer the traditional woman police role. She concluded that while supervisors were trying to meet the goals of integration, they should consider the desires of the women in maintaining a gender-restricted role.

Hybrid Regimes: Reform in Fiji and Bangladesh

Fiji is an island in Oceania with a population of just under one million people (Central Intelligence Agency 2020). The dominant ethnic groups are iTaukei (56.8 percent) and Indo-Fijian (37.5 percent). English and Fijian are the official languages and Christianity (64.4 percent) and Hinduism (27.9 percent) are the dominant religions (Pew Research Center 2020; Central Intelligence Agency 2020). Fiji is a parliamentary republic that obtained independence in 1970 after over 100 years of colonization by the U.K. The legal system is based on the English common law model, and the Fiji Police Force is centralized. There is not much research on women police in Asian and Oceania hybrid regimes. In a 2004 news story, the Police Commissioner was reported as stating that Fiji, with only 10 percent women officers, needed more women to change the "male-dominated organization with macho-culture" (BBC Monitoring Asia Pacific 2004). Fiji's Police Commissioner declared that he would increase women's representation to 25 percent, believing that women would improve the police culture, "It makes for a much healthier organization with a better decision making, compassionate and empathetic management culture, breaking down the negative aspects of a male-dominated hierarchy" (BBC Monitoring Asia Pacific 2004). He also intended to give women frontline police duties, reporting that they played a supportive role. However, research could not be found to examine the results of these promises.

The Fiji Police Force first recruited women police in 1968 in response to pressure to recognize the work that women were doing in the community. In 1968, a pilot project was initiated in which eight women were recruited into the Special Constabulary. By the mid-1970s, women were finally allowed to work in the general police force. In an international review, the only information Prenzler and Sinclair (2013) provided for Fiji was that women represented 19 percent (740) of the police force in 2012. This data showed that the Police Commissioner did in fact follow through with his plans to recruit more women. However, the Fiji Police Force has a long journey to reach integration of women with only 0.7 percent serving at the Inspector level, 1.8 percent as UN peacekeepers, and the majority serving in the lowest levels of policing.

Bangladesh is also a parliamentary republic. The nation gained independence from Pakistan in 1971. However, it was initially colonized by the British (1700–1947), resulting in a mixed English common law and Islamic law system. Bengali (98 percent) is the dominant ethnic group and Islamism (90.8 percent) and Hinduism (8.2 percent) are the dominant religions (Pew Research Center 2020; Central Intelligence Agency 2020). Following the British model, Bangladesh has a centralized police organization. In Pakistan, from which Bangladesh seceded, police recruitment of women began in 1952 (Afroze 2017). This movement did not reach Bangladeshi practice while under Pakistani rule. However, Pakistani women police did not make strong inroads, as they only represented less than 1 percent of the police force by 2015. In Bangladesh, 14 women were appointed to the police force in 1973, and there were 10,000 women police by 2016.

Women police were first hired to serve as security to the wives of the President and Prime Minister (Afroze 2017). Similar to India, Bangladesh enacted quotas. Unlike the quotas of the 1970s, current quotas are often intended to increase women's representation in policing. At higher levels of the police organization, 10 percent of supervisory positions are reserved for women. Fifteen percent are reserved for women at the entry level. The government also initiates recruitment campaigns for other positions when needed. In order to increase retention and job satisfaction for women police, Bangladesh gave women six months maternity leave, established childcare centers in major cities, and prioritized family issues in considering women's assignments. The police force also established a unit to handle workplace sexual harassment.

The Bangladesh police have also improved their responses toward violence against women and children. In Dhaka, the all-female Women Support and Investigation Division was created in 2009. The nation's Police Reform Programme also developed the Community Police Forum and reserved 33 percent of the seats for women. The Police Reform Programme also created the Bangladesh Police Women Forum to give support to women police. Data reveal that since the 1976 Dhaka Metropolitan Police Act was passed, the annual percent increase of women in policing through 2014 was over 100 percent. However, there were still only 6,857 women police. Afroze (2017) found that women were assigned to every police unit. Their duties included traffic, detective and investigative work, supervision, operational units, court security, and UN peacekeeping, yet their representation in nonadministrative work is low. Most women work at the Dhaka Metropolitan Police department where 25 percent of their work involves traffic duty. Only 19 percent engage in crime fighting duties and 13 percent work as peacekeepers for the UN or study abroad. As much as 43 percent work in administrative jobs. These data reveal that Bangladeshi women police have a long way to reach equality and integration.

Authoritarian Regimes: From Inspectors to Women Police in China

China is the most populous nation in the world. A communist nation, China gained independence in 1949 after a civil war between the Nationalist Party and the Chinese Communist Party. China's legal system is civil law influenced by a mix of Soviet and continental European civil law systems, and the legislature has the power to interpret statutes (Central Intelligence Agency 2020). The largest ethnic group is Han Chinese (91.6 percent). Over fifty percent of the population are religiously unaffiliated; however, 21.9 percent of the people follow folk religions and 18.3 percent are Buddhists (Pew Research Center 2020). While current China did not experience mass colonization, the Opium Wars with the British resulted in the end of the Qing Dynasty, colonization of Hong Kong, and trading rights over the ports of Canton and Shanghai (Ma 2008). France, Germany, and Japan also had concessions in Chinese cities and ports. Under these concessions, the European powers were able to establish their own judicial systems and laws. It was at this time that European powers developed modern policing in China. Unlike many of the Western nations, China does not have a police academy. Training involves completing four years at a police university or two years at a technical college.

Women inspectors were first hired in Shanghai in 1919 in response to smuggling (Chan and Ho 2017). Inspectors were not police officers. However, in 1929, Shanghai did hire the first women police (Shen 2020). Women were hired into the Capital Police Department in Nanking in 1931 (Chan and Ho 2017). Beijing hired women in 1932. Also in 1932, four female police officers graduated from the Chekiang Police College. By 1933, women police were being hired around the country. Early women police, as in so many nations, were assigned mostly clerical work (Chan and Ho 2017), to protect women and children, and to engage in crime prevention and intelligence work (Chu and Sun 2006; Shen 2020). However, during the Japanese invasion and Communist uprisings of the 1930s, the

Central Police College in Nanking began hiring young pretty girls under the age of 17 as cadets. It is speculated that they served as spies, though the information is classified. Reviewing the limited past research, Shen (2020) found that women's representation increased from 5.6 percent in 1982 to 13.7 percent in 2011. Currently, China places a 15 percent quota on female recruits. However, their duties remain mostly separate from those of male police. Furthermore, Chu, Cretacci, and Jin (2019) found that female cadets have lower self-efficacy. That is, they are less likely than men are to believe themselves capable of doing the job. The lack of research in this area allows only for the speculation that this finding could be a result of the perceived treatment that female cadets receive as well as deployment practices. We can apply Tu and Liao's (2006) finding that the men and women of China hold strongly to traditional gender roles, because they strongly view women as natural caregivers who feel a sense of achievement through their husband's career achievements.

Sub-Saharan Africa

African countries are typically organized by region: MENA and Sub-Saharan Africa. Seven African countries comprise MENA: Algeria, Djibouti, Egypt, Libya, Morocco, Sudan, and Tunisia. The remainder comprise Sub-Saharan Africa. Table 3.3 reveals the democracy regimes for 44 countries in the Sub-Saharan African region for which The Economist (2020) was able to gather data. Half of the countries have authoritarian regimes. The region experienced a decline in democracy largely as a result of a deterioration of electoral processes in Benin, Comoros, Niger, Rwanda, Senegal, and Zambia.

Table 3.3 Democracy Regimes in Sub-Saharan Africa

Regime type	*Country*
Full democracy	Mauritius
Flawed democracy	Botswana, Cabo Verde, Ghana, Lesotho, Namibia, South Africa
Hybrid regime	Benin, Burkina Faso, Côte d'Ivoire, Gambia, Kenya, Liberia, Madagascar, Malawi, Mali, Nigeria, Senegal, Sierra Leone, Tanzania, Uganda, Zambia
Authoritarian	Angola, Burundi, Cameroon, Central African Republic, Chad, Comoros, Congo (Brazzaville), Democratic Republic of Congo, Djibouti, Equatorial Guinea, Eritrea, eSwatini, Ethiopia, Gabon, Guinea, Guinea-Bissau, Mauritania, Mozambique, Niger, Rwanda, Togo, Zimbabwe

Source: The Economist. 2020. Democracy Index 2019. *A Year of Democratic Setbacks and Popular Protest*. New York: The Economist Intelligence Unit Limited.

Police research focusing on women police is sparse for this region and Africa in general and even harder to find in English. The UNODC collects annual data on crime and criminal justice (2020). The UNODC was able to collect data for most of the available nations for 2015 (2016 and 2017 did not yield much data). However, it was only able to gather data on female police personnel for Kenya (13 percent), Madagascar (4 percent), and United Republic of Tanzania (20 percent) (see Table 3.4). Tanzania is a hybrid regime (a presidential republic) and was ranked 13th on the Sub-Saharan democracy index for 2019 (The Economist 2020). The dominant religions in Tanzania are Christianity (63.1 percent) and Islamism (34.1 percent) (Pew Research Center 2020). Tanzanian women suffer high rates of teenage pregnancy (27 percent), lack of formal education (24 percent), violence (57 percent), and female genital mutilation (10 percent) (UN Women Africa n.d.). The UNODC data, however, revealed Tanzania as reaching what Brown (1997) and Brown and Silvestri (2020) identified as the tip-over stage for women in policing. I must caution accepting this conclusion without supporting research as many studies find women serving administrative civilian roles. Furthermore, what does tip over mean if women are hired to work in areas considered beneath "real" police work? Tip over should mean balanced representation as well as equality in work.

Full and Flawed Democracies: Women Police in Mauritius and South Africa

Mauritius is a parliamentary republic island country east of Madagascar and is the only country recognized as a full democracy by The Economist (2020) within the Sub-Saharan region. Mauritius gained independence from British rule in 1968 and has a national law enforcement system (Becker and Becker 1986). The nation gained independence through decades of negotiation not political struggle. At the time of Independence, 44 percent of the people opposed independence (Kasenally 2018). According to Ramtohul (2018), Mauritius is a pluralistic society, making mobilization difficult. Two thirds of the population are Indo-Mauritian, followed by Creole, Sino-Mauritian, and Franco-Mauritian (Central Intelligence Agency 2020). Eighty seven

Table 3.4 Women Police in Sub-Saharan Africa, 2015 (UNODC)

Country	*Regime*	*Number*	*Percent*
United Republic of Tanzania	Hybrid	9,197	20%
Kenya	Hybrid	5,038	13%
Madagascar	Hybrid	303	4%

Source: United Nations Office of Drugs and Crime. 2020. *Administration of justice*. www.unodc.org/unodc/en/data-and-analysis/statistics/crime.html (accessed May 11, 2020).

percent of the population speaks Creole, although the official language of the National Assembly (less than 1 percent) is English. The country's major religions include Hinduism (48.4 percent), Christianity (32.8 percent), and Islamism (17.4 percent) (Pew Research Center 2020).

Married women were legislated the status of "minor" with Napoleon's Civil Code of 1804. This Code relegated women to the private domestic sphere. Only health, fertility, and welfare were a focus of improvement, not legal rights. As a British colony, the British male hegemonic ideology was imposed and the workforce, including government and policing, were male dominated. It was not until the 1970s, with the setup up of the Export Processing Zone, that women with little education gained mass employment opportunities. Ramtohul (2018) argued that this provided women with economic empowerment and autonomy. The political corruption that ensued with Mauritius' Independence in 1968 and the rise of political consciousness allowed for the start of a feminist movement, and by 1980, 68 women were part of a new women's police service (Roth 2007). By the 1990s, the women's police service was a parallel service to general police services. Still "women [were] very slow to make a move, to distance themselves from traditions which sometimes oppress them. . . . They are not sufficiently interested in events outside their daily life" (Baudot 1976, as cited in Ramtohul 2018, p. 142). Today, women only represent 11.4 percent of parliament, although since 1997, the law mandated that they represent 30 percent. Mauritius holds strongly to cultural distinctions between men and women in the home and in the workplace.

There is no research on the role and conditions of women police in Mauritius. However, Mauritius government records provide some police data. Mauritius employs women in policing, and according to the Police Commissioner, women are equal to their male counterparts (The Mauritius Police Force 2019). Nevertheless, female police positions are legally separate from male positions (Government of Mauritius 2019a, 2019b). The Ministry of Finance and Economic Development for Mauritius (2019) reported that between 2015 and 2018, the number of females employed within the police force only increased from 1,021 to 1,214. Women currently represent 9 percent of the police force. In 2018, there were 112 police stations with 3.9 percent of the leadership roles filled by women. For example, there was one Woman Police Chief Inspector, six Women Police Inspectors, and 55 Women Police Sergeants. Women represented 5 percent of all police sergeants. However, the majority of women served as Women Police Constables/Trainees. They represented 8.4 percent of the entire Mauritius Police Force, only slightly more than their 7 percent representation in 2011 (Gokulsing and Tandrayen-Ragoobur 2014).

Gokulsing and Tandrayen-Ragoobur (2014) found that the national gender pay gap for Mauritius was 36 cents with a 13-cent pay gap in the public sector, even though women tend to be more academically qualified than men are. The Woman Police Constable is a position legally established separate from the (male) Police Constable. Similar to Police Constable recruits, Women Police Constable recruits must be between the ages of 18 and 30. Regulations also give them the same salary brackets. Both can be appointed by completing training or by completing a Cambridge School Certificate and having good physique. Both are required to have the same Body Mass Index (18.50–27.50). However, men are required to have a height of at least 5 ft. 5 in. while women's height must be 5 ft. 3 in. Men are also required to have a minimum chest measurement while women are not. The small numbers of women police are not surprising given the continued traditional cultural stress on gender role differences. Additionally, the establishment of the position as a "women's" position provides evidence that Mauritius defines women police as fundamentally different from male police. Their small numbers tell us that policing is a man's job.

South Africa is a parliamentary republic and is the sixth largest populated country in Africa. Black African is by far the largest ethnic group (80.9 percent) (Central Intelligence Agency 2020). This is followed by Colored (8.8 percent), White (7.8 percent), and Indian/Asian (2.5 percent). The dominant religions include Christianity (80.8 percent) with 15.3 percent of the population unaffiliated (Pew Research Center 2020). South Africa has 11 official languages, but the most widely spoken language is isiZulu (24.7 percent). The Economist (2020) identifies South Africa as a flawed democracy. The nation established its first police force in 1913 as a national police force. As discussed in Chapter 2, South Africa was colonized by the British as a trade colony. As such, the police force was established in order to protect economic interests and became brutal in the process (Cole 1998). The police played a central role in upholding apartheid. Therefore, when South Africa had its first democratic elections in 1994, the government determined that the police required structural change and created the South African Police Service (SAPS) in 1995 (formerly SAP) (Steyn 2015). It was not until 1996 that the Bill of Rights brought to the forefront gender discrimination.

SAP hired the first two women in 1972, but this was quickly followed by the hiring of 100 additional "policewomen" in that same year (Morrison 2004). As is commonly the practice in the early stages of women in policing, SAP policewomen were hired on a different police structure than policemen competing only with other policewomen. However, in 1989, this dual structure was eliminated. Furthermore, Act 108 of the new Constitution (1996) and the Bill of Rights eliminated unfair discrimination. Nevertheless, policewomen are still held to a different standard (Morrison 2004). While equality exists on paper, policewomen still find little opportunity for advancement when competing with their male counterparts in some jurisdictions (Morrison and Conradie 2006). Adding to this knowledge, Steyn (2015) found that policewomen tend to develop a strong belief in the police culture. In response to the Convention on the Elimination of all Forms of Discrimination against Women, the SAPS established the Office on the Status of Women that promised to have a "gender focal point" (Denney 2019).

In 1997, SAPS created a target of 30 percent women officers and raised the quota to 40 percent in 2002. In 2003, SAPS established the Women's Network to provide support, mentoring, and leadership training. It also established Men for Change in 2004 in order to create a culture of change. By 2017, women represented 27.5 percent of the SAPS, surpassing the tip-over point in policing. Women also achieved tip over in leadership roles. In 2015, they represented 37.5 percent of top management and 34.8 percent of senior management positions. Unlike research in many nations, race is addressed when examining women police in SAPS. In 1995, over half of all women police were White (53 percent) and only a third were African (36 percent) (Ulicki 2011). In an effort to increase racial representation, 52 percent of women police were African by 2004. By 2008, African women made up 68.9 percent of the SAPS, and White women were 18.2 percent, while Colored women were 10.5 percent and Indian women were 2.3 percent of the SAPS. Only 1.5 percent African women served as commissioned officers in 1995 but this increased to 15.2 percent by 2008. However, these numbers mask the gendered structure of the SAPS and its masculinized environment, as seen in the sexual harassment of women police discussed in Chapter 6. More research is needed to understand how this tip over has manifested for women police in the SAPS.

The Hybrid Regime: Women in the Nigeria Police Force

Nigeria is a federal presidential republic and is the most populated nation in Africa with over 214 million residents. The Economist (2020) ranks Nigeria 20th on the Sub-Saharan 2019 democracy index, with a substantial increase in democracy since 2006. The legal system of Nigeria is a mix of English common law, Islamic law in 12 northern states, and traditional law (Central Intelligence Agency 2020). The largest ethnic groups in Nigeria are Hausa (30 percent), Yoruba (15.5 percent), and Igbo (15.2 percent). There are 250 ethnic groups in Nigeria but English is the official language. However, Nigeria also boasts having over 500 indigenous languages including Hausa, Yoruba, Igbo, and Fulani. Islamism is the dominant religion (51.1 percent), followed by Christianity (46.9 percent) (Pew Research Center 2020).

By 1914, Nigeria was under British control for purposes of trade, and by 1930, the various police forces in the nation were integrated into a national police force called the Nigeria Police Force (NPF). Nigeria gained independence on October 1, 1960. A dual police system operated at the local and national levels until 1972, when the NPF absorbed local police forces (Alemika 1988). As was the case for most African colonies, the police functioned as a paramilitary hand to protect the British economic infrastructure (Aderinto 2012). Also in line with most nations, women entered the NPF in an effort to deal with women's issues. The Lagos Ladies League first unsuccessfully petitioned the government to hire women police in 1923 (Aderinto 2012). The Lagos Women's Party revived this call in 1944 using the argument that women police would be more effective at helping female offenders and keeping them safe (from male police). At this time, the focus was on prostitution. As a result, "the history of women police in Nigeria is therefore closely connected to the history of prostitution" (Aderinto 2012, p. 72).

Women were finally hired as female constables in 1955, and the Women's Police Branch was developed with 20 women (Akinjobi-Babatunde 2015). Their duties included working with women and children in a social worker role, including: investigation of sexual offenses against women and children; recording statements from women and children; being in attendance when women and children were being interviewed; searching, escorting and guarding women prisoners; school crossing duties; crowd control where women and children were present in any numbers; and clerical work (Nigeria Police Act 1967). The Women's Police Branch also created juvenile welfare centers where they worked as arbitrators and counselors. However, while women were hired on the platform of morality, the recruitment process did not reflect this as it is focused heavily on physical agility (Akinjobi-Babatunde 2015).

Women trained similar to men in many ways including lifesaving, first aid, fire and ambulance drills, police duties, and field training. However, they were initially not given arms training as it was believed that they were too weak to handle a firearm. By the 1980s, women pushed back and are now able to train with and carry firearms. However, this is not a right and has not been institutionalized. Additionally, female recruits had to be unmarried and were not allowed to marry without permission from the commissioner after no less than three years of service (Nigeria Police Act 1967). It was not until 2012 that the Federal High Court in Lagos declared the marriage provision unconstitutional. In an attempt to further increase equality, the Nigeria Police Act of 2018 mandated that all training programs be made available to women and prohibited gender discrimination in the performance of one's functions within the NPF (Nigeria Police Act 2018). The most current research finds that gender discrimination is still rampant in the NPF (Akinjobi-Babatunde 2015).

There is not much data on women in the NPF. However, Prenzler and Sinclair (2013) found that in 2010, women made up 12.4 percent of the NPF. In that same year, women were 5 percent of senior officers but had no representation in top ranks. An NPF report, *A Gender Policy for the Nigeria Police Force*, claimed that the NPF would increase women's representation in police to 35 percent by 2015 (NPF/UN Women/UNFPA 2010 as cited in Prenzler and Sinclair 2013). However, in 2017, only 11.3 percent of recruits enrolled in the Nigeria Police Academy in Wudil were women (National Bureau of Statistics 2019). With the lingering gender discrimination, it is unlikely that the NPF will ever be able to reach this threshold.

Women Police in Sub-Saharan Authoritarian Regimes

There is little research on women police in Sub-Saharan authoritarian regimes. Women's rights and women's involvement in male work is strictly curtailed. For example, in the Sudan, although women contributed to the Sudanese war effort (MENA region), there is little effort to include women in the police force (Lokuji, Abatneh, and Wani 2009). However, there is considerable violence against women, even at the hands of the police. These patterns are strongly linked to the traditional gender role ideology in many African authoritarian regimes. When we examine the research, however, we find more reference to women as peacekeepers. For example, in 2014, woman represented 41 percent of Zimbabwean peacekeepers (Dzinesa 2015). *Providing for Peacekeeping* (n.d.) provides data for peacekeeping efforts and found that in 2009, of the authoritarian regimes in this region, Rwanda had the most women peacekeepers (n = 172). The efforts by Rwandan women to stop future atrocities against women speak to this high number. Other authoritarian regimes with female peacekeepers were Burundi, Cameroon, Chad, Egypt (MENA), Guinea, Niger, Togo, and Zimbabwe. Zimbabwe does employ female police; however, the research is sparse. By 2018, there were 1,198 women police serving as UN peacekeepers, most from Africa (United Nations Peacekeeping 2018). Again, Rwanda ranked first of the top five contributing nations of women police (n = 216) to the UN. Cameroon was ranked fifth with 61 women UN police.

Middle East and North Africa

Twenty nations comprise the MENA. However, depending on where one gathers the information, Turkey and Sudan may not be listed as countries within MENA. In this examination, I use The Economist's organization and include Sudan but place Turkey into the Eastern European region. The examination into this region reveals more countries with the lowest democracy index scores, including political turmoil and public unrest (The Economist 2020). As with the Sub-Saharan authoritarian regimes, there is not much research on women in policing in MENA. As a result, when examining hybrid and authoritarian regimes, I provide the little information gathered from several countries. Table 3.5 shows the regime types for the 20 countries in MENA. The Economist (2020) did not find any full democracies but did list Israel and Tunisia as flawed democracies. In this section, I will look at Israeli women police. Three countries were found to have hybrid regimes (Algeria, Lebanon, and Morocco). The rest of the

Table 3.5 Democracy Regimes in the Middle East and North Africa

Regime type	*Country*
Flawed democracy	Israel, Tunisia
Hybrid regime	Algeria, Lebanon, Morocco
Authoritarian	Bahrain, Egypt, Iran, Iraq, Jordan, Kuwait, Libya, Oman, Palestine, Qatar, Saudi Arabia, Sudan, Syria, United Arab Emirates, Yemen

Source: The Economist. 2020. Democracy Index 2019. *A Year of Democratic Setbacks and Popular Protest*. New York: The Economist Intelligence Unit Limited.

countries are authoritarian regimes. Not enough UNODC data could not be gathered for this region within a reasonable time frame to include a table.

Flawed Democracy: Women in the Israel National Police

Israel is a parliamentary democracy that gained independence from the U.K. in 1948. The nation's legal system is a mix of English law and Jewish, Christian, and Muslim law (Central Intelligence 2020). Hebrew is the official language with a Jewish population of 74.4 percent. Arabic is also commonly spoken with an Arabic population of 20.9 percent. Shadmi (1993) reported that Israeli women began joining the Israel National Police (INP) in real numbers in 1948 (5.5 percent). Women represented 7.8 percent of the INP in 1966 and 18.9 percent in 1986 (Shadmi 1993). By 2015, women represented 25 percent of the INP (Geva 2019). Current data are hard to obtain, as most research and government statistics focus on women in the Israel Defense Forces (IDF). Furthermore, research on women in the INP is also hard to find in English. According to Geva (2019), most accounts of women in the INP reference the first women's unit established in Tel-Aviv in the 1960s. However, examining the history of women in the INP, Geva eloquently tells the story of Zipporah Fell-Shik, the first female Chief of the INP (1948–1951). Unfortunately, after three years, the female chief position was eliminated. Geva blames the patriarchal nature of the police organization for this elimination.

Similar to other countries, women's entry into the INP occurred in phases. Geva refers to women's earliest entrance as the "years of establishment." Shadmi (1993) refers to this stage as segregation (1948–1959), similar to Brown (1997). During this stage, their numbers were small and their duties were limited. Women's initial entry was divided into three sub-periods (Geva 2019). In the first period (1948), women were encouraged to join the INP. The War of Independence (1948–1949) required the INP to turn to women to fill police ranks left open by men who went to war. Recruitment stressed height, weight, and education. Most women police were given

Figure 3.1 Israeli Police Women in Tel Aviv, 1948.

Source: Photo used with permission from the Israel Police Heritage Center.

clerical work with some assigned traffic duty (Figure 3.1). Geva states that the preoccupation with the design of the woman's police uniform was evidence that the INP intended women to stay with the force long term. However, between 1949 and 1952 (second sub-period), the INP developed policies that limited women's roles; and by 1953 (third sub-period), these policies were strongly enforced (Figure 3.1).

Not receiving the full duties of an officer, women police were marginalized. The position of women in the INP was similar to that of the woman in the IDF in that women were given auxiliary roles so as not to impede women's ability to become mothers. They were given day shifts only, lighter duties, mostly office work, and lower wages. Additionally, when policemen married, their salary was increased. This did not occur for policewomen who married. In fact, the INP did not believe that married women would or could commit to a career in policing so they tended to hire single women. Soon policy required women to obtain permission from National Headquarters to marry, or at least to submit notification. By the end of the War, the national emergency was over and so was the enthusiasm for women in policing. Still, by 1951, there were 420 women police. Yet, as with the backlash that follows initial inroads in most countries, their numbers quickly decreased.

The INP soon created positions they deemed only appropriate for women. Shadmi (1993) tells us that this occurred in 1960 and labeled this era breakthrough (1960–1969). Geva (2019) reports this as occurring a few years earlier. During the breakthrough era, women were relegated to such duties as searching and guarding women suspects, detainees, and prisoners and interviewing women regarding sex crimes. In fact, women police were integral to the fight against sex crimes, including those committed on the black market. However, they were often used as bait. It was the first time that women were given typical police jobs. Moreover, in 1960, an all-female police unit responsible for traffic control was established in Tel-Aviv.

Shadmi (1993) identified the last era of women in policing as partial integration (1970–present). In the 1970s, the INP started to recruit male and female college graduates and former army officers. Many women were recruited as commissioned officers. Additionally, the investigations into juvenile and sex offending opened the doors to other investigative work. Today, all police jobs are open to women in the INP. Shadmi presented data that revealed women working in all areas expect dealing with bombs. Yet, sexism and discrimination limits women's movement toward equality. Nevertheless, more current research is needed to determine if partial integration is still in place or if women police have moved forward or backward. For example, the Deputy Commissioner for Women Affairs position was created after a critical 2012 State Comptroller Report. The position was created in order to create equal opportunities and safer conditions for women in the INP (Ashkenazi 2019). Unfortunately, colleagues in Israel could not find research on the gains of this position.

Women Police in Hybrid Regimes: Algeria, Lebanon, and Morocco

According to The Economist (2020), Algeria is a hybrid nation whose legal system is a mix of French civil law and Islamic law (Central Intelligence Agency 2020). Algeria, a former French colony, gained independence in 1962. It is currently a presidential republic. The country is made up mostly of Arab-Berber (99 percent) and Arabic and Berber or Tamazight are the official languages. Additionally, 97.9 percent of its citizens are Muslim (Pew Research Center 2020). UNODC (2020) data reveal that there were 8,896 (6 percent) female police personnel in 2010 and 11,005 (6 percent) in 2015. There are no social science studies of women police in Algeria. However, news accounts reveal that women are perhaps recruited into the field because they proved their capability fighting alongside men against the French (1958–1962) (Lowe 2009; Donadio 2019). Nevertheless, women police typically work office jobs and traffic duty. Similarly, Algerian women have served in the military since 2000. By 2013, women made up 18 percent of military recruits (Donadio 2019).

Lebanon is a parliamentary republic that gained independence from France in 1943. The legal system is a mix of French civil code, Ottoman legal tradition, and religious laws. Arabic is the official language with 95 percent of the population of Arabic ethnicity; 61.2 percent are Muslim (Central Intelligence Agency 2020; Pew Research Center 2020). The first two women joined Lebanon's Interior Security Forces (ISF) in 2001 and 2003. The UNODC (2020) data only reported two women police personnel in Lebanon by 2010 but has no data for the following years. In 2010, women represented 0.01 percent of the ISF. As a result, Lebanon started active recruitment of women into its police forces. In 2012, 610 Lebanese women were given full police responsibilities through the establishment of an all-woman police unit within the ISF (Thomas 2013). However, ISF code does not allow the display of religious symbols, which also applies to Muslim women who wear a hijab.

In 2017, Al Mina, a municipality in Lebanon, started recruiting its first female officers (Government of Canada 2018). Women police state that they have the same duties as men in the Al Mina police force. Not much is known about Lebanese women police in the research; however, it is obvious that women police still experience second-class status. In order to entice tourism in the Christian town of Broumana, Lebanon, the mayor hired young women as police officers and required that they dress in "black hot pants" (The Economist 2018; McKernan 2018). These police served as traffic wardens. The mayor's decision sparked debate over sexism with many arguing that this decision would increase sexual harassment of women on the street. One critic stressed that women's choices were taken away from them by powerful men.

Morocco is a parliamentary constitutional monarchy. The country gained independence from France in 1956 and bases its legal system on French civil law and Islamic (*shari'a*) law (Central Intelligence Agency 2020). The country is composed of 99 percent Arab-Berber and 99 percent Muslim, with Arabic as its official language. Morocco also employs women police, though not much is known in the research. News accounts tell us that in 2014, policewomen were already in the field and that 21 female officers joined the motorcycle unit alongside male police officers (Morocco World News 2014). Another news story detailed the work that female officers accomplished within a three-year period, including 2,486 robbery arrests, 15,883 illegal immigrant attempt preventions, and 783 human smuggler arrests (Ben Saga 2019).

Authoritarian Regimes: Women Police in the Gulf Cooperation Council

Because so little is known about most nations in the authoritarian regimes of MENA, I focus on the Gulf Cooperation Council (GCC). Six nations comprise the GCC: Bahrain, Kuwait, Oman, Qatar, Saudi Arabia, and the United Arab Emirates (UAE). The formation of the GCC was conceptualized by

Kuwait with the British intention to leave the Gulf region in the 1960s (Christie 1986). With Kuwait's independence in 1961 and the development of the oil industry in the Gulf, Kuwait proposed the union. However, it was not until 1981 that the GCC was chartered. The purpose was to unify based on common political and cultural ideologies and to be able to compete in the global economy (Christie 1986; World Bank Group 2016).

By the 1970s, all of the countries of the GCC gained independence, mostly from the British (Central Intelligence Agency 2020). Oman gained independence from Portugal by expulsion in 1650 and later became a protectorate of the British but was not colonized, as were the other countries of the GCC. All of the countries have a monarchy. Bahrain and Kuwait have constitutional monarchies, while Oman, Qatar, and Saudi Arabia have absolute monarchies. The UAE has a federation of monarchies. Each nation has a legal system that is a mix of Islamic (*shari'a*) law and English, Egyptian, French and/or customary laws. In each nation, Islam is the dominant religion (73–85 percent) and Arabic is the official language.

Countries in MENA have historically maintained gender inequality. Like most nations around the world, countries in MENA consider women to be delicate and in need of protection. As such, women are not seen as capable of executing the duties of the police. However, in most countries in MENA, religious edicts accompany tribal laws and do not allow women to speak to or spend time with unrelated men (Strobl 2020). This is also where guardian laws come into play. These laws require females to have male guardians (*wali*) which include a father, brother, uncle, or husband. Guardians make life decisions for women including giving them permission to work or denying them that ability. Recently some countries have allowed women to join male-dominated occupations such as policing. The Arab Gulf States Institute in Washington, a think tank that examines diversity in the Arab Gulf States, reported that in 2018 Saudi Arabia opened some male-dominated occupations to women such as air traffic control, traffic police, military, and investigators for prosecution (Alhashmi 2018). Furthermore, in 2019, Saudi law amended its guardianship law to exclude women over 21 years of age. The previous guardianship law made it impossible for women with traditional guardians to work in policing.

Gender segregation and prohibition of physical contact between unrelated men and women in Gulf Arab states led to the hiring of women to work in women's jails, schools, customs, and border patrols as early as 1970 (Alhashmi 2018). Gulf Arab states developed police academies to train women. In 1970, two women were hired in Bahrain after completing a 6-month field training. In 1974, 17 women enrolled in Oman's police training academy. In 1977, 18 women in Dubai (UAE) enrolled in the police training academy, and in 1978, Abu Dhabi (UAE) created a women's police academy. In that same year, 24 women police officers were hired. Yet, it was not until 2008 that Kuwait, with a lot of push back, enrolled 40 women into the Saad Abdullah Police Academy for a 1-year training. By 2009, 27 Kuwaiti women were sworn in as police officers (Strobl 2020). In fact, Bahraini women police trained the first women police in Kuwait. Saudi Arabia opened its first women's police stations in Riyadh and Jeddah (Alhashmi 2018). However, women were only allowed to work on personal, financial, and real estate cases. In 2013, Qatar established a women's police section within its police academy and graduated 107 women. Nevertheless, it is still considered inappropriate for women to work in frontline policing. Their jobs mostly remain gender segregated. Gains have been made toward female designed uniforms (Bahrain and Dubai) and the ability to wear the hijab in Bahrain. Additionally, the Dubai Police established childcare centers at work and allow for flexible hours in order to breastfeed.

Dubai has opened traditional policing positions to women allowing them to work in the areas of human trafficking and forensics and as dog handlers and medical doctors. They also allow women police to study abroad in order to specialize in cybersecurity, digital crime, and forensic investigations (Alhashmi 2018). Today, there are over 1,500 women police (10 percent), with 93 in senior positions.

Eastern Europe

Much of Eastern Europe is composed of flawed or hybrid democracies (see Table 3.6). Most countries struggling over basic democratic rights are found within the Commonwealth of Independent States, or CIS region of the continent, most of which are authoritarian regimes. Eastern Europe experienced the largest decline in democracy between 2008 and 2019 (The Economist 2020). Research has revealed that the region is plagued with corruption, an unstable political culture, no safeguarding of the rule of law, rejection of liberal democratic values, and a preference for leaders who circumvent political institutions.

Table 3.6 Democracy Regimes in Eastern Europe

Regime type	*County*
Flawed democracy	Bulgaria, Croatia, Czech Republic, Estonia, Hungary, Latvia, Lithuania, Poland, Romania, Serbia, Slovakia, Slovenia
Hybrid regime	Albania, Armenia, Bosnia and Hercegovina, Georgia, Kyrgyz Republic, Moldova, Montenegro, North Macedonia, Ukraine
Authoritarian	Azerbaijan, Belarus, Kazakhstan, Russia, Tajikistan, Turkmenistan, Uzbekistan

Source: The Economist. 2020. Democracy Index 2019. *A Year of Democratic Setbacks and Popular Protest*. New York: The Economist Intelligence Unit Limited.

The UNODC (2020) obtained more data for Eastern European nations than for African and Asian nations. Overall, data revealed that women have reached the tip-over stage in four flawed nations (Table 3.7). Latvia, Lithuania, Estonia, and Slovenia each have 25 to 36 percent female representation, while Hungary and Serbia are approaching the tip-over stage with 23 percent female police representation in each country. Countries with flawed democracies are more likely to employ women police, while some of the hybrid and authoritarian regimes listed in the table have negligible representation. Poland employed the largest number of women police among the flawed nations shown in the table (15,227). Yet, this still only represented 15 percent of the total Polish police force.

Flawed Democracy: Women Police in Poland

Poland is a parliamentary republic that experienced partitioning in 1795 by Russia, Prussia, and Austria (Central Intelligence Agency 2020). The country gained independence in 1918 but became a Soviet satellite state in 1945. Poland finally had free elections in 1989 and now has a legal system that consists of civil law and the power of judicial review. By 1925, Poland joined the world's international policewoman movement, seeing women's entry into the police as necessary in order to save children and women, especially prostitutes. Petruccelli (2015) argues that while nations like the

Table 3.7 Women Police in Eastern Europe, 2015 (UNODC)

Country	*Regime*	*Number*	*Percent*
Latvia	Flawed	3,236	36%
Lithuania	Flawed	3,220	36%
Estonia	Flawed	1,360	35%
Slovenia	Flawed	2,076	25%
Hungary	Flawed	8,443	23%
Serbia	Flawed	9,852	23%
Bulgaria	Flawed	4,693	19%
Croatia	Flawed	3,645	18%
Slovakia	Flawed	3,805	17%
Russian Federation	Authoritarian	112,972	17%
Czech Republic	Flawed	6,034	15%
Poland	Flawed	15,227	15%
Romania	Flawed	7,347	14%
North Macedonia	Hybrid	1,148	12%
Albania	Hybrid	945	10%
Montenegro	Hybrid	375	9%
Bosnia and Herzegovina	Hybrid	1,129	7%
Kazakhstan	Authoritarian	2,983	7%

Source: United Nations Office of Drugs and Crime. 2020. *Administration of justice*. www.unodc.org/unodc/en/data-and-analysis/statistics/crime.html (accessed May 11, 2020).

U.S., the U.K., Germany, India, China, and Uruguay hired women for preventative purposes (i.e., moral police), Poland focused on the male function, or "repressive" tasks, for its women police. However, Levine (1994) found that policewomen in countries like the U.K. were more controlling than preventative.

Poland first hired women police in 1924 in order to fight the growing plague of the trafficking of women and children in Central Europe. Many women were recruited from the Legion of Women Volunteers (*Ochotnicza Legia Kobiet* or OLK), an all-female paramilitary group who fought alongside men in the 1918 fight against Partition. By 1925, 24 women police were hired in Warsaw and five in Lodz. Stanislawa Paleolog, who served in the OLK, was hired in 1925 to lead the Polish Women Police in Warsaw and in 1935 was appointed to head the central office of Women Police in Warsaw. Paleolog's Polish Women Police led investigations, raids, and arrests of traffickers, pimps, procurers, and brothel operators. Petruccelli (2015) describes that while women's organizations selected women police in the first wave of hiring, by 1928, the selection of women was institutionalized. Similar to all nations, female candidates were required to be in good physical health, unmarried, and complete a minimum number of years of school. However, the age requirement was more generous and resembled today's standards (21–35 years of age). Initially, women police served alongside policemen. However, the successes of women police in their fight against human trafficking pushed many policemen out of those areas.

Under Paleolog's leadership, new women divisions were established to handle juveniles on the street and in detention centers. This was the time that social welfare replaced repressive policing as women's primary focus. By 1935, with the decreasing concern over sex trafficking, the number of women police decreased, and by 1945, most of the gains women made within the police were lost with the invasion by the Soviet Union. In 1953, the Polish police again appointed a woman as a station commander (Basinska 2015). Yet, it was not until Poland was free of Soviet rule in 1989 that women once again made inroads into the Polish Police. By 1990, women represented 10 percent of the police force and by 2010, 13 percent. Today, women represent 15 percent of the police force in Poland and are able to work in all areas of policing. However, Basinska (2015) found that women's discrimination in policing is found in the unequal access to managerial positions, longer wait times for promotion, and lower pay. Additionally, Poland still holds to a strong belief that women's main role is in the home.

Women Police in Hybrid Regimes: Albania and Ukraine

Albania is a parliamentary republic with a mostly civil law system. The population is mostly Albanian (82.6 percent) and predominantly Muslim (Central Intelligence Agency 2020). Albania gained independence from the

Ottoman Empire in 1912 but later experienced occupation by Italy (1939) and Germany (1943). It became a communist nation in 1944 and allied itself with the Soviet Union and China. The Albania State Police (ASP) is a national police force that was met with fear from the people, as it was a communist agent enforcing strict Soviet rule (Gibbs, Ruiz, and Klapper-Lehman 2015). However, in the 1990s, Albania established a multiparty democracy and reformed the ASP. Among the changes was a promise to end gender discrimination. As Gibbs and colleagues (2015) described, in 1992, the ASP required police to have military experience. Since the military did not allow women, they were unable to join the police force. Beginning in the late 1990s, Albania adopted gender equality legislation but did not adopt more progressive legislation until joining the European Union in 2006.

Recent legislation focuses on access to jobs, remuneration, working conditions, and career advancement (Gajic et al. 2013). In 2006, women represented 0.5 percent of the police force (Gibbs, Ruiz, and Klapper-Lehman 2015). By 2010, women's representation increased to 10 percent. The Women Police Officers Network (2012) found that many nations in Eastern Europe hold to quotas for hiring women, limiting their numbers. However, the ASP has made strong efforts to recruit women police in drafting a personnel regulation mandating that 50 percent of basic police training candidates be women. This resulted in an all-woman basic police training class in 2011 (Women Police Officers Network 2012). The ASP also found that the driver's license requirement prior to training hindered many women from joining so it postponed the requirement until the completion of training. The ASP also recruits through woman-focused media and provides preparatory training for women in order to increase enrollment.

However, prejudice is reported as one of the biggest obstacles to women's career advancement. Most women in the ASP are civilian staff (51.5 percent), with women represented only 6.5 percent of all uniformed ASP (Women Police Officers Network 2015). Considering the female population in the ASP, 55.5 percent of all women are uniformed police, and 60.2 percent of all uniformed women hold lower-level positions. The nation has made little progress in integrating women into law enforcement. There remains a lack of incentives for empowering women within the ASP and a failure to implement much of the gender equality legislation within police activities (Gajic et al. 2013). In fact, the nation's culture still holds to traditional roles for women.

An overwhelmingly Christian country, the Ukraine is a semi-presidential republic that gained independence from Russia in 1991 (Central Intelligence Agency 2020). The nation's legal system is composed of civil law and judicial review of legislative acts. The nation's population is mostly Ukrainian (77.8 percent) and Russian (17.3 percent). Over 85 percent of the country is Christian, many orthodox (Pew Research Center 2020). Women have been a part of the Ukrainian police organization for over 100 years (Spasic

2011). They make up about 8 percent of the police force (Beck, Barko, and Tatarenko 2003). However, women tend to work in support roles in offices such as issuing passports and visas (65 percent), investigations (43 percent), and human resources (41 percent). Most hold lower ranks with only a few reaching the ranks of lieutenant colonel (7 percent) or colonel (1 percent). Spasic (2011) found that women police were less satisfied with their jobs in policing and reported that their male supervisors had an authoritarian style of policing toward them than toward their male counterparts. Spasic argues that the male-dominated organizational culture coupled with the larger Ukrainian culture promulgates gender stereotypes that keep women in domestic roles. Additionally, the Ukraine is still plagued with gender discrimination with a high rate of violence against women (UN Women 2019a).

Authoritarian Regimes: The Women of Russia, Tajikistan, and Uzbekistan

There is not much research on authoritarian nations within Eastern Europe. The little information found is predominantly from news accounts of women in police. For example, in a news conference, the Ministry of Internal Affairs of Russia claimed that the number of women in policing was growing and that women work in all areas of policing including investigations, injury, criminalistics, and operational work (Bragina and Jones 2017). Women have definitely made inroads into police as they currently represent 17 percent (112,972) of all police in Russia (United Nations Office of Drugs and Crime 2020). In one analysis, women police were compared to women in the Soviet Army (Regamey and Schechter 2016). Specifically, the authors argued that women in uniform had maternal responsibility because gender equality was viewed as harmful.

We do not speak of colonialization when referring to Russia as Russia was an empire itself. Russia broke off from the USSR, along with 14 other nations, in 1991 and is currently a semi-presidential federation. However, the dominant gender ideologies of the former Soviet Union appear to persist and most women police are given administrative and low-level education duties (Bragina and Jones 2017). In a review of Russian policing, Roudik (2008) found that women's representation in the Russian police has been decreasing because they are the first to be fired during reductions. Roudik also found that women tend to be assigned clerical duties, as well as administrative work in issuing passports and visas. They are also assigned to work with minors and engage in searches of women. Women are also more likely to engage in research within the police force and serve as forensic experts. However, with so little research on Russia, Roudik's findings must be followed by more current research.

In Tajikistan, the Ministry of Interior claimed to encourage women to join policing and praised them for their work in crime fighting and security (Direnberger 2016). Tajikistan is a Muslim nation (96.4 percent) (Pew Research Center 2020) with little ethnic diversity (Central Intelligence Agency 2020). Tajiks comprise 84.3 percent of the population, with 13.8 percent Uzbeks. It is a presidential republic. Having gained independence from Russia in 1991, Tajikistan has a civil law system. The recruitment of women is viewed as a rejuvenation of the nation as women are viewed as having "natural characteristics" that will improve the police and the nation (Direnberger 2016, para. 38). However, like everywhere around the world, Tajik women do not have equal access to the highest positions in policing. Additionally, it is not uncommon for women to claim that women in general have maternal problem-solving traits that qualify them for high leadership roles.

Uzbekistan also has no identifiable research on women police. One news report claimed that women have increasingly joined the Uzbekistani police force, working alongside men and performing the same duties (Yeniseyev 2016). The Uzbek government claims not to discriminate. The academy requirements are also the same for men and women, although women are given a modified physical fitness test. Additionally, special women's councils have been established in order to help women cope with work and family. However, Uzbekistan does not release their women police personnel statistics and no research could verify the news account. Uzbekistan is a predominantly Muslim (97.1 percent) country (Pew Research Center 2020) with one of the lowest democracy index scores in the world with a civil liberties score close to zero (The Economist 2020). The Central Intelligence Agency (2020) lists it as a highly authoritarian nation with a presidential republic government. It gained independence from Russia in 1991 and has a civil law system. According to Amnesty International (2020), 30 percent of elected officials in 2019 were women. This bodes well as research has found that in some countries, when women and other minorities hold office more women police are hired (Belknap 2015).

Conclusion

The chapter opened with a discussion on the integration of women in policing. Western models of integration propose a near linear progression of women into policing. Women are integrated when they reach the tip-over point of 20 to 25 percent representation in the police organization (Brown 1997; Brown and Silvestri 2020). On the other hand, Natarajan (2008, 2014), Strobl (2010, 2020), Shen (2020), and Chu (2020) provide evidence for another model. Natarajan (2008) started the conversation that integration should not be presumed. Strobl (2020), Shen (2020), and Chu (2020), provide evidence for Strobl's circular country-specific model. While the chapter was not an empirical study and the research is sorely lacking for so many countries, it is apparent that in much of the Eastern Hemisphere, integration may not be as simple as gaining numbers.

For many of the Muslim nations, for example, religious edict requires that women maintain a separate domestic focus. In non-Muslim countries, however, we still see strong traditional gender ideologies that stress family and motherhood above paid labor and a frowning upon women engaging in man's work. Most of the countries in the Eastern Hemisphere have allowed women to work in law enforcement, and as time progresses, their numbers have increased. We have also witnessed increased legislation to increase their numbers as well as to improve working conditions such as reducing harassment, and providing maternity leave and childcare. However, while there has been activity in many countries to give equal treatment in pay, deployment, and promotion, the evidence reveals that gender ideologies get in the way of equality for women. Women and men are not equal in any nation. Furthermore, gender ideologies stress difference, presenting this difference as strengths for each gender. However, the value placed on each gender is unequal and so *equity* is the language we should use. Some nations have legislated gender-hiring quotas and address women's issues in work in attempts to gain gender equity. In the coming chapters, I will examine how effective these attempts have been and how much more needs to be done. However, I first examine women police in the Western Hemisphere of the world.

Chapter 4

Past and Current Status of Women Police in the Western Hemisphere

When discussing policing in the Western Hemisphere of the world, many refer to policing in the U.S. and the U.K. However, there are many countries in this region of the world, many with governments similar to those in the Eastern Hemisphere. Similar to many of the Eastern European, MENA, and Sub-Saharan countries, there is sparse research on women in policing in Latin American and Caribbean countries. What we do know is that gender ideologies are similar. That is, most of the world still views women as having natural traits that make them nurturers and the only logical solution to handling cases involving women and children. Many claim that Islamic law and gender ideologies are what hold women to the private/domestic sphere of existence. However, we will see that the largely Christian nations in Latin American and Caribbean countries hold those same ideologies. We will see in the following discussion that many of the countries in the Western Hemisphere still see policing as a man's job too dangerous for women. I begin my examination with Latin America and the Caribbean.

Latin America and the Caribbean

The Caribbean, Central America, and South America comprise Latin America. In all, there are 33 countries. The Economist (2020) was able to gather data for 24 countries and listed Chile, Costa Rica, and Uruguay as full democracies (see Table 4.1). Most of the countries in this region fall into the flawed democracy category, with only four hybrid regimes (Bolivia, Haiti, Guatemala, and Honduras) and three authoritarian regimes (Cuba, Nicaragua, and Venezuela). The Economist found that Latin American countries had the largest decline in democracy in 2019 with its largest decline in civil liberties. Major protests in Bolivia, Chile, Colombia, Ecuador, Haiti, and Venezuela erupted in response to corruption, electoral fraud, and various government policies. Additionally, there was an increase in authoritarianism in Bolivia, Nicaragua, and Venezuela. Chile (full democracy) and El Salvador (flawed democracy) were the only countries that experienced an increase in democracy.

Table 4.1 Democracy Regimes in Latin America and the Caribbean

Regime type	*Country*
Full democracy	Chile, Costa Rica, Uruguay
Flawed democracy	Argentina, Brazil, Colombia, Dominican Republic, Ecuador, El Salvador, Guyana, Jamaica, Mexico, Panama, Paraguay, Peru, Suriname, Trinidad and Tobago
Hybrid regime	Bolivia, Haiti, Guatemala, Honduras
Authoritarian	Cuba, Nicaragua, Venezuela

Source: The Economist. 2020. Democracy Index 2019. *A Year of Democratic Setbacks and Popular Protest*. New York: The Economist Intelligence Unit Limited.

As Walsh points out, "democracy promises equal rights to all citizens, yet a range of women's rights outcomes is found in democratizing states" (2012, 1324). Walsh found that women' rights advanced in Chile after the first democratic election because women's access, voices, and capacity for debate in public institutions pressured politicians to endorse their demands. Similarly, Nicaraguan women's protests in response to the government's removal of protections against intimate partner violence (IPV) resulted in the reopening of all-women's police stations (Canal 4 2020; Neumann 2018). The Economist includes not only civil liberties among the categories within the democracy index but also political participation. Latin America experienced increased participation by women in electoral government (31.6 percent) following imposed gender quotas (UN Women 2020). However, women in police have a long way to go.

Table 4.2 shows the UNODC data for women police in Latin America, the Caribbean, and North America in 2015. The only nations to reach tip over in the 2015 data were Guyana (29 percent) and Trinidad and Tobago (25 percent). These are flawed democracies according to The Economist (2020). Canada and Mexico, both full democracies, had over 20 percent female representation in policing. Furthermore, we see that the U.S., a flawed democracy and world power that tends to boast democracy and equality, is near the bottom of female representation in policing for data in this region.

Full Democracy: Women's Police Stations in Uruguay

Throughout its early history, Uruguay was colonized by Spain, Portugal, Great Britain, Argentina, and Brazil. In early colonial days, the Spanish created the *Blandengues Corps* (1797), a brutal rural military patrol force, in order to control crime and squash native uprisings. However, these *Blandengues* joined with Portuguese Brazilian forces to push Spain out in 1811. Still, in 1821, Uruguay was annexed by Brazil. Uruguay finally declared

Table 4.2 Women Police in Latin America, the Caribbean, and North America, 2015 (UNODC)

Country	*Regime*	*Number*	*Percent*
Guyana	Flawed	1,057	29%
Trinidad and Tobago	Flawed	1,636	25%
Uruguay	Full	5,460	24%
Canada	Full	14,331	21%
Mexico	Flawed	71,786	18%
Barbados	—	231	16%
Costa Rica	Full	2,099	16%
Chile	Full	7,688	15%
Peru	Flawed	16,512	15%
Grenada	—	136	14%
El Salvador	Flawed	2,789	12%
United States of America	Flawed	73,800	12%
Honduras	Hybrid	1,228	10%
Colombia	Flawed	16,190	9%
Paraguay	Flawed	1,294	8%

Source: United Nations Office of Drugs and Crime. 2020. *Administration of justice*. www.unodc.org/unodc/en/data-and-analysis/statistics/crime.html (accessed May 11, 2020).

independence in 1825 and gained it in 1828 (Central Intelligence Agency 2020). Today, Uruguay is a presidential republic with a civil legal system based on Spanish law. With 3.3 million people, 87.7 percent of Uruguayans are white, 4.6 percent are black, and Spanish is the official language. Christianity (57 percent) is the dominant religion, with 41.5 percent of the people unaffiliated (Pew Research Center 2020). Established in 1929, Uruguay has a national police force.

There is evidence of women joining the ranks of the Uruguayan police forces in the 1920s. Entry of women into the Montevideo Police Department documents Jeanette Johnson, Special Police Officer, as the first female appointment as of 1923 (Montevideo Police Department 2020). There were two female officers by 1924. However, recruitment of women was not a focus until 1966 when 21 women were hired into policing (Sherman 1977). Women police assisted tourists but otherwise performed police duties. Their police work, like so many early and current women police around the world, consisted of protecting and guarding women and children. Montevideo held the belief that women possessed skills most effective when working with these populations. This ideology still exists and Uruguay still operates Women's Police Stations (WPSs)(Immigration and Refugee Board of Canada 2002b; Brysk 2018).

In 1985, WPSs in Montevideo focused specifically on IPV, as did most WPSs around the country. The *Instituto Nacional de la Mujer y Familia* (National Institute of Women and Family) in Uruguay reported that police departments in Montevideo currently operate WPSs tasked with investigating violence against women. In 2001 alone, these stations received almost 1,000 complaints and filed charges in half of these cases. There are also WPSs in Soriano, Cerro Largo, Flores, Florida, and Maldonado (Immigration and Refugee Board of Canada 2002a). Today, women police represent 25 percent of Uruguay's police force. However, there is no research to inform us of the conditions of their work and how much equality they have gained.

Flawed Democracy: Police Women of Sao Paulo, Brazil

Brazil is a federal presidential republic with a new civil law code enacted in 2006 (Central Intelligence Agency 2020). With over 211 million people, Brazil is the largest country in South America. Almost half of the population is White (47.7 percent), closely followed by Mulatto (43.1 percent). Brazil was under Portuguese rule for more than 300 years before it gained independence in 1822. As a result, Portuguese is the official and mostly spoken language, and Christianity (88.1 percent) is the dominant religion (Pew Research Center 2020).

Colonial policing (1500–early 1800s) consisted of public police working with the military in order to protect the territory while private police protected plantations (Ellison and Pino 2012). Colonial police had unchecked power in its brutality. By 1930, when the first police academy was established, the civilian police force operated under Dictator Getuilo Vargas. He led the police in a coup as a secret police eliminating adversaries through death squads. A second military coup in 1964 incorporated the police into the military. Even after Brazil's transition to democracy in the 1980s, its police force maintained the same civilian-military organization. The State Military Police are uniformed and patrol the streets, while the Civil Police (a.k.a. Judicial Police) wear civilian clothing and investigate crimes (Ellison and Pino 2012; Verguiero 2008). Brazil also has a federal police force.

Brazil is the nation most referred to when discussing women's police stations. Sao Paulo established its first WPS in 1985 (Santos 2005). Before this time, women only represented 1 percent of the police force. Sao Paulo hired the first woman into the police department in 1959 as a police clerk (*escriva*). Santos' research found that the *escriva* was consistently harassed. With progress still the aim, the first woman officer (*delegada*) was hired in 1970. Before the WPS was opened in 1985, Sao Paulo had 16 officers. By August of that year, the department hired 26 *delegadas*, 418 *escrivas*, 628 *investigadoras*, and 229 *carcereiras* (jailors). However, women could no longer work in general police stations. Today, Brazil has almost 500 WPSs (UN Women 2011b). Unfortunately, although WPSs were created to help fight violence against women, the research shows that most of the women police hold to the same traditional gender views as male police and do not help most of the women (Santos 2005; Hautzinger 2007). Hautzinger (2020) found that these ideologies and practices are changing in Bahia, Brazil. I will briefly discuss WPSs in Chapter 6.

The Hybrid Regime: Women in the National Police of Haiti

Haiti gained independence from France in 1804, and underwent occupation by the U.S. in 1915 until 1934 (Central Intelligence Agency 2020). Today, Haiti is a semi-presidential republic, but it experienced a repressive and corrupt regime from 1971 until 1986. The legal system is based on civil law strongly influenced by the Napoleonic Code. Ninety five percent of Haitians are black, and French is the official language. Christianity is the predominant religion (87 percent) while 10.7 percent are unaffiliated (Pew Research Center 2020). In 1789, slaves outnumbered the free population by ten to one. As a result, the colonial militia's main task was to protect the colony from the slave population (Dubois 2012). Unsurprisingly, Haiti gained independence after a revolution of nearly half a million slaves. Much of Haiti's history from that point involves U.S. occupation, self-proclaimed dictatorships, and military coups. The military was finally disbanded in 1995 and replaced with the newly created civilian controlled National Police of Haiti (referred to as PNH). Amid political corruption and mass killings by gangs, the UN sent troops into Haiti in 2004 to aid in bringing down violent gangs. Additionally, in 2012, President Martelly unsuccessfully proposed reviving the army to deal with these problems. Haiti's police force is still a civil agency.

Haiti does not have large representation of women in policing. A 2013 news story reported that women have worked in the PNH since its creation in 1995 (Haiti Libre 2013). Admission into the police academy requires passing a general knowledge test, physical exercises, psychological and medical examinations, and an interview. Applicants must train for seven months, complete a one-year internship at a police station along with continuing education, and pass a test. Training for everyone involves gender violence, handcuffing techniques, and defensive tactics, among other disciplines. The PNH declared that men and women are treated the same and trained the same. However, in an attempt to "feminize the police institution," some women undergo a one-year special training in Colombia on sexual and gender-based violence, at which point they must manage these types of cases within their appointed police stations. In 2013, women police represented 8 percent of the PNH. By 2016, there were 1,747 (12.6 percent) women in the PNH.

In 2012, Haitian females in low-income urban areas were 27 times more likely to be sexually assaulted than were wealthier females in non-urban locations (Caparini and Osland 2016). Furthermore, police were likely to blame the victim and the judiciary frequently dismissed the few cases that made it that far. As a result, the United Nations Mission for Justice Support in Haiti (UN MINUJUSTH) sent a team to examine the conditions in Haiti and aid in reforming the PNH. In a 2018 news story, the Minister for the Status of Women reported that there were only 10 percent female staff in the PNH (Haiti Libre 2018). Under the 2017 MINUJUSTH, the PNH declared that by 2020 it would increase its female representation to 15 to 20 percent. Research has yet to be conducted to learn if the MINUJUSTH was effective in aiding this goal.

The Authoritarian Regime: From Sandista Guerillas to Nicaraguan Women Police

Nicaragua is a presidential republic (currently a dictatorship) that gained independence from Spain in 1821 (Central Intelligence Agency 2020). However, the British controlled the Caribbean Coast until 1860. Nicaragua has a civil legal system with Supreme Court review of administrative acts. Similar to many other countries, the current president has control of all branches of government. Nicaragua has 6.2 million people; 69 percent are Mestizo. Spanish is the official and most spoken language (95.3 percent), and 85.3 percent of the people are Christians (Pew Research Center 2020).

In 2011, women represented 30 percent of the Nicaraguan police force (Verfurth 2011). Women are deemed necessary for frisking females and handling gender-based violence. Following the overthrow of Dictator Anastasio Somoza Debayle in 1979, Marxist *Sandista* guerillas, many of them women, replaced the national security. At that time, women comprised 35 percent of the new police force. However, by the 1990s, the government downsized and cut many welfare programs, including child daycare centers. As a result, women's representation dropped to 17 percent. Additionally, men were usually promoted over women, even when less qualified. After a campaign to hire more women, lowering of the height requirement, and greater fairness in promotions, the representation of women police in 2008 reached nearly 30 percent. Furthermore, from 2006 until 2018, Aminta Granera served as the National Police Chief of Nicaragua. Under her tenure, she helped create special units designed to help female victims of violence and increase the number of women on the police force.

Nicaragua established WPSs, known as *comisarias de la mujer*, in 1993 (Neumann 2018). *Comisarias* were run by women in order to help female victims of violence. Unfortunately, this was not identified as desirable work and many of the officers desired deployment to other posts as soon as they were able (Matamoros 2016). Neumann (2018) reported that women police at the *comisarias* were marginalized. Within District 6, for example, there were no working bathrooms, no internet, computers were old, and ten women shared one vehicle. By 2016, most of 162 *comisarias* were closed (Neumann

2018). However, recent news stories tell of the reopening of the *comisarias* around the country (Canal 4 2020).

North America

Two countries comprise North America: Canada and the United States. The Economist (2020) listed Canada as a full democracy and the U.S. as a flawed democracy. Between 2006, the first year of the democracy index, and 2015, the U.S. was listed as a full democracy. However, it has been a flawed democracy with decreasing scores since 2016, with its lowest scores in the functioning of government, political participation, and political culture. Within the U.S., the increased partisan politics and Mr. Trump's undermining of the judicial branch decreased the public trust in political institutions and the political culture. On the other hand, Canada is a full democracy with increasing scores. Its lowest score is in political participation (the same score as in the U.S). Within Canada, the electoral process and pluralism and the functioning of government have always been high. While Canada's equality is strong, its declining score in civil liberties reflects its Holocaust denial laws, which limit free speech. Regardless, Canada's women represent 21 percent of its police force, while the U.S. only has 12 percent female representation (see Table 4.2).

The Full Democracy: Canadian Women Police and Mounties

Canada is one of two nations in North America. With a population of 37 million, 32.3 percent of the population is Canadian (Central Intelligence Agency 2020). The nation is also composed of large populations of English (18.3 percent), Scottish (13.9 percent), French (13.6 percent), Irish (13.4 percent), and German (9.6 percent). Chinese, Italian, North American Indian and East Indian each comprise just under 5 percent of the population, and 51.6 percent are listed as other. As in the U.S., Canadians are able to identify with more than one ethnic group. English and French are official languages. According to the Pew Research Center (2020), Christianity is the dominant religion (66.4 percent) but a quarter of the population is unaffiliated (24.5 percent).

Canada was once colonized by France and Great Britain. The French ceded most of their territory to Great Britain after the Seven Years' War and the signing of the Treaty of Paris in 1763 (Augustyn 2020). In 1867, upper and lower Canada united and in 1931, Canada declared independence from the U.K. (Central Intelligence Agency 2020). By 1982, Canada was completely free of the U.K. Colonial policing in Canada was similar to the U.S. Urban areas were first to develop formal police organizations, largely in order to control Indigenous peoples (Mawby 1999). French settlements adopted homeland forms of policing in which landowners formed night militia. In British Canada, an unpaid constable system was first developed in Newfoundland in 1729, and Upper Canada established the night-watchman system in 1793. As Mawby described, North American policing systems were power systems in which slaves, Indigenous peoples, and workers were controlled in protection of land and settlements. Adopting the decentralized policing structure, Canada's current police system operates much like the U.S. Canada has three levels of police organizations: municipal or city police, provincial police, and federal police.

Canada has a long history of employing women in policing. The country documents the first woman in policing in the early 1800s. Rose Fortune, a Black Loyalist born into slavery, imposed curfew in Annapolis, Nova Scotia (Schmidt 2016; International Association of Women Police 2018). In 1887, Mrs. Whiddon was Toronto's first police matron. Similar to other countries, she only had the authority to arrest women. Additionally, the Calgary Police Service, created in 1885, records hiring the first female employee to serve as a juvenile matron in 1905 (Calgary Police Service 2018).

The first documented female police officers in Canada were Constables Lurancy Harris and Minnie Miller, hired in Vancouver in 1912 (International Association of Women Police 2018) and Annie Jackson in Edmonton in that same year (Schmidt 2016). Policewomen in Canada wore plain clothes and served in a social worker role dealing with women and children. They also patrolled "areas of amusement where women might get into trouble," such as parks, dance halls and bars (Schmidt 2016). However, Constable Jackson worked with prostitutes, as was a common focus for women police around the world. Pushing reformer agendas, Toronto developed the Morality Bureau in 1933 in which policewomen engaged in undercover work. By the 1940s, the idea that women could serve as police started to take hold. In 1943, Calgary hired Mrs. Vera Bell and Mrs. Mowat as temporary policewomen, and in 1946, Vera Russell was hired as the first full-time policewomen (Calgary Police Service 2018).

In the Canadian federal system, the wives of male Royal Canadian Mounted Police (RCMP) were referred to as the "unpaid Mountie" or "second man" (Schmidt 2016). These women served as unpaid support staff keeping the detachments running in the early 1900s. It was not until 1974, after 101 years of establishment, that the RCMP recruited the first 32 women. Aside from some of the physical requirements, training was the same for men and women, including training in firearms, self-defense, swimming, drill, and academics. Six months later (1975), 30 women successfully completed training and were sworn in as Mounties. The swearing in occurred at the same time across the nation so that no one woman would be harassed for being the first women to break the gender barrier. In that same year, the title "policewoman" was eliminated. In her research, Schmidt learned that female Mounties were harassed by men in the community and sexually harassed by male coworkers and superiors.

Almost 20 years later, Lenna Bradburn became Canada's first female police chief (Ontario), and Christine Silverberg became Calgary's first female Police Chief in 1995. These gains in leadership roles followed the 1993 election of Canada's first female Prime Minister, Kim Campbell (BBC News 2012). Reaching higher ranks, Gwen Boniface became the first female commissioner of the Ontario police in 1998, and Beverley Busson was appointed Interim Commissioner of the RCMP. By 2016, women's representation in Canada's police was 21 percent. The RCMP appointed the first permanent female Commissioner in 2018. In May of 2020, with the increase in violence against women during the COVID-19 pandemic, victim's advocates were calling for the government to create women's police stations (Gillis and Hasham 2020).

A Flawed Democracy: Women Police in the United States

The U.S. has a population of over 332 million (Central Intelligence Agency 2020). The U.S. is very diverse compared to many countries. However, Whites still represent 72.4 percent of the population with African Americans representing 12.6 percent and Asians representing 4.8 percent. Hispanics comprise 18.3 percent of the population, though this category is considered an ethnicity and not a race. Ethnicities from all over the world can be found within the White, Black, and Asian races. However, Native Americans only comprise 0.9 percent of the U.S. population. English is the dominant language but 13.4 percent of the population speak Spanish, and 8.4 percent speak other languages. Christianity is the dominant religion (75.5 percent) with less than two percent representation of other major religions such as Buddhism, Hinduism, Islamism, Judaism, and folk religions (Pew Research Center 2020). As many as 18.6 percent of the population is unaffiliated.

The U.S. is a constitutional federal republic with a common law legal system based on English common laws at the federal and the state levels of government (Central Intelligence Agency 2020). However, the law of the state of Louisiana is based on Napoleonic civil code. The Spanish were among the first to colonize the U.S. However, the nation was also colonized by the British, French, and Dutch. As history reveals, the British gained the most territory and influence within U.S. history as well as within U.S. policing. As Mawby (1999) described, U.S. policing reflected the systems of the countries colonizing the territory, the most prominent being the English night-watchman system. This system continued even after U.S. independence in 1776. Along with night watchmen, frontier territories relied on U.S. Marshals and vigilantes, while the southern states formed slave patrols.

Modern policing was structured after the Metropolitan Police of London. With all structures of policing, crime control and minority population control has been the primary focus, from Native Americans to slaves to immigrants and other minorities. Following most early policing, U.S. policing operates with a paramilitary structure, which is masculinized.

Women first entered policing as jail and prison matrons when New York hired two female matrons in 1845 (National Center for Women in Policing 2013). Widows were also sometimes appointed with the rank of policeman as a type of death benefit. Mary Owens was hired with the Chicago Police Department under such conditions in 1893. She was the first woman to have arrest powers. In 1905, Lola Baldwin was hired as a safety worker in Portland, Oregon. However, Alice Stebbens Wells was the first sworn policewoman in 1910 (Garcia 2003; Heidensohn 1992). Wells helped establish the International Association of Policewomen in 1915 and led a policewomen's movement that aided entry. By 1925, 210 cities employed 417 policewomen but still employed 355 female matrons (Heidensohn 1992).

As discussed in Chapter 2, women's movement into policing in the U.S. and the U.K. occurred in stages (Martin 1980; Heidensohn 1992). In the first stage, women began as self-proclaimed moral reformers (1840–1910/15) and as such they entered policing with the skills that allowed them to help women and children (Barlow and Barlow 2000; Schulz 1995). As I have discussed with other nations in this book, this seems to be the first stage of entry for all women police, no matter the year of entry. In the second stage, women became specialists and pioneers (1910/15–1930). Here, women's maternal, nurturing skills were deemed necessary to protect women and children (Martin 1980). Women won the right to work with women and children as officers, but not as police, and women's police precincts were created (Martin 1980; Schulz 2004). Many nations, such as India and Brazil, have maintained the specialist model for women in their police forces. The number of policewomen during this stage in the U.S. increased to 417. Latency and depression (1930–1945) is the third stage, in which in the hiring of women police slowed down. In the U.S., the Great Depression was a major cause for this stagnancy (Horne 1980; Schulz 1995). Women were let go and women's precincts/stations were closed. Additionally, the role that policewomen claimed for themselves did not solidify their needed presence in a masculine and dangerous organization (Garcia 2003; Heidensohn 1992). This pattern is also common in nations throughout the world. Stricter standards and small quotas for women was also a major barrier for increased numbers. Informal expansion (1945–1970) occurred next and was the result of needed bodies caused by World War II. For the first time, women were assigned general police duties, such as traffic and patrol, and their numbers increased from 2,610 in 1950 to 11,234 in 1970. By this time, however, the specializations of policewomen moved to the social welfare field, leaving women to find another purpose for their presence in the police force.

The civil rights movement and laws of the 1960s gave women the tools they needed to claim the ranks within policing and the organization moved into the integration and afterwards stage (1970s to present). Specifically, Title VII (1972) outlawed discriminatory practices in the workplace, while the Crime Control Act (1973) banned sexual discrimination in policing (Bell 1982). Additionally, a number of lawsuits broke down some of the barriers that women faced in the field. Women represented 12 percent of the U.S. sworn police in 2015 (UNODC 2020) and 12.6 percent in 2018 (Statistica 2020). In 2013, women comprised 9.5 percent of first-line supervisors and 2.7 percent of chiefs and executives (National Institute of Justice 2019). In 2019, in New York City, the largest police department in the country, women comprised 18 percent of sworn personnel but 68 percent of civilian personnel. The U.S. has a long road ahead to reach the tip-over point and even further to obtain equity in promotion for women (Garcia 2017, 2020).

Western Europe

The number of countries that comprise Western Europe is different depending on the source. The Economist (2020) gathered data from 21 countries in this region (see Table 4.3). Most countries in Western Europe are full democracies. Turkey is the only hybrid regime. While Western Europe has a strong democracy index, it has fallen since 2006. As with the U.S., dissatisfaction with traditional mainstream political parties is strong. This has resulted in political wins for anti-establishment parties in Austria, Belgium, Italy, and Spain. Parliament's attempts to sidetrack Brexit created some government dysfunction, but conservative wins in elections helped to counterbalance the disruption. These events have increased political participation, and Portugal saw a rise in confidence in political parties. Finally, Malta dropped to a flawed democracy after the government assassination of a journalist and corruption found at the bloc's border.

Table 4.4 reveals UNODC data for 16 nations in Western Europe. Compared to Eastern Europe, we see fewer countries that have reached tip over:

Table 4.3 Democracy Regimes in Western Europe

Regime type	*Country*
Full democracy	Austria, Denmark, Finland, France, Germany, Iceland, Ireland, Luxembourg, Netherlands, Norway, Portugal, Spain, Sweden, Switzerland, United Kingdom
Flawed democracy	Belgium, Cyprus, Greece, Italy, Malta
Hybrid regime	Turkey

Source: The Economist. 2020. Democracy Index 2019. *A Year of Democratic Setbacks and Popular Protest*. New York: The Economist Intelligence Unit Limited.

Table 4.4 Women Police in Western Europe, 2015 (UNODC)

Country	*Regime*	*Number*	*Percent*
Netherlands	Full	18,916	32%
Sweden	Full	6,252	31%
Cyprus	Flawed	1,214	25%
Belgium	Flawed	8,154	22%
Germany	Full	49,976	20%
Malta	Flawed	417	19%
France	Full	38,828	19%
Finland	Full	1,253	16%
Austria	Full	4,380	16%
Iceland	Full	95	15%
Denmark	Full	1,520	14%
Greece	Flawed	7,054	13%
Luxembourg	Full	230	12%
Spain	Full	18,455	11%
Portugal	Full	3,500	7%
Italy	Flawed	19,489	7%

Source: United Nations Office of Drugs and Crime. 2020. *Administration of justice*. www.unodc.org/unodc/en/data-and-analysis/statistics/crime.html (accessed May 11, 2020).

the Netherlands, Sweden, and Cyprus. Overall, five nations have 20 percent or more female representation in policing. In comparison, Eastern Europe does better at bringing women into policing than Western Europe. However, Western Europe has overall higher representation at the bottom ranks. Interestingly, most of the hybrid and authoritarian nations in Eastern Europe have higher representation than we find in Western Europe. Western European nations also have more equality in this area than most of the Americas, with the exceptions of Guyana and Trinidad and Tobago. In the following discussion, I examine the U.K. and Ireland (full democracies), Greece (flawed democracy), and Turkey (hybrid democracy). Western Europe does not have any authoritarian regimes.

Full Democracies: Women Policing the United Kingdom and Ireland

The United Kingdom has a population of 65.7 million people with 84 percent of the population in England, 8 percent in Scotland, 5 percent in Wales, and 3 percent in Northern Ireland. Britons are predominantly White (87.2 percent) followed by Asian/Asian British (9.9 percent), and Black (3 percent). Fifty nine percent of the population are Christians, 6.1 percent Muslims, and 31.2 percent are unaffiliated (Pew Research Center 2020). The U.K. has a common law system that has been adopted by many post-colonized nations around the world and a nonbinding judicial review of Acts of Parliament. The U.K. served as a world leader and imperial power for centuries and annexed countries on every continent. As a result, the U.K. does not celebrate a national independence day. Currently the U.K. still has rule over territories.

As discussed in Chapter 2, the U.K. had several forms of policing that it imposed on its colonies, including the military/quasi-military and night watchmen systems and the Royal Irish Constabulary system. Modern policing within the U.K. was the result of the introduction of the Metropolitan Police Act by Robert Peel in 1829 (Heidensohn 1992). The Act organized the police under a central government and focused on crime fighting and prevention, collectivity, and visibility. England, Wales, and Northern Ireland have 44 police forces and Scotland has eight (Beckley 2007).

The history of women's entry into the U.K. police forces is similar to that of the U.S. Heidensohn's (1992) research found the same stages of movement in the U.K. police as she did in the U.S. police, with subtle differences. In the U.K., the moral reformers stage (1840–1910/15) came with more struggle. Women's initial roles were as female searchers and police matrons. Levine (1994) noted an 1892 letter from Inspector Herbert Croft of the Hereford Constabulary. Upon his inspection of nine towns in the 1890s, Inspector Croft noted the presence of policemen's wives serving as matrons without pay. Additionally, from the mid-1860s through the mid-1880s, in response to the Contagious Diseases Act, women in plainclothes patrolled the streets for prostitutes. It was believed that a woman's presence would protect female prostitutes from male police.

By 1893, most major constabularies in England, Scotland, and Wales employed females as matrons, warders, and searchers. However, the centralized nature of the police organization, as compared to the decentralized U.S. police, required reformers to gain approval to appoint policewomen from various committees and the Royal Commissions. Like the U.S., U.K. moral reformers joined policing in order to do a different job, i.e., protect women and children. Unlike policewomen in the U.S., policewomen in the U.K. had a greater role as "moral police" enforcing curfews and controlling provocative behaviors of women. Many claim that policewomen actually engaged in control over women instead of their protection. In other words, policewomen of the U.K. and U.S. joined the oppressors of women and children and solidified their traditional gender role.

During U.K.'s specialists and pioneers stage (1910/15–1930), English women fought harder than U.S. women to gain entrance into policing. Most women still served on a voluntary basis but fought hard on moral grounds. The first woman to be officially sworn in as a policewoman in the U.K. was Edith Smith in 1915 (Heidensohn 1992). While English policewomen experienced greater possibility for promotion, their numbers decreased during the latency and depression stage (1930–1945). Only 25 percent of the constabularies employed women. However, some gains were made during informal expansion (1945–1970). In England and Wales, marriage bars were removed and the number of policewomen about doubled. By 1966, women represented 5 percent of the police force. During the integration and afterwards stage (1970s to present), like in the U.S., women police in the U.K. experienced a decline in their specialist role and they were integrated into the general duties of the police. Their numbers continued to increase. In the U.K., the Sex Discrimination Act of 1975 eliminated discrimination in the workforce and applied to police organizations. While integration in the U.S. is questionable with their 12 percent representation, women police made up 30.4 percent of the U.K. police force in 2019 (Home Office 2019). This represented a 3 percent increase from 2018 and a 4.7 percent increase from 2010. While women are more likely to hold constable rank (32.2 percent), their leadership positions have also reached tip over in the positions of chief inspector (26 percent), superintendent (27.6 percent), and chief officers (27.4 percent).

The Republic of Ireland has a population of 5.1 million people with 82.2 percent Irish (Central Intelligence Agency 2020). English and Irish (Gaelic) are official languages and 89.7 percent are Christians, mostly Roman Catholic (78.3 percent) (Central Intelligence Agency 2020; Pew Research Center 2020). Ireland came under British control in the twelfth century after Norse control; however, it was never a colony. After centuries of struggle, British rule ended in 1921. In 1922, Ireland established itself as the Irish Free State, and in 1949, it legislated itself the Republic of Ireland.

Policing in Ireland cannot be understood unless one considers the evolution of policing in the southern and northern regions of the island. The Constabulary of Ireland was established in 1836, after prior failed attempts with the Baronial Police and the Peace Preservation Force in 1814 (Police Service of Northern Ireland 2020a). The Constabulary was centralized and controlled all aspects of the lives of policemen. It was a colonial as well as a quasi-military force that focused on controlling crime and nationalist insurrection. In 1867, it became the Royal Irish Constabulary (RIC) after putting down the Fenian Rising. This police force was modeled in many of the colonized lands, as discussed in Chapter 2. However, discontent with British rule and years of conflict persisted, and Ireland partitioned with the Government of Ireland Act in 1920. Partition created Northern Ireland (six counties that are part of the U.K.) and Southern Ireland or 26 counties (known as the Republic of Ireland). After the partition, the Civic Guard (now An Garda Siochana) was created to police Ireland (Republic of Ireland) and the Royal Ulster Constabulary (RUC) was formed in 1922 to police Northern Ireland, which is part of the U.K. The RUC was now concerned with Irish Republican Army terrorism. However, by 1968, the RUC's military duties were eliminated and the Police Authority for Northern Ireland was established.

The RIC began to appoint women police in 1917 in the Dublin Metropolitan Police (Holmes 2018). The RIC hired four women to patrol the streets between 7 pm and midnight in order to protect society against "khaki fever," the extreme attraction and promiscuity of women toward military men during World War I (Clancy 2009). These women were paid and wore uniforms but did not have arrest powers as they were not actual members of the police force. However, in 1917, there were two female constables already part of the police force. Most of the women did not have police powers and held the title women police assistants. Most retired from service over time and were not replaced. By 1955, only one woman patrolled the streets.

The Republic of Ireland's An Garda Siochana established a women's division in 1959. Northern Ireland's RUC, on the other hand, established a women's division in 1943. It would seem that as part of the U.K., Northern Ireland moved more in line with the policies of England. These units were tasked with handling cases dealing with women and children. As in the U.K., the fight to appoint women police was an arduous one. An Garda Siochana hired its first 12 women police when it opened the women's unit. When determining who should be hired it was stated, "While recruits should not be actually horse faced, they should not be good looking. They should be just plain women and not targets for marriage" (Clancy 2009). By the 1970s, women held the rank of officer and gained the right to carry firearms in 1994. Additionally, the marriage ban was eliminated in 1973. In 1959, there were 12 female Gardas; by 1991, there were 419. In 2009, 3,074 women served as police for An Garda Siochana. In 2019, there were 3,780 female Garda representing 27 percent of the entire force. The Police Service of Northern Ireland (2020b) reported that women in the RUC were 29.7 percent of police officers and 58.4 percent of female staff.

A Flawed Democracy: Women in the Greek Hellenic Police

Current Greece was established in 1830 after shedding rule from the Ottoman Empire but was invaded by Italy in 1940 and occupied by Germany from 1941 to 1944 (Central Intelligence Agency 2020). The nation has undergone dictatorship and is now a parliamentary republic. Greece has a civil law legal system based on Roman law. The nation has a population of 10.6 million, 91.6 percent of whom are Greek, and Greek is the official language. The Pew Research Center (2020) reported that 87.6 percent of

Greeks were Christians in 2020, 5.9 percent were Muslim, and 6.1 percent were unaffiliated.

Greece initially had a dual police system, the national gendarmerie and the municipal police, influenced by Ottoman rule (Farsedakis 2006). However, over time and reorganization, the two systems joined to create the Hellenic Police in 1984. The Hellenic Police is a national centralized police force with regional services. Women first entered the police force in Greece in 1969 (Hellenic Police 2011). At this time, 69 women were appointed to the former City Police Force (1921–1984), and by 1971, women police were under with the status of "special women staff" in the Gendarmerie Service. More than ten years later, women were allowed to attend the police academy but were held to a 10 percent quota. However, by 2003, the quota limits were eliminated. By 2006, women represented 11 percent of the Hellenic Police (Farsedakis 2006). Yet, in 2011, women's representation decreased to 10 percent (Hellenic Police 2011). According to the Hellenic Police, women are recruited without quotas and attend the same academies with the same training. Furthermore, women are not restricted to any position and all ranks are open. In 2020, a woman was promoted to Police Major General for the first time. Women of the Hellenic Police are experiencing the same drop that most women police around the world are experiencing.

Hybrid Regime: Women in the Turkish National Police

The Republic of Turkey declared independence in 1923, shortly after the fall of the Ottoman Empire (Central Intelligence Agency 2020). Turkey is currently a presidential republic with a civil law system based on various European legal systems. The population of Turkey is 82 million with over 70 percent Turks and 19 percent Kurds. Turkish is the official language and 98 percent of Turks are Muslim (Pew Research Center 2020).

Turkey's police system is a national police made up of the Turkish National Police (TNP), the General Directorate of Police, and the local branches (Gültekin, Leichtman, and Garrison 2010). There is not much research on women police in Turkey. A news story tells us that the first traffic police officer in Istanbul's police force was Fikriye Yavuz (Pancar 2020). She served as a female traffic police officer. So unusual was this that she made headlines. She was later appointed to several branches of the TNP and eventually became chief inspector. However, there was no systematic effort to recruit women into the TNP until 1979 (Gültekin, Leichtman, and Garrison 2010). In their research, Gültekin, Leichtman, and Garrison found that women's representation in the TNP was 4.9 percent in 2001 and 5.5 percent in 2005. The lowest rank within the police is constable, or police officer, which is unranked. Women constables represent 5.2 percent of all TNP officials. Seen another way, among all constables (unranked officers), women represent 86.8 percent of this group. Women have a small representation in each of the ranks: sergeant, lieutenant, captain, major, and one- to four-star police chiefs. Gültekin and colleagues also found that women police face discrimination in recruitment, promotion, and deployment.

Conclusion

The analysis of the Eastern and Western Hemispheres reveals various patterns when examining women in policing. First, in each nation, women joined under the assumption that women are innately qualified to work with women and children. With earlier entry, the focus was on prostitution. Whether to protect women or to control them, reformers and police alike defined this as a woman's job. With later entry, the focus was on searching and guarding females or on responding to gender-based violence. All nations relegated cases involving children to the women's sphere of work with the tasks of protecting, guiding, interviewing, and guarding juveniles, often within juvenile detention centers. These duties resulted in the second commonality among most nations, the WPS. Most police forces created WPSs in order to work with women and children. However, more recently, these stations have been designed specifically to deal with gender-based violence. In most cases, these stations have been all-women stations.

A third pattern found with almost all nations was that women entered as civilians before they became policewomen and then became women police. Most nations denied women full police powers upon entry. When women gained police power, it was typically when dealing with women, children, and traffic. Some police forces still do not allow women officers to police men. Fourth, in all nations, women police have had to deal with resistance from male coworkers. Resistance takes the form of negative attitudes, verbal abuse and sexual harassment, and assault. As a male-dominant masculine occupation, women who have broken the gender barrier have had to grow a "thick skin" in order to work within the organization. Fifth, recruitment, training, and deployment for women has gone from avoidance to creating legal barriers to acceptance with altered gender-specific requirements. Initially, the possibility of a woman police was not a concept. Later, legal barriers were erected. From gaining parental permission to height requirements, women have had to battle many hurdles in order to find a place in the police organization. Once women gained entry, training was altered to accommodate the height and build of women. When finally sworn in as a police officer, women have had to face legal barriers that limited hours and the times of day they could work as well as how strenuous the work given them was. Last, but certainly not the end, women have faced hurdles in gaining promotions. In some police forces, superiors initiate promotion.

In all police forces, men tend to be given priority in most cases of promotion. The six commonalities outlined here are experienced with variation throughout the world. The next two chapters will examine these issues in detail. In Chapter 5, I will examine the gendered organizational structure that tends to create barriers for women police in the areas of recruitment, training, and promotion. In Chapter 6, I will focus on the resulting stress of these barriers, as well as sexual harassment and the gendered work of women police.

Chapter 5

Recruitment, Training, and Promotion of Women in the Gendered Police Organization

In 2002, Anastasia Prokos and Irene Padavic published a study about the hegemonic masculine hidden curriculum in the U.S. police academy. The main title of their article was "There Oughtta Be a Law Against Bitches." This title has been a favorite title of mine because it tends to epitomize the attitudes of many men in policing. The researchers in this article explained that cadets borrowed this term in a "joking" manner from a *COPS* television show they viewed during training. From that point on, cadets would yell out the phrase "there oughtta be a law against bitches" when joking about a woman or about something a female cadet did. While the phrase was used in jest, the woman who shared the story felt ostracized. This article used 1997 data. The question we must ask is how much has the police organization changed since this time. In countries, such as Canada, Poland, Germany, the U.K., and the U.S., where women joined the ranks of police prior to the 1920s, one would think that the police culture would accept women. However, the phrase referenced above came from a study conducted in the U.S., 92 years after the first sworn policewoman was hired within that country. The U.S. has made a lot of improvement, giving women general police duties in the 1970s. Nevertheless, not enough improvement has been made. Women still represent only 12 percent of U.S. police forces and this representation is decreasing. In many nations, women remain separated in specialized police duties or in civilian positions pointing to the belief that they cannot or should not engage in general policing. I stress that in many countries, women hold to these beliefs as well. This is not a condemnation of traditional gender roles. It is, however, a condemnation of the value given to women and "women's work."

In Chapters 2 through 4, I asked if we can truly consider women integrated into policing if their duties are still predominantly segregated and devalued. In her discussion of integration, Heidensohn stated of women police in the U.K. and U.S. after the 1970s, "[T]hey no longer have their own bureau and most discriminatory recruiting practices are, or are being, removed" (1992, p. 56). While she recognized that male colleagues' rejection of integration is much more problematic, Heidensohn stated that integration was achieved in the U.S. and U.K. in the 1970s because women were given equal ranks and general police duties. For other researchers, integration has been a consideration of numbers. In 1997, Jennifer Brown discussed tip over, three stages beyond integration, as the point when women's representation moves from a minority to gender-balance. Many scholars have run with Brown's discussion of tip over as 25 percent representation. I reject 25 percent as the telltale sign of tip over for women police, as it represents a much lower representation than that of the larger female workforce. Instead, I will hold to Brown's statement that with tip over and women's growing leadership within the police organization, "there appears to be a need to maintain external scrutiny through some watch-dog mechanism, policing the organization and making remedial interventions once policies and procedures have had a chance to influence the internal organization culture" (1997, p. 15). Brown recognized that numbers were not enough. In a later work, Brown and Silvestri (2020) argued that, along with tip over numbers, the police structure and culture need to change. They also emphasized the need for greater police accountability, a balanced ratio of gender in all areas of policing, and greater gender equality legislation.

In a previous policing book, I concluded that for many nations, integration is not necessarily the ultimate goal (Garcia 2020). Given what we know about women policing around the world as discussed in Chapters 3 and 4 and given what we know about current gender ideologies around the world, one might claim that true integration has never been the goal of any police organization. We can point to individuals, even groups of individuals both men and women, who hail the entry and work of women as equals in policing. However, as we examine the gendered substructure and subtext of police organizations (Acker 2012), we see the lack of true effort to create effective equality policies and the lack of enthusiasm to enforce these policies. Gendered substructures are the ongoing processes that produce and reproduce gender and gender inequalities within an organization, while the subtext includes the written or common practices that shape the gendered processes and structures of the organization. These two social facts make policing gendered organizations and reveals that discussions of integration are premature. After describing the entry and current status of women police throughout the world in Chapters 3 and 4, we must return to our discussion of the sociology of gender that opened this book.

The sociology of gender requires that we acknowledge that gender is a master status and is understood and defined through a patriarchal system. This patriarchal system stratifies gender in a way that places males in power, giving them a higher status and marginalizing females. It also creates policing as a gendered organization. As Herbert (2001) describes, policing is a masculinist organization that suppresses any non-masculine reforms. Policing does gender, or rather hegemonic masculinity, on a daily basis, and thus recreates hegemonic masculinity on a daily basis. To introduce women defies this work, especially since within the hegemonic masculinity, women must be protected by men (Messerschmidt 2016). Thus, the police organization becomes a gendered organization. One that is structured to reproduce hegemonic masculinity. Returning to the gendered organization discussion, I turn my examination to these structural practices and barriers. Specifically, I examine how the gendered substructure and subtext of police resists women in policing via legal barriers, recruitment, training, and promotion.

Recruitment/Inroads Into Policing

Recruitment of women into policing is the first activity of a gendered organization. The police organization is a gendered organization that has formal and informal rules of masculinity and femininity (Acker 2012; Garcia 2017; Herbert 2001; Martin and Jurik 2007). Furthermore, the organizational logic (i.e., common understandings of how organizations work) is premised in masculinity (Acker 2012). In policing, this is seen in its military or paramilitary structure, a structure where few women fit. Additionally, gender inequalities are found within the gendered subtext (i.e., the written or common practices that shape the gendered processes and structures of the organization), organizing processes, organization culture, and interactions on the job (Acker 2012). These are all part of the gendered substructure (i.e., the ongoing processes that produce and reproduce gender and gender inequalities within an organization). In a modern gendered organization, substructure and subtext appear to be gender neutral, or abstract, without taking into account the gender inequalities that already exist as well as the non-work obligations held by workers. For women, these are usually family obligations. Considering this gendered organization in light of gender ideologies, we see barriers within recruitment and training.

Policing has become increasingly crime-control oriented in the war on terror and in conflict and post-conflict nations. For some nations, this reflects no change in policing as the crime-control ideology did not waver much. For other nations, this means a decreased focus on community-based policing and a decreased concern for the conditions of women in policing. As a result, the "cult of masculinity" remains or increasingly becomes the face of policing (Silvestri 2003, p. 33). This cult of masculinity in a gendered organization results in a continued belief that police work, which is task oriented, dangerous, and physically hard, is men's work. This invariably affects women's abilities to enter the organization and gain positions of leadership (Figure 5.1).

Legislative Labor Restrictions for Women

Entry itself can be difficult when considering labor laws that restrict women's work. These laws represent the gendered subtext of the gendered organization. They are the written practices that shape the gendered substructure.

Figure 5.1 Israel Border Police, 2020.

Source: Photo used with permission from the Israel Police Heritage Center.

Women, Business and the Law (2020b) of the World Bank collected data on labor laws for 190 countries and found that 102 countries did not have a law that mandated equal remuneration for women for work of equal value. These countries are located in all regions of the world. Twenty-six countries did not allow women to work the same night hours as men and 56 countries did not allow women to work jobs deemed dangerous in the same way as men.

Table 5.1 reveals the legislated workplace limitations for women by region. Countries in the MENA region tend to place the greatest restrictions on women. For example, within MENA, 54.5 percent of the countries do not allow women to work the same night hours as men, and 72.7 percent do not allow women to work in dangerous jobs in the same way as men. In these countries, you find more women working in administrative or traffic duties or with women and children. These data tell us that women are limited from entering the field of law enforcement. However, 29.5 percent of the countries worldwide place limits on women's ability to work dangerous jobs. This has real repercussions for women in policing in that in some countries, such as those within the GCC, women are relegated to handling cases involving women and children only, or they may be denied the right to carry a firearm or to serve in quasi-military units (Strobl 2016, 2020). In the same fashion, countries in MENA are least likely to allow women to

Table 5.1 Labor Laws Constraining Women's Movement in the Workplace, 2020

	Asia	*Eastern Europe*	*Latin America and the Caribbean*	*MENA*	*North America*	*Oceania*	*Sub-Saharan Africa*	*Western Europe*	*Total*
Women cannot work the same night hours as men	15.4%	14.8%	6.1%	54.5%	0.0%	16.7%	4.3%	0.0%	13.7%
Women cannot work in jobs deemed dangerous in the same way as men	23.1%	25.9%	18.2%	72.7%	0.0%	8.3%	42.6%	0.0%	29.5%
Women cannot work in hazardous jobs in the same way as men	19.2%	25.9%	12.1%	54.5%	0.0%	0.0%	36.2%	0.0%	23.7%
Women cannot work in jobs considered arduous in the same way as men	11.5%	25.9%	9.1%	59.1%	0.0%	8.3%	34.8%	0.0%	22.8%
Women cannot work in jobs deemed morally inappropriate in the same way as men	0.0%	0.0%	12.1%	31.8%	0.0%	0.0%	19.6%	0.0%	10.6%

Source: World Bank Group. 2020b. *Women, Business and the Law*. https://wbl.worldbank.org/en/data/exploretopics/wbl_sj (accessed June 3, 2020).

work in jobs deemed hazardous (54.5 percent) or arduous (59.1 percent) in the same way as do men. These data were 23.7 percent and 22.8 percent for the world's nations, respectively. In the latter category, in early policing for women, most countries did not allow women to lift heavy objects. From Table 5.1, we see that a quarter of the countries in Eastern Europe do not allow women to work in dangerous, hazardous, or arduous jobs in the same way as do men. We also see that North America and Western Europe are the least restrictive. However, from our earlier examinations, we also saw that many of the other regions have higher percentages of women in policing.

Tables 5.2 and 5.3 show the labor restrictions for the countries examined in Chapters 3 and 4. The data are organized by the year of entry. We can see that all of the countries in the Western Hemisphere examined in Chapter 4 had laws that allowed women to work night hours and dangerous, hazardous, and arduous jobs in the same way as men. However, three countries did not have legislation that guaranteed equal pay for women: Brazil, Nicaragua, and the U.S. All of these countries are located in North America and South America. While the U.S. does have laws requiring equal pay, exceptions are allowed for equal pay and large gender pay gaps exist. The presence of these laws, however, does not affect female representation as Greece, Haiti, Poland, Turkey, and Uruguay all have low female representation and also have equal pay laws. On the other hand, Nicaragua restricts equal pay but has one of the highest female representations, as shown in the Table 5.2. The year of entry also does not appear to be a factor. Additionally, as we saw in Chapters 3 and 4, while laws may appear to provide equality, practices often find ways around them (Acker 1992). We see this in all nations. Identifying some of these countries found in the research, we see this in Australia (Fleming 2020), Bangladesh (Afroze 2017), Brazil (Santos 2005), Canada (Langan, Sanders, and Gouweloos 2019), China (Shen 2020), India (Natarajan 2014), Israel (Shadmi 1993), Nicaragua (Verfurth 2011), Nigeria (Akinjobi-Babatunde 2015), South Africa (Morrison 2004), the U.K. (Brown and Silvestri 2020), and the U.S. (Garcia 2017).

Table 5.3 provides these data for the Eastern Hemisphere countries examined in Chapter 3. From this table, we see that countries with the most legislative restrictions have the least amount of female representation in policing and are predominantly in the MENA, or the GCC to be more specific (Strobl 2020). The exception is Ukraine, which has five of the six legislative restrictions presented in the table and is in Eastern Europe. Within the Ukraine, women cannot work the same night hours as men or dangerous jobs in the same way as men. Laws also prohibit women from working in some industries, such as mining. Additionally, the law does not provide equal remuneration for work of equal value. Women have entered policing within the Ukraine; however, they only represent 8 percent of the police force. Additionally, they tend to work in support roles, as discussed in Chapter 3.

Table 5.2 Labor Laws Hindering Women's Movement into Policing in the Western Hemisphere, 2020

	Region	*Equal Pay*[1]	*Night hours*	*Dangerous jobs*	*Hazardous Jobs*	*Arduous jobs*	*Year Entered*	*% Police*
U.S.	NA	No	Yes	Yes	Yes	Yes	1905	12%
Canada	NA	Yes	Yes	Yes	Yes	Yes	1912	21%
U.K.	WE	Yes	Yes	Yes	Yes	Yes	1915	30.4%
Ireland	WE	Yes	Yes	Yes	Yes	Yes	1917	27%
Brazil	LAC	No	Yes	Yes	Yes	Yes	1924	14%
Uruguay	LAC	Yes	Yes	Yes	Yes	Yes	1924	24%
Poland	WE	Yes	Yes	Yes	Yes	Yes	1926	13%
Turkey	WE	Yes	Yes	Yes	Yes	Yes	1932	5.5%
Greece	WE	Yes	Yes	Yes	Yes	Yes	1969	13%
Haiti	LAC	Yes	Yes	Yes	Yes	Yes	1995	10%
Nicaragua	LAC	No	Yes	Yes	Yes	Yes	—	30%

Source: World Bank Group. 2020b. *Women, Business and the Law*. https://wbl.worldbank.org/en/data/exploretopics/wbl_sj (accessed June 3, 2020).

[1] See https://wbl.worldbank.org/en/methodology#3 for definition. Considers exceptions written into the law.

Table 5.3 Labor Laws Hindering Women's Movement into Policing in the Eastern Hemisphere, 2020

	Region	*Equal Pay*[1]	*Night hours*	*Dangerous jobs*	*Hazardous Jobs*	*Arduous jobs*	*Year Entered*	*Percent Police*[2]
Australia	Oceania	Yes	Yes	Yes	Yes	Yes	1915	32%
Nigeria	SSA	No	Yes	Yes	Yes	Yes	1923	35%
China	Asia	No	Yes	No	Yes	No	1929	19%
Hungary	EE	No	Yes	Yes	Yes	Yes	1935	23%
India	Asia	No	No	Yes	Yes	Yes	1938	7.3%
Israel	MENA	Yes	Yes	No	No	Yes	1948	25%
Fiji	Oceania	No	Yes	Yes	Yes	Yes	1968	10%
Bahrain	MENA	No	No	No	Yes	No	1970	10%
South Africa	SSA	Yes	Yes	Yes	Yes	Yes	1972	27.50%
Bangladesh	Asia	No	Yes	No	No	Yes	1973	10%
Oman	MENA	No	No	No	No	No	1974	5%
UAE	MENA	No	Yes	Yes	Yes	Yes	1977	5%
Qatar	MENA	No	Yes	No	No	No	1980s	5%
Lebanon	MENA	No	Yes	Yes	Yes	Yes	2001	0.01%
Albania	EE	Yes	Yes	Yes	Yes	Yes	2006	10%
Kuwait	MENA	No	No	No	No	No	2009	5%
Russia	EE	Yes	Yes	No	No	No	—	17%
Tajikistan	EE	Yes	Yes	No	No	No	—	—
Ukraine	EE	No	No	No	No	No	—	8%
Uzbekistan	EE	No	Yes	Yes	Yes	Yes	—	—
Algeria	MENA	Yes	No	No	Yes	No	—	6%
Mauritius	SSA	Yes	Yes	Yes	Yes	Yes	—	9%
Saudi Arabia	MENA	Yes	No	No	No	Yes	NA	0%

Source: World Bank Group. 2020b. *Women, Business and the Law.* https://wbl.worldbank.org/en/data/exploretopics/wbl_sj.

[1] See https://wbl.worldbank.org/en/methodology#3 for definition. Considers exceptions written into the law.

In most countries, whether labor restrictions or equality is legislated, there are often exceptions to allowing women to work in particularly closed or open fields of employment. For example, bona fide occupational qualifications (Title VII, S703(e)(1)) in the U.S. allow for an employer to reject an applicant based on sex, religion, or national origin only if the applicant's group affiliation would make it impossible to perform the job being considered (U.S. Equal Employment Opportunity Commission 2000). In the case of criminal justice and gender, employment is limited in how men and women work in prisons. In China, women cannot be denied employment based on gender. However, Chapter II, Article 13 specifies that women must be given equal rights in employment, "with exception of the special types of work or post unsuitable to women as prescribed by the State" (Congressional Executive Commission on China 2016). Taiwan enacted gender equality legislation in 2001 and created the Gender Equality Department (Chu 2020). Taiwan began hiring women police in 1949. By 1952, Taipei created an all-women police unit, and by 1977, women were regularly recruited. Today, Taiwanese women police represent 10.62 percent of the police force and are allowed to work in general policing but tend to have greater representation in gender-restricted duties working with women and children and in support roles to men.

Within the GCC, most of the countries have four to six restrictions. The UAE only restricts equal pay, but women only represent 5 percent of the police force and 10 percent in the Dubai police (Chu 2020). Dubai first hired women police in 1977. However, following the 2015 establishment of the UAE's Gender Balance Council, which is tasked with implementing the Gender Inequality Index, recruitment of women in traditionally male occupations has started to increase substantially. Saudi Arabia only has three restrictions (night hours, dangerous jobs, and hazardous jobs). Saudi Arabia has only recently started to allow women to apply for positions in traffic police; however, there were no statistics on their representation in the police force as of 2020. Moreover, Lebanon only restricts pay, and women represent 0.01 percent of the police force. Furthermore, most of the countries that legally allow women to work duties outside of cases involving women and children or administrative tasks place informal restrictions on women police by relegating them to these fields by practice. This is widely practiced in both hemispheres. For example, although women are allowed regular police duties, women police in India and Brazil tend to be appointed to women's police stations, limiting their exposure to more high-profile cases (Natarajan 2008; Santos 2005). Additionally, in China, promotions are initiated by supervisors, who acting through the edicts of culture, tend to select men (Ding 2020).

Recruitment Efforts

Recruitment efforts tend to reflect the gendered subtext by their written and informal practices. Many countries are increasing their recruitment efforts of women. Some countries, like Turkey, place maximum quotas on the number of women that can be hired into the police force (Gültekin, Leichtman, and Garrison 2010). However, under reform efforts, many countries have imposed quotas that dictate the minimum number of women to employ within the police force. In Fiji, the police Commissioner declared a quota in order to increase women's representation in policing from 10 percent to 25 percent (BBC Monitoring Asia Pacific 2004). In Bangladesh, quotas require that 15 percent of entry-level police positions and 10 percent of supervisory positions must be reserved for women (Afroze 2017). Recruitment campaigns are then initiated for mid-level positions. The Hellenic Police in Greece eliminated its 10 percent maximum quota in 2003 (Farsedakis 2006), and China has a 15 percent national recruitment quota (Shen 2020). In a comparative study, Van der Lippe, Graumans, and Sevenhuijsen (2004) found that the Netherlands adopted a 25 percent quota and Austria adopted a 40 percent quota but Sweden and Catalonia, Spain did not impose quotas or goals. The NPF declared an increase in women's representation to 35 percent (Prenzler and Sinclair 2013). Following UN peacekeeping recommendations, the Timor-Leste police adopted a 20 percent quota (Karim et al. 2018).

In post-conflict Liberia, with only 2 percent women police, a quota was set at 15 percent in 2008. The Liberia National Police (LNP) then increased its quota to 20 percent and then to 30 percent by 2010. Very few countries, however, ever meet their quotas. By 2015, women police only represented 19 percent in the LNP. While this is far from its 30 percent goal, it is a large improvement from the 2 percent representation in 2005. Albania State Police's (ASP) mandate that 50 percent of new recruits be women resulted in an all-women basic police training class in 2011 (Women Police Officers Network 2012). The ASP also loosened the driver's license requirement for women and instituted preparatory training classes for women in order to increase their enrollment. Following Taiwan's gender equality legislation, recruitment brochures specified that all cadets would be given first-line duty (Chu 2013). By 2007, the recruitment brochures stated that female and male cadets would receive identical duties.

In a brief review of women in policing, Resetnikova and Schulz (2004) examined the recruitment of women into policing around the world. They found that many countries gave preferential treatment to women or initiated quotas in order to increase their representation. In Norway, women were given preferential treatment when their representation dipped below 40 percent. Belgium specified the number of women to be hired as constables (600) and officers (40) in the late 1990s, while Finland and Greece set their quotas to a minimum of 15 percent. The Netherlands set a quota of 25 percent minimum, while Turkey, a country that typically limits the number of women in policing, set a quota of 5 percent. However, the following research discussion finds that this tends to limit women's entry. Research revealed that Turkish officials who did not believe that women belong in policing were able to get around quotas by subjecting female candidates to illogical and difficult questions (Gültekin, Leichtman, and Garrison 2010). Female recruits, on the other hand, viewed recruitment to be fair and equal. However, they believed quota limits that specified a maximum number of women hired per cohort worked against them. Gültekin and colleagues concluded that the police culture in Turkey has a foundation of male supremacy.

These kinds of loopholes in the implementation of the law allow for the continuation of institutional discrimination. These are the less obvious forms of institutional discrimination and are found in gendered forms of recruitment. In an examination of the lack of diversity within the New York Police Department (NYPD), the U. S. Commission on Civil Rights (2000a, 2000b) found that the lack of women in the NYPD began with the application process and recommended a more targeted recruitment campaign. Additionally, attrition of women was a problem. Women had less trust in the police, lacked promotional opportunities, and psychological tests were culturally and gender biased. However, the NYPD refused to examine this problem. The U.S. Commission on Civil Rights (2000b) found that the cultural diversity training within the NYPD's police academy perpetuated stereotypes of ethnic and religious minorities and women. Among stereotypes of women, police were taught that women are weak and incapable.

In the U.S., many police departments give hiring preference to military veterans (Patterson 2002). Research shows that in the U.S., veterans preference results in a higher percentage of men hired in federal civil service jobs (Lewis 2013). Additionally, these men tend to be less educated and less qualified than non-veterans are, yet they receive higher pay. In a domestic war on terror, who better to investigate and apprehend terrorists than soldiers who have engaged in the same work during times of war and conflict? So the argument goes. However, we see in Nicaragua and Israel, women moving from the military into policing do not receive equal treatment even with superior training (Haberfeld 2020; Verfurth 2011). As with other forms of work, military service is also gendered. As a hypermasculine organization, the military does not see many women joining their ranks. In fact, in 2015, women represented only 15 percent of the U.S. military personnel, and over 60 percent of female veterans worked in the private sector (Department of Veterans Affairs 2017). This leads to a focus on hiring men. Unfortunately, deployed and non-deployed veterans tend to engage in more police shootings (Reingle Gonzalez et al. 2019). With compulsory military service in Israel, women represent 56 percent of military junior officers and 14 percent of those with ranks from major to colonel (Karazi-Presler, Sasson-Levy and Lomsky-Feder 2018). However, this does not appear to transfer to the police force (Geva 2019; Shadmi 1993). In fact, research shows that female military officers felt a level of shame for crossing cultural gender boundaries by working jobs reserved for men (Karazi-Presler, Sasson-Levy, and Lomsky-Feder 2018). Furthermore, once military women enter policing, there is an expectation to engage in women's work.

Institutional discrimination is revealed in other forms of recruitment as well. Up until the 1970s, police organizations in the U.S. incorporated height and weight standards impossible for most women and many ethnic minorities to meet (Birzer and Craig 1996). However, the courts ruled that these standards were discriminatory. There was no evidence that the height and weight minimums were required to perform the job effectively. Most nations have altered their height and weight requirements as well as their physical fitness requirements, thus opening the doors for more women. For example, in Mauritius, male candidates must have a minimum height of 5.7 feet, while women's height must be no less than 5.3 feet (Gokulsing and Tandrayen-Ragoobur 2014). In India, the Delhi Police set height and chest requirements for men at 5.4 feet and 29–31 inches, respectively (Delhi Police 2019), whereas women's height requirement is 5.15 feet with no chest requirement. In Turkey, women have lower standards for running and push-ups compared to men (Gültekin, Leichtman, and Garrison 2010).

In the place of height and weight requirements, police agencies required physical agility testing in the U.S. (*Dothard v. Rawlinson* 1977) and most other nations. Physical agility testing, it is argued, weeds out those who will not be able to handle the physical dangers of policing and protects departments from liability in the event that an unfit officer is injured on the job. However, similar to the height and weight standards, U.S. departments were sued on the basis that the physical agility tests were not job related, and similar to the height and weight standards, they adversely affect women. Physical agility tests in the U.S. also required applicants to run 200 yards, climb through a window, and drag or pull a 158-lb. dead weight for 30 feet in nine seconds. Focus on upper body strength and a myth that policing is riddled with extreme violence and the need to fight drives these requirements. Most physical agility tests today concentrate on push-ups, sit-ups, and running, tests that measure muscular endurance and power testing.

In Delhi, physical endurance entrance tests require men up to 30 years of age to race 1,600 meters (roughly one mile) in 7 minutes but require women to race 800 meters in 5 minutes (Delhi Police 2019). The long jump is 12 feet 6 inches for men but 9 feet for women and the high jump is 3 feet 6 inches for men and 3 feet for women. It should also be noted that Delhi has different standards for male and female candidates within age groups of 30 to 40 and over 40. In Portugal, the selection process results in the success of 6 percent for women compared to 25 percent for men (Castelhano et al. 2012). In their research, Castelhano et al. (2012) found that, although it did

Figure 5.2 Israeli YASAM (SWAT) Operative, 2005.

Source: Photo used with permission from the Israel Police Heritage Center.

not reflect the major role of policing, the physical test for the Portuguese Public Security Police had a high failure rate for both men and women, but twice as much for women. Where 38 percent of the male applicants failed the physical test, 63 percent of the women failed. Furthermore, the researchers found that male officers equate the lower physical capability of female officers with an inability to do the job because the police culture strongly values strength (Figure 5.2).

Research has found that women's abdominal strength is 75–80 percent of men's and their upper-body strength is 55 percent of men's (Augustsson et al. 2009). In comparing women and men, Augustsson and colleagues found that there was no difference in the sit up testing between men and women but that men are able to execute twice as many pushups as women. Pushups are a test of strength relative to body weight so it would make sense that men, who are on average taller and heavier than women, would fare better. In an earlier study of physical ability testing for recruits in the U.S., Birzer and Craig (1996) found that officers rated as absolutely necessary some activities that were not very common in the actual job but that were tested for during recruitment and training. These activities included such things as long distance running, lifting, dragging or pulling, crawling, jumping, and other extreme activities. The research has revealed that while much of the testing does not reflect real police work, women do not do as well as men on these activates. In their study, Birzer and Craig found that 72 percent of the female candidates failed the test while only 7 percent of the males failed. Since we know that police work does not involve much need for these physical activities, Silvestri pointed out that physical agility testing is a test for women (2003). Furthermore, Lonsway (2003) found that within the U.S., there is no standardized test or one that was used by the majority of the police departments. There was also no standard for success. Yet, the tests tend to eliminate more female candidates.

Thus, we see the formal recruitment process reflects a gendered subtext that gives preference to men, while loopholes ensure that few women make it through this process. Furthermore, the gendered interactions during recruitment, such as in Turkey, reinforce the male preference. This reinforces the organizational logic that policing is men's work and it reinforces the ongoing processes that produce and reproduce gender and gender inequalities within policing (i.e., the gendered substructure). Still, many nations are increasing their female representation and we must ask why. Tajikistan views the increased presence of women as a way to increase the moral compass of its police force. Uruguay increased recruitment of women to work in WPSs (Immigration and Refugee Board of Canada 2002b; Brysk 2018). As we saw throughout the world, the increase of women in policing often follows a concern over prostitution or general cases involving women and children. This reinforces the organizational logic that women police must engage in women's work, while male police engage in crime fighting. We then must ask: if women are recruited for specific women's work, how are they trained and how does that training affect female self-efficacy?

Gendered Training

When women entered police forces in the early 1900s, their primary focus was on the morality of women and children. As a result, they did not undergo the same training as men in most countries. In fact, in countries like the U.S., the focus was on women's schooling and the social work skills necessary to interview and investigate troubled women and children (Hutzel 1933). However, as women police gained more powers, their training started to resemble that of men. In earlier years, the NPF trained women and men equally, in lifesaving, first aid, fire and ambulance drills, police duties, and field training (Akinjobi-Babatunde 2015). Firearms training was not included until the 1980s. However, this was not a right that women police had until the Nigeria Police Act of 2018. Not much is known about training in the GCC; however, Abu Dhabi, UAE created a separate women's police academy in 1978 (Alhashmi 2018).

Most women police in Argentina receive the same training as men (Carrington et al. 2020). However, there is specialist training for women assigned to work with women and children. Additional specialist training is also provided for women in the ASP, as mentioned earlier. Haiti stated that it trains men and women the same (Haiti Libre 2013). However, some women receive special training overseas on gender-based violence so that they are prepared to work these cases upon deployment. In Kosovo, women have the right to equal training (Vrajolli 2011). However, watchdogs on these measures are inactive. Canada, on the other hand, trains women and men the same in firearms, self-defense, swimming, drill, and academics (Schmidt 2016). The Hellenic Police in Greece also trains women in the same academies as men with the same training (Hellenic Police 2011). In Tamil Nadu, India, when women started to enter policing, all new recruits were required to undergo six years of training in the armed reserve before they could be assigned full police duties. In China, training for women is the same as for men (Ding 2020; Chu, Cretacci, and Jin 2019). Kuwaiti policewomen undergo a six-month police academy training in police and legal studies followed by field training. Kuwaiti women describe their training as military training, which involves firearms and physical combat training (Strobl 2016).

Regardless of the type of training women police receive, whether it involves equal, separate, or additional training, they experience pushback for stepping out of traditional gender roles (Castelhano et al. 2012; Garcia 2017; Strobl 2016). Within Kuwait, women police may be trained with firearms but they are not deployed with firearms so their gender role breach only goes so far. Much of the research examines the explicit attitudes of male police in order to understand women's integration in policing. A few studies, however, have examined the gendered nature of training (Castelhano et al. 2012; Prokos and Padavic 2002) or the effects training has on cadets (Chu, Cretacci, and Jin 2019).

Research has found that police training is gendered and devalues women and qualities associated with femininity. In this way, training reinforces the gendered organizational logic that policing is man's work, through gendered subtext (written and informal processes) and through gendered interactions, thus reproducing the gendered substructure. Reaction training, such as physical training, was more desirable among Portuguese police students and better performed by men (Castelhano et al. 2012). However, the researchers stressed that the communication portions of training were more in line with daily policing and that women showed greater capacity here. In sum, the Portuguese Public Security Police gave greater value to physical strength and equated this with men and a perceived greater capacity to perform the job well. On the other hand, lack of male strength was stigmatized as were the interpersonal relations and receptive skills associated with women. Research has revealed that sex discrimination experienced during training is one reason for female recruits to drop out (Haarr 2005). Recruits tend to experience a dissonance between their cognitions of what policing is and the reality exposed to them during training.

Haarr's (2005) study supports Prokos and Padavic's (2002) research that found a hidden curriculum within the police academy in the U.S. supporting hegemonic masculinity. Curriculum and interactions tended to exclude and disparage women and exaggerated gender differences. Similar to Portuguese female recruits who feel like "guests" within the police organization (Castelhano et al. 2012), female cadets in the U.S. felt ignored, excluded, and isolated (Prokos and Padavic 2002). The findings of these studies can perhaps explain why the female cadets in China had a lower self-efficacy upon completion of training than men did (Chu, Cretacci, and Jin 2019). Specifically, female cadets had less confidence than men did in their ability to effect an arrest or use physical strength during policing. They also had lower self-efficacy in filing reports, using police equipment, and being able to mentally handle the job. Thus, we see that gendered training not only makes female recruits feel "other" but it can also diminish their confidence to successfully do the job.

Barriers to Promotion

Just as recruitment and training reproduce hegemonic masculinity so does promotion. In a last-ditch effort to ensure that policing and the power that accompanies this activity remains masculine, the promotional process is gendered. In countries like China, promotion is administrator initiated (Ding 2020). In other countries, such as Mauritius, the legislated separation of female and male positions creates a separate promotional process for women in an organization that does not hold women's work as equal (Government of Mauritius 2019a, 2019b). However, in most countries, promotion is merit-based and seemingly gender-neutral yet women find barriers to promotion. In every country examined in this book in which statistics could be found, women represented a very small portion of the top hierarchy of the police force. For example, in Nicaragua, men were more likely to be promoted over women, even when less qualified (Verfurth 2011). In China, promotion is supervisor initiated but men are usually selected over women (Ding 2020). In Bangladesh, 10 percent of supervisory positions are reserved for women but almost half of the women police work in administrative roles (Afroze 2017). In Poland, women's discrimination in promotion is likely because Poland still holds strongly to the belief that women's main role is in the home (Basinska 2015). In Kosovo, women have the right to equal training and promotion is based on merit (Vrajolli 2011). Women police represent 14 percent of the Kosovo Police. However, they have a higher representation in civil service positions. While measures were put into place to ensure higher representation and equality, they are not actively enforced. In addition, in Turkey, sex discrimination was found in all aspects of policing, including promotion (Gültekin, Leichtman, and Garrison 2010).

Box 5.1 Women Police in China: Recruitment, Training, and Promotion

Ruhan Ding joined a southern Chinese police department in 2013 and currently holds the rank of Sergeant 2nd Class. She graciously agreed to the interview for this book but asked that her name and place of employment remain confidential. Because there is so little information on the Chinese police and even less on women police in China, Ruhan provided details of current police recruit requirements and training. In order to become a police officer in China, one must be a minimum of 18 years of age, have a clean criminal and political background check, and be willing to uphold the Constitution. Any negative findings will disqualify the applicant. China does not have police academies. Instead, applicants must hold an associate's or bachelor's degree in a related field, although some jurisdictions accept just the high school diploma. While in Police College, students receive course work and physical training. Police work is considered very demanding for women so there are very few in the field. Ruhan's jurisdiction has about 5 percent female representation. However, women are more frequently assigned to the provincial ministry or city police administration.

Once the recruit is on the job, there are special task force officers who provide special training; however, they do not drill regularly. Promotions require drills and a performance assessment, including an 800-meter run, target shooting, and other professional tests. Men and women train together but the passing standard for physical assessment, i.e., running and shooting, is higher for males. Ruhan stated that treatment during training is different in that it is less intense for women. Furthermore, women can ask for leave during training if they begin menstruating, while men are expected to maintain consistent attendance.

Currently, Ruhan supervises the legal side of cases. She reviews the cases for progression, approval, etc., and may offer directional advice for the next steps. Ruhan stated that female officers assigned to local departments face the same expectations from their supervisors that males do, though it depends on the leadership. However, she personally believes that female officers should be respected more and given more *soft work*, such as household registration administration, general order maintenance, public safety tip promotion work, and personnel work. Furthermore, when working with minors, female officers are an asset and are usually present during conversations. In China, correctional police officers are under the umbrella of the police. Additionally, female correctional facilities are staffed by an all-female correctional officer staff with male administrators. In this way, the Chinese police does have all-female police units. Promotions are based on accrued years, performance as reflected in one's record, and identification by leadership. However, males have a better chance at promotion. Female officers at local departments rarely receive promotions. Women only represent about 0.2 percent of higher-ranking positions.

Furthermore, benefits are the same for men and women but tasks vary by gender.

Ruhan reports that she receives respect from the public. She believes that respect depends on how you carry yourself as an officer. She also receives support from her family, including her husband, though they worry for her safety. While Ruhan does not have children, she stated that in China women receive five months maternity leave. Ruhan reports being happy with her job in general, and she most enjoys interacting with experienced professionals. However, she often feels ostracized in her department. She feels that her supervisor has no compassion and fellow officers at times do not understand or receive her work well. She believed that it is possible that many feel this way because they have not yet accumulated the knowledge and skills. In addition to barriers to promotion, Ruhan stated that female police do not perform the job in the expected aggressive manner as their male counterparts. Ruhan stated that this is expected but the difference may be due to their gender. It is likely that Chinese female officers are held to the same male standards the world over, and they suffer in promotions when they do not meet those standards.

Source: Ruhan Ding. 2020. Personal communication.

In the U.S., promotion is merit based but emphasizes a policing style more likely to be valued and used by men (Garcia 2017). The U.S. Commission on Civil Rights (2000b) found that promotion within the NYPD was linked to higher arrests instead of protecting citizens' civil rights. This is a barrier for women, as they tend to view arrests and other aggressive behavior as less necessary when dealing with the public (Morin et al. 2017). Morin et al. (2017) found that female police are more likely than men to report that fellow officers do not spend enough time diagnosing a situation before acting; while male police are more likely to report that fellow officers take too much time (Figure 5.3). Additionally, female police are less likely than men are to believe that aggressive tactics (versus courteous tactics) are needed in some neighborhoods (48 percent vs. 58 percent, respectively). They are also less likely than men are to believe that some people can only be brought to reason through physical aggression (33 percent vs. 46 percent, respectively). Yet, recruitment, training, and promotion emphasize physical policing as good policing.

Overall, women police experience discrimination in promotion in a good old boys network in which networking often occurs during male-bonding events or through nepotism (National Institute of Justice. 2019). Returning to veterans preferences, some U.S. departments give promotional points for military service (Archbold and Schulz 2008). As in China, reputation and popularity in the department also influence promotional

Figure 5.3 Colonel Sigal Bar Tzvi, Commander of Ayalon Sub-Division.

Source: Photo used with permission from the Israel Police Heritage Center.

opportunities for evaluators. Additionally, as with Chinese female cadets, female police in the U.S. tend to possess lower self-efficacy concerning promotion.

Another barrier to promotion is pregnancy and motherhood. In a study on maternity leave and policing, Schulze (2020) found that the presence of a national maternity leave policy was correlated with higher representation of women police but the amount of time and pay that mothers receive was not. The International Labour Organization (ILO) (2017) drafted maternity leave recommendations during the Maternity Protection Convention of 2000. Among its recommendations, the ILO recommended that national laws should be set and that mothers should receive a minimum of 14 weeks leave with 6 weeks of compulsory leave after childbirth. Schulze was able to gather data for 97 countries and found that 43 countries did not meet ILO's 14-week minimum, including the U.S. What has been important for women is returning to work after maternity leave to the same or equivalent position. Only 39 countries in Schulze's sample provided women this protection. In most countries, policing requires women to work full time making this provision vital, especially when the importance of motherhood is stressed. However, all women officers in India are allowed to work part-time (Natarajan 2014). As noted in Chapter 3, most women police work in all-women police stations and often prefer gender-specific policing roles. Even with these allotments, Indian policewomen tend to experience high role conflict between work and family. Married women experience more stress trying to balance professional and family roles. The research found that they have difficulty adjusting to the police work environment. Policewomen experience greater feelings of role stagnation and feel more isolated and hostility for joining a male-dominant organization (Bano and Talib 2014). The problem that women police encounter is when pregnancy comes to be treated as an imposition, an illness, or a problem. While laws may exist to protect women's right to work, the implementation of those laws do not always reflect the written word.

In Turkey, pregnancy is seen as an inconvenience (Gültekin, Leichtman, and Garrison 2010). A pregnant woman is seen as useless and must often forfeit her position. Promotion is automatic in rank with increase years on the job and this increases job satisfaction. However, maternity leave delays promotion. While men's military leave does not affect their promotion track, maternity leave stops the promotion track for women. Turkey places a strong emphasis on motherhood as women's primary role. However, the police organization does not provide for time for family or daycare centers. Women police have reported being treated like second-class citizens. If they make a mistake, they are labeled as clumsy and uniforms are designed for men. The negative attitudes that women police receive from their male coworkers and supervisors make the job more difficult. Additionally, while the motherhood role is highly valued, some women police feel that their male coworkers and supervisors do not acknowledge their roles as mothers and wives. In this way, the Turkish woman police is treated as an abstract or neutral worker (Acker 2012) while discriminating against her gender.

In Canada, as in most countries, pregnant police are immediately pulled from active duty as it is seen as a liability (Langan, Sanders, and Gouweloos 2019). Pregnant women are usually assigned to the front desk, which was coined the P.I.L.L. squad by one male officer (i.e., pregnant, injured, lazy, or lame). In this way, pregnancy was a liability by women who could not and would not do a good job in real policing. Langan, Sanders, and Gouweloos found that women police were told that pregnancy ruins their careers. This leads to withdrawing pregnant women from training courses that could bolster their careers or not assigning them because they are on desk duty. Van der Lippe, Graumans, and Sevenhuijsen (2004) found that Sweden publicly funds childcare helping to decrease the role strain that women police with children experience. Furthermore, Sweden and the Netherlands allow for flexible working hours and part-time shifts. While women have a high representation in higher positions (30 percent), a large number of women work part-time. Catalonia, Spain, on the other hand, does not have public childcare or allow flexible working hours. In Austria, public childcare facilities are only found within large cities and there is no possibility of flexible working hours.

Conclusion

Chapters 3 and 4 revealed many patterns among police forces worldwide. This chapter revealed that these patterns point to a strong and thriving gendered organization. In all nations, women police experience resistance resulting from the gendered substructure and subtext of policing with an organizational logic that functions on hegemonic masculinity. As a paramilitary organization, or military in some nations, most women do not benefit. The gendered subtext in some police forces officially separates women from men, and while the rhetoric claims equality, the research clearly shows that women are not equal. However, we have seen that, in most nations, it is the institutional discrimination in the subtext that addresses a gender-neutral worker that is clearly not neutral. Plato wrote, "for when equality is given to unequal things, the resultant will be unequal, unless due measure is applied" (Bury 1967/1968). Imposing physical agility tests and training for a job that typically does not warrant these activities institutionally eliminates women. If the job truly required such strength and fitness then all police would be required to pass such tests continuously throughout their careers. The family responsibilities that most women tend to have in most countries, as compared to men, tend to either be overlooked or over treated thus hindering women's movement into and through the police career. Promotions based on merit that give points for military service and felony arrests, jobs most likely to be given to men, also exclude women.

Research has revealed that women must have high self-efficacy in order to change their status and rank within the police organization (Morabito and O'Connor Shelley 2018). Yet, the gendered nature of training and police work tends to break down women's self-efficacy (Chu, Cretacci, and Jin 2019; Morin et al. 2017; Prokos and Padavic 2002). Morabito and O'Connor Shelley (2018) found that authority can act as a potential restraint, as the examples in Canada, China, and Turkey reveal. However, in order for authority to serve as a potential resource to agency, "slippage" needs to occur. This slippage allows women to assert agency in order to change institutionalized gendered practices. Women police find that strong female support, such as role models, mentors, and colleagues, help provide this slippage. Research finds that women still tend to have token status in policing and this tends to hinder their upward mobility (Archbold and Schulz 2008). In the complex way that tokenism works, some women do not apply for promotion when encouraged by male supervisors if they feel that they would only be promoted because of their sex. This, again, brings us back to women's self-perception. The gendered nature of policing works to remind women of their place in the organization. Nothing is a stronger reminder of token status and devalued worth than policing gender-based violence. Chapter 6 examines violence against women and how the police organization responds. I start with sexual victimization of women police within the organization itself.

Chapter 6

Gendered Policing

Working Conditions and Gender-Based Violence

The gendered nature of policing works to remind women of their place in the organization. The institutionalized gendered practices can be seen in the policies and practices when recruiting, training, and promoting women police. These gendered practices also exist in how policing is done. In this chapter, I examine gendered policing in relation to violence against women. As we have seen throughout the world, women initially joined police forces in order to protect, and control, women and children. These police tasks worldwide have been defined as women's work and so when women joined police forces, they were still doing gender. Without women police, in most cases, violence against women has largely been ignored. The establishment of women's units or specialist positions gives the police organization a way to continue hegemonic masculinity while allowing women to do women's work. I focus on these gendered practices within this chapter. Gendered practices also exist in the interactions within the organization, specifically in the ways that male coworkers and supervisors receive women police. There is ample research to show that women are largely not accepted by their male colleagues and are subjected to organizational violence. This rejection comes in the form of subtle and not so subtle language and actions from male police. I begin the chapter examining gendered policing through the resistance by men within the organization.

Doing Policing/Doing Gender: Resistance to Women Police

I have demonstrated thus far that although there has been progress in almost all countries, women police still hold token status. This is reflected in their small numbers around the world. The small number of women applying to the police organization is likely more of a reflection of cultural gender role expectations and doing gender around the world. However, once the application process begins, we see institutional sexism within this gendered organization. The research shows that when women join the police force to do a "man's job" they encounter resistance. However, when women join in an attempt to do "woman's work" there is also resistance (Garcia 2003, 2017; Heidensohn 1992; Brown 1997; Brown and Silvestri 2020). Feminist scholars have argued that this resistance reflects the rejection of women's initial entry into the workforce as can be seen by the many labor restrictions discussed in the first two chapters. However, Chapter 5 shows that governments continue to place labor restrictions on women making equality in any occupation difficult but making it especially difficult to infiltrate historically male occupations.

Some research has found that the hegemonic masculine culture of policing decreases women's self-efficacy (Chu, Cretacci, and Jin 2019; Morin et al. 2017). Other research has found that women police have strong confidence in their fit with the job, agency, and police workgroup unless experiencing incivilities. Resistance can be subtle manifesting as workplace incivilities (Rief and Clinkinbeard 2020) or it can be severe manifesting as sexual harassment, assault, and even rape (Garcia 2017; Kringen and Novich 2020). Incivilities are defined as behaviors that violate workplace norms such as putting someone down or condescending a person (Rief and Clinkinbeard 2020). Women police are more likely than men to experience incivilities and this works to lower their perceived fit in the workgroup. As we saw with the cadets who felt isolated after repeated jests that "there oughtta be a law against bitches" (Prokos and Padavic 2002), incivilities can be experienced as jokes or as straight talk. Box 6.1 reveals straight talk in incivilities in the Israel National Police. Box 6.1 features the story of former Israeli National Police Officer, Dr. Maria (Maki) Haberfeld, who experienced sexual harassment and gender discrimination in the gendered organization.

In Portugal, research has found that many women police feel like "guests" within the police force (Castelhano et al. 2012). In order to fit it, some women take on the characteristics associated with men. Regardless, women police are viewed as fragile and are distrusted for this reason. They find themselves having to prove themselves. In an earlier study, I found that women police in the U.S. felt that they had to prove themselves capable of doing the job effectively on a day-to-day basis (Garcia 2017). These women claimed that they had "thick skin," making them ready for the challenge. Hautzinger (2007) found that in Bahia, Brazil, many policewomen engaged in masculinized policing when dealing with victims and suspects in WPSs in efforts to prove themselves. Policewomen reported countless incidents where male coworkers did not trust their abilities to handle tougher cases. As a result, many policewomen engaged in violence or threatened violence and often blamed the victim. They resented being assigned to "dry" police stations and being associated with "a woman's place" in the "kitchen of the police" (Hautzinger 2007, p. 224). In Bahia, Brazil, women saw assignments to women's work as a hindrance to their careers.

Box 6.1 Dr. Maria (Maki) Haberfeld, The Life of a Military Trained Israeli Policewoman: Sexual Harassment and Sexual Discrimination on the Job

During the COVID-19 pandemic stay-at-home order, I had the pleasure of virtually meeting Dr. Maria R. (Maki) Haberfeld. As a former Israeli police officer and current academic, Maki agreed to a Zoom interview and shared her fascinating story. Maki was born in Poland and immigrated to Israel when she was 14 years old. From 1975 to 1977, she joined the *HIBA* Unit (translated as "Soldier in the Service of the Israel Police") of the Israel Defense Forces (Figure 6.1). This female unit received specialized anti-terrorist training and was tasked with mitigating terrorist activities in urban environments. Stationed at the Headquarters in Jerusalem, Maki was a junior commanding officer who supervised 30 female officers. They wore the military uniform with police patches. After her two years of military service, Maki received her Bachelor's and Master's degrees at The Hebrew University of Jerusalem (1977–1983). Because she had special training with the military, Maki knew that she would do well in the Israel National Police (INP). She joined the police force in 1981, where she worked as a Lieutenant in

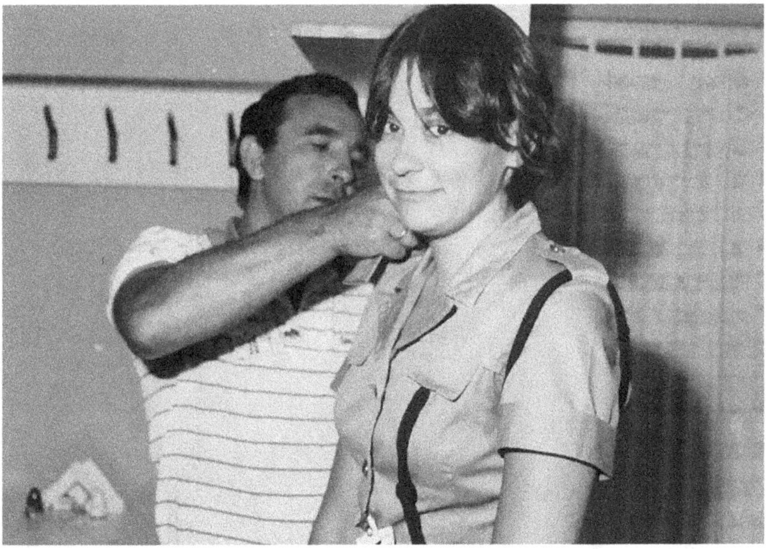

Figure 6.1 Dr. Maki Haberfeld, Former Israeli Officer, Being pinned with Second Lieutenant Rank by Her Commanding Officer.

Source: Photo used with permission by Dr. Maki Haberfeld.

the Division of Investigations in Jerusalem. She then moved to the Juvenile Unit (1981–1985). She wore plain clothes and drove a car. She was proficient in firearms and highly trained in crime fighting.

As Maki described, women were not restricted in the work they could do, officially. However, she had to deal with a lot of sexual harassment, as was very common for women in law enforcement. She stated that you had to swallow it if you wanted to continue in your career. When she complained, she was given desk duty the next day or told that she would be dropped at home. Men of higher and lower ranks sexually harassed women of all ranks regardless of age. Maki described that men felt threatened by women in the field, "To listen to a woman and a commanding officer invalidated their manhood."

On her first day of work with the new unit in the INP, Maki was directed to the forms and office supplies. She was then taken to the coffee table and told that it was the most important place for her. The next day a male officer was heard saying, "Whose stupid idea was it to attach a woman to our team?" You had the opportunity to complain but there were consequences. Maki aspired to become the Chief of Police but was told that it would never happen (Figure 6.2). Moreover, if it did happen, it would be a "token appointment." In December of 1984, she and a colleague relocated to the United States to work at the Israel Police Representative Office attached to the Israeli Consulate in New York City.

Figure 6.2 Dr. Maki Haberfeld, Former Israeli Officer, Being Congratulated on Promotion to Second Lieutenant by the General in charge of the INP Human Resources.

Source: Photo used with permission by Dr. Maki Haberfeld.

She had to take a staff position as a civilian employee of the INP (due to consular restrictions), keeping her rank informally for the dealings with U.S. law enforcement agencies. She was told that she would be formally given back her rank when she returned to Israel. She never went back.

During her time with the Consulate, Maki worked with many police agencies across the U.S., including the New York Police Department, Los Angeles Police Department, Los Angeles Sheriff's Department, U.S. Department of Justice, Drug Enforcement Administration (DEA) and the Secret Service on extraditions, counterfeiting, and bringing down drug cartels. Among many other cases, she was involved in three prominent ones: extradition to Israel of accused WWII Nazi criminal "Ivan the terrible," search for missing New York child Etan Patz, and the arrest warrant for the notorious Colombian drug dealer and co-founder of the Medellin Cartel, Carlos Lehder Rivas.

When Maki became a mother, her Commanding Officer harassed her about her inflexibility. It seemed that Maki was required to set her daughter's needs aside in order to do her job at all times. She finally left the INP position at the Consulate in 1989 and was hired as a consultant, translator, and interpreter to the DEA to work on cases involving Israeli drug smugglers (1989–1993). With conflict in Israel, Maki did not want to bring her family back to Israel, so she went back to John Jay College of Criminal Justice to complete her Master's and PhD degrees in criminal justice (1985–1992). Surprisingly, I learned that she taught criminal justice at my current place of employment, New Jersey City University (1994–1997). Ultimately, in 1997, she took a position with the John Jay, where she is currently employed as a full professor.

Had Maki not experienced sexual harassment and discrimination in policing, she would never have entered the world of academia, teaching at one of the more prestigious criminal justice colleges in the U.S., receiving several research grants, publishing 25 police books, 27 book chapters, and many more peer reviewed articles, reports, and academic presentations and working with other world-famous police researchers. Today, the INP has finally acknowledged the hostile conditions that women police still experience. The Deputy Commissioner for Women Affairs position was created after a critical 2012 State Comptroller Report, in order to create equal opportunities and safer conditions for women in the INP. Research has yet to be found on its impact.

Source: Haberfeld, M. R. 2020. Personal Communication.

Some women police in Portugal tend to emphasize their difference by working in community-based services (Castelhano et al. 2012). In this way, the skills they display in policing reflect the skills associated with women as caretakers for the family. Yet, the Portuguese Public Security Police stigmatizes the interpersonal relations and receptive skills associated with women. Rabe-Hemp found that women police in the U.S. believed that they were better at "feminized forms of police work" (2009, p. 124). Her research revealed that many women police rejected the aggression and violence associated with policing and adapted their more feminine characteristics of caretaking and empathy to community policing. However, there was still a tendency for male officers to reject women police and even ostracize and isolate women who socialized with other female police. This would definitely hinder the slippage that Morabito and O'Connor Shelley (2018) found aided women's agency when attempting to advance in policing.

Research found that male police in Dubai, New South Wales, and Taipei did not support women's work in general policing roles (Chan, Doran, and Marel 2010; Chu 2017). Additionally, male police were less receptive to partnering with female police in Dubai than in Taipei. In Dubai, both male and female officers believed that women should be assigned to gender-restricted policing duties. In Brazil, WPSs were created in the backdrop of a sexist male-dominated criminal justice system (Nelson 1996). However, the masculine nature of policing and the resistance to women as equal to men does not start in the police organization. Research continues to find that the police organization still recruits candidates who display hypermasculine traits that are in line with the "crime-fighter" model of policing (Brown et al. 2020).

Research has found that students and recruits believe that women are less capable than men (Austin and Hummer 1999; Chu and Tsao 2013; Prokos and Padavic 2002). Chu and Tsao (2013) found that male cadets in Taiwan did not have confidence in women's competence as officers or their physical ability to perform the job. Female cadets did have this confidence but preferred to engage in gender-specific roles while males preferred that females engage in equal or similar duties. In China, Kim and Gerber (2019) found that both male and female cadets had less confidence in the competence of women police. The researchers reported, however, that Chinese male and female cadets had higher self-efficacy than Taiwanese cadets did (see Chu and Tsao 2013). Kim and Gerber also found that male cadets who view females as less competent are more likely to support gender-specific policing.

Many women police hold strong to the gender-specific model of policing. Natarajan's (2008) research in Tamil Nadu, India found that males preferred equal assignments, while many women police preferred gender-specific assignments. Her later research in India found that both men and women believed that men were more competent with most police tasks (Natarajan 2014). Natarajan's research revealed that younger women police are more likely to support equal integrated policing for women. Sahgal (2007) found that male police in Delhi, India believed that they experienced more discrimination than did women. They believed that women were in the position to demand more because of their sex. Women police, on the other hand, felt stereotyped by men who treat the job as too hard for women. Additionally, men's belief that the family is the primary duty for women increased their belief that women were not committed to the job. Strobl (2008) found that many of the policewomen in Bahrain preferred gender-segregated duties. She did not find evidence that policewomen would publicly demand gender integration. In fact, when women were deployed to mixed-gender traffic patrols in 2001, many protested the decision.

Sexual Harassment and Assault in the Police Force

Legislative Prohibitions Against Sexual Harassment

Nothing makes resistance to women in policing more obvious than gender discrimination, sexual harassment, and assault in policing. Here sexual harassment is defined as,

> unwelcome, uninvited, coercive, or threatening sexual attention, often in a non-reciprocal relationship [and] includes unwanted sexual or suggestive comments, attempts to coerce a sexual relationship, punishment or threats of punishment for refusal to comply, a demand for sexual favors in return for jobs or the creation of a hostile, intimidating, and offensive work environment.
>
> (Huang and Cao 2008, p. 325)

Although we see that officials find ways around legislated protections for women in policing, the existence of these laws is evidence that countries are at least starting to work toward improvement. The labor law database compiled by the Women, Business and the Law division of the World Bank Group (2020b) discussed in Chapter 5 includes evidence of national laws on gender discrimination and sexual harassment for 190 countries. Table 6.1 presents these data by region. Gender discrimination in the workplace is prohibited in 154 nations. Most countries within each region prohibit gender discrimination except Oceania. Furthermore, with the exceptions of North American and Oceania, countries within each region were less likely to legislate sexual harassment prohibitions than they were gender discrimination prohibitions.

The Women, Business and the Law 2020 report found that 50 nations still do not have legislation protecting women against sexual harassment in the workplace (World Bank Group 2020b). Between 2017 and 2019, Bahrain, Djibouti, Saudi Arabia, Tunisia, UAE, and Barbados passed legislation

Table 6.1 Labor Laws on Discrimination and Sexual Harassment in the Workforce by Region, 2020

	Region								*Total*
	Asia	*EE*	*LAC*	*MENA*	*NA*	*Oceania*	*SSA*	*WE*	
Does law prohibit gender discrimination in employment?	26 76.5%	19 100.0%	24 72.7%	15 75.0%	2 100.0%	5 45.5%	40 83.3%	23 100.0%	154 81.1%
Is there legislation on sexual harassment in employment?	25 73.5%	18 94.7%	23 69.7%	11 55.0%	2 100.0%	5 45.5%	35 72.9%	21 91.3%	140 73.7%
Criminal Penalties	14 41.2%	9 47.4%	18 54.5%	10 50.0%	1 50.0%	2 18.2%	28 58.3%	12 52.2%	94 49.5%
Civil Remedies	19 55.9%	16 84.2%	17 51.5%	3 15.0%	2 100.0%	5 45.5%	23 47.9%	20 87.0%	105 55.3%

Source: World Bank Group. 2020b. *Women, Business and the Law*. https://wbl.worldbank.org/en/data/exploretopics/wbl_sj (accessed June 3, 2020).

Note: EE=Eastern Europe; LAC=Latin America and the Caribbean; MENA=Middle East and North Africa; NA=North America; SSA=Sub-Saharan African; WE=Western Europe.

for the first time prohibiting sexual harassment in the workplace, which included criminal and/or civil remedies. France, Sao Tome and Principe, and South Sudan implemented laws that allowed civil remedies in these cases, and Gabon, Montenegro, and Peru implemented laws that enabled criminal penalties. The table reveals that countries were less likely to legislate criminal penalties (n=94) than they were to legislate civil remedies (n=105). In other words, sexual harassment in the workplace is not serious enough to warrant criminal charges, including within the U.S. Perhaps this is the message that perpetrators take away.

Tables 6.2 and 6.3 present evidence of legislation for the countries examined in Chapters 3 and 4. The data show that all of the countries presented in the Western Hemisphere have legislation prohibiting gender discrimination and sexual harassment in the workplace, except for Haiti which does not prohibit sexual harassment in the workplace. Additionally, all but Haiti legislate criminal penalties or civil remedies for sexual harassment in the workplace. Civil remedies are slightly more likely to be legislated (73 percent) than are criminal penalties (64 percent). In Haiti, sexual exploitation of females has been defined as a social problem. In 2000, the Commission on Human Rights of the UN released a report on violence against women with the finding that Haiti was a structurally and inherently violent society with 90 percent of females experiencing violence (United Nation 2020a). Among their recommendations, the Commission recommended that the UN peacekeeping mission in Haiti train a young and brutal police force on human rights and violence against women and provide other support. However, it was recently revealed that UN Peacekeepers (i.e., UN police) had sexually exploited and abused women and girls in Haiti and fathered and abandoned hundreds of children (United Nations 2020b).

Training in gender and sexual harassment was found lacking in the U.S. The U.S. Commission on Civil Rights (2000b) found that NYPD sexual harassment training officially included the laws and materials needed to teach officers. However, trainers were typically ranked NYPD police who did not have the qualifications to teach the materials with any effectiveness. When non-NYPD trainers taught the classes, officers slept, ate, talked, groaned, and threw objects at the instructors.

Table 6.3 reveals data for the Eastern Hemisphere countries featured in Chapter 3. While we did not discern any patterns for the Western Hemisphere data presented in Table 6.2, we can see a pattern in Table 6.3. With the exception of Nigeria, which began hiring women police in 1923, we see that nations that hired women police between 1915 and 1972 are more likely to have workplace gender discrimination laws in place. Bangladesh, which began hiring women in 1973, does not protect women against gender discrimination in the workforce. We also see that Kuwait (2009), Qatar

Table 6.2 Labor Laws Prohibiting Gender Discrimination and Sexual Harassment in Employment in the Western Hemisphere, 2020

	Region	*Law prohibits gender discrimination*	*Law prohibits sexual harassment*	*Remedies for sexual harassment*	*Criminal penalties*	*Civil remedies*	*Year Entered*	*Percent Police*
U.S.	NA	Yes	Yes	Yes	No	Yes	1905	12%
Canada	NA	Yes	Yes	Yes	Yes	Yes	1912	21%
U.K.	WE	Yes	Yes	Yes	Yes	No	1915	30.4%
Ireland	WE	Yes	Yes	Yes	Yes	Yes	1917	27%
Brazil	LAC	Yes	Yes	Yes	Yes	Yes	1924	14%
Uruguay	LAC	Yes	Yes	Yes	No	Yes	1924	24%
Poland	WE	Yes	Yes	Yes	No	Yes	1926	13%
Turkey	WE	Yes	Yes	Yes	Yes	Yes	1932	5.5%
Greece	WE	Yes	Yes	Yes	Yes	Yes	1969	13%
Haiti	LAC	Yes	No	No	No	No	1995	10%
Nicaragua	LAC	Yes	Yes	Yes	Yes	No	—	30%

Source: World Bank Group. 2020b. *Women, Business and the Law*. https://wbl.worldbank.org/en/data/exploretopics/wbl_sj (accessed June 3, 2020).

Note: LAC=Latin America and the Caribbean; NA=North America; WE=Western Europe.

Table 6.3 Labor Laws Prohibiting Gender Discrimination and Sexual Harassment in Employment in the Eastern Hemisphere, 2020

	Region	*Law prohibits gender discrimination*	*Law prohibits sexual harassment*	*Remedies for sexual harassment*	*Criminal penalties*	*Civil remedies*	*Year Entered*	*Percent Police*
Australia	Oceania	Yes	Yes	Yes	No	Yes	1915	32%
Nigeria	SSA	No	Yes	Yes	Yes	No	1923	35%
China	Asia	Yes	Yes	Yes	Yes	Yes	1929	19%
Hungary	EE	Yes	Yes	Yes	Yes	No	1935	23%
India	Asia	Yes	Yes	Yes	Yes	Yes	1938	7.3%
Israel	Asia	Yes	Yes	Yes	Yes	Yes	1948	25%
Fiji	Oceania	Yes	Yes	Yes	No	Yes	1968	10%
Bahrain	MENA	Yes	Yes	Yes	Yes	No	1970	10%
South Africa	SSA	Yes	Yes	Yes	No	Yes	1972	27.5%
Bangladesh	Asia	No	Yes	No	No	No	1973	10%
Oman	MENA	Yes	Yes	Yes	No	Yes	1974	5%
Ukraine	EE	Yes	Yes	Yes	No	Yes	1977	5%
Qatar	MENA	No	No	No	No	No	1980s	5%
Lebanon	MENA	Yes	No	No	No	No	2001	0.01%
Albania	EE	Yes	Yes	Yes	Yes	Yes	2006	10%
Kuwait	MENA	No	No	No	No	No	2009	5%
Algeria	MENA	No	Yes	Yes	Yes	No	—	6%
Mauritius	SSA	Yes	Yes	Yes	Yes	Yes	—	9%
Russia	EE	Yes	No	No	No	No	—	17%
Tajikistan	Asia	Yes	No	No	No	No	—	—
UAE	MENA	Yes	Yes	Yes	Yes	No	—	8%
Uzbekistan	Asia	Yes	No	No	No	No	—	—
Saudi Arabia	MENA	Yes	Yes	Yes	Yes	No	NA	0%

Source: World Bank Group. 2020b. *Women, Business and the Law*. https://wbl.worldbank.org/en/data/exploretopics/wbl_sj (accessed June 3, 2020).

Note: EE=Eastern Europe; MENA=Middle East and North Africa; SSA=Sub-Saharan African.

(1980s), and Algeria do not protect against gender discrimination in the workforce. The representation of women in policing does not seem to be affected. The table shows that nations that began hiring women police after the 1980s have prohibitions against sexual harassment in the workplace. However, a few nations have only recently added this legislation between 2017 and 2019 (Bahrain, Djibouti, Saudi Arabia, Tunisia, UAE, and Barbados). Additionally, while Bangladesh legally prohibits sexual harassment in the workplace, there are no criminal penalties or civil remedies, which effectively nullifies the law. Kuwait, Lebanon, Qatar, Russia, Tajikistan, and Uzbekistan do not provide for any legal protections against sexual harassment in the workplace. Interestingly, slightly more of the countries presented allowed criminal penalties (48 percent) than civil remedies (44 percent), making sexual harassment more serious.

A sampling of laws that specify how employers must develop compliance procedures include: Australia's Sex Discrimination Act (Australian Human Rights Commission 2004); Brazil's Law 3488/2006: Framework on Equal Treatment of Men and Women (UN Women 2016); Taiwan's Sexual Harassment Prevention Act (Republic of China 2009); the Equality Act of 2010 in the U.K. (United Kingdom 2020); and the 1972 Title VII of the Civil Rights Act of 1964 in the U.S. (U.S. Equal Employment Opportunity Commission 1997). Statistica (2020) found that in Brazil, 7 percent of women were sexually harassed in the workplace in 2017. In Chile, 9 percent of women experienced such sexual harassment, and in Mexico, this statistic was 15 percent. Women who work in male-dominated fields are more likely to experience sexual harassment than women who work in gender-balanced fields (Gruber and Morgan 2005; Jackson and Newman 2004). Brown and Heidensohn's (2000) comparative analysis found that within 35 countries, 77 percent of women police were sexually harassed by coworkers. However, sexual harassment in the workplace, including within policing, often goes unreported. Their study revealed that sexual harassment is used to reinforce women's token status.

Sexual Harassment and Assault as a Form of Organizational Violence

The sexual harassment of women police by the men they work with has always been a problem throughout the world. Through her research, Anderson found in the U.S. that, "[Policewomen] were cautioned that they may often be the only women among men and thus may be pinched, patted, or played with. Therefore, they should not wear excessive makeup, suggestive clothing, or use abrasive language" (1973, cited in Bell 1982, pp. 113–114). Sexual harassment research in Australia, England, France, and the U.K., as well as comparative studies in Europe were more frequent in the 1990s

(Brewer 1991; Brown 1997, 1998, 2000; Dene 1992; Heidensohn 1992; McKenzie 1993). Overall research found a significant amount of sexual harassment of women police. In a comparative study of the U.K. and Ireland, Brown (2000) found that female police were more likely to experience sexual harassment in England and Wales (over 85 percent) followed by women in the Royal Ulster Constabulary of Northern Ireland (about 80 percent). Roughly, 70 percent of women police in Scotland experienced sexual harassment, while the women police from An Garda Siochana (Ireland) experienced the least amount of sexual harassment (63 percent).

More recent sexual harassment research in Europe can be found in the Netherlands and Iceland. de Hass et al. (2010) examined sexual harassment policies in Dutch police forces that were substantially revised between 2004 and 2005 (Figure 6.3). They found that there was no significant decrease in sexual harassment after the changed policies. In 2000, 69 percent of women police reported sexual harassment, while 64 percent reported this victimization in 2006. Instead, de Hass et al. found that men were more likely to report sexual harassment after the change (44 percent in 2000 and 48 percent in 2006). They speculated that men might try to mask their perpetrator status by claiming to be victims. Additionally, departments with comprehensive policies did not have significantly different reporting than

Figure 6.3 Dr. Maki Haberfeld, Former Israeli Officer.

Source: Photo used with permission by Dr. Maki Haberfeld.

those with less comprehensive policies. Obviously, more research in needed to unravel this complex crime.

Steinþórsdóttir and Pétursdóttir (2018) examined sexual harassment in the Icelandic police force. They found that women police (31 percent) are ten times more likely to experience sexual harassment than are men (4 percent). Women are more likely than men are to be sexually harassed by male supervisors (32 vs 5.6 percent). However, one's power was not the driving force of this crime since women police are also sexually harassed by male colleagues (48 percent) and male subordinates (8 percent), as compared to 5.6 percent and 0 percent, respectively, for male police. Twelve percent of sexual harassment perpetrators for women police were the male public, compared to 16.7 percent for male police (Steinþórsdóttir and Pétursdóttir 2018). This supports research in the U.S. that shows that women police receive more resistance from within the organization than outside of it (Garcia 2017). Male police also experience sexual harassment from female colleagues (11 percent) and the female public (61 percent) (Steinþórsdóttir and Pétursdóttir 2018). Female officers do not experience sexual harassment from any females.

Examining bullying, Steinþórsdóttir and Pétursdóttir (2018) found that women police are more likely than men to experience bullying from female supervisors (9.5 vs 8.2 percent), male colleagues (33.3 vs 19.2 percent), female colleagues (4.8 vs 4.1 percent), male subordinates (9.5 vs 4.1 percent), and female subordinates (4.8 vs 1.4 percent). Male police were more likely than females to be bullied by male supervisors (47.9 vs 38.1 percent), the male public (8.2 vs 0 percent), and the female public (6.8 vs 0 percent). The abuse was rarely reported for fear of retaliation, especially since so much of it was perpetrated by male supervisors. The researchers concluded that females are more likely to experience bullying and sexual harassment as forms of exclusion and coercion, which can be seen in their high rates of resignation. Sexual harassment and bullying are defined as gendered phenomena that represent, "a form of organizational violence that maintains a gender hierarchy within an organization" (Steinþórsdóttir and Pétursdóttir 2018, p. 172). They also concluded that within the Icelandic Police, there is organizational tolerance of organizational violence.

Unfortunately, there is not much research on gender and sexual harassment outside of a few Western nations. This research is a common focus in the U.S. Lonsway, Paynich, and Hall (2013) found that 9 out of 10 women experience gender harassment in the U.S. military and federal law enforcement as a way to drive them out of the job. Furthermore, this behavior is more likely to be perpetrated by male coworkers and not supervisors or citizens. Most sexual harassment and assault go unreported. However, women are more likely to report the abuse when the harassment turns to assault or in quid pro quo situations, which are more likely to be committed by male supervisors. Unfortunately, retaliation is common when women report these crimes. As Haarr and Morash (2013) point out, sexual harassment diminishes health and mental well-being as well as work productivity, turnover, and absenteeism. They examined discrimination and harassment in police work and found that many women put a stop to sexual harassment, especially women with higher rank, using straight talk. However, many women police put up with harassment early in their careers. Because women who complain experience retaliation through poor evaluations, being used as "practice" chopping bags, and having their desks searched, Haarr and Morash stated that straight talk as opposed to seeking help from male officers tends to work better for many women police. However, this does not change the organizational violence found in most police organizations around the world.

Brown et al. (2020) found sexual teasing and sexual harassment alive and well within the U.S. police culture. Sexual teasing refers to behavior that is harmless and mutually receptive. However, in some cases, women neutralize less severe sexual harassment taking "paths of least resistance" and relabeling, or neutralizing, it as sexual teasing. In a two-stage process of legitimation, women first undergo basic training and second must prove that they fit into the masculine police culture. Neutralizing sexual harassment and sexual teasing is a way to fit in. The researchers argued, "one's mere existence in the patriarchal society forces one to participate in it" (Brown et al. 2020, p. 165). In this way, women police are forced to participate in their own oppression. Some women feel coerced or pressured to ignore the sexual teasing for fear of retaliation or rejection. Some see the sexual teasing as an occupational necessity. Although sexual harassment was not a frequent occurrence among the women in their study, women police often did not report this offense (Brown et al. 2020).

Among the women police in my study, I found that almost 25 percent of the women were sexually harassed by male coworkers (Garcia 2017). Women police experienced being slapped on the butt, and men showing the women nude selfies and walking around naked in coed locker rooms. Women were invited to join in the nudity and told to quit if they did not like it. This sexual harassment was perpetrated in obvious attempts to drive the women from the job. In response to the crimes, women claimed that they could handle it because they had "thick skin" (Garcia 2017, p. 182). While much of the research tends to reveal decreased sexual harassment the longer women are employed in a male-dominated field, I found slightly more sexual harassment committed against more recently hired women. Furthermore, racial and ethnic minority women were more likely to experience sexual harassment: 33 percent Hispanic, 28 percent Black, and 22 percent White. This finding speaks to the intersectionality at play in U.S. policing that has not been addressed within this book. The lack of diversity among women police is not part of the research for most nations outside of the U.S. Ulicki (2011) examined race and sexual harassment in South

Africa, while Fleming (2020) examined the double marginality that Indigenous women police experience in Australia. However, Fleming did not address sexual harassment.

Sexual harassment, however, must be considered within the cultural context of the nation (Huang and Cao 2008). For example, in Thailand, explicit language and jokes are perceived to be very offensive and a form of sexual coercion among students. Employees in China, however, define sexual harassment as physical sexual coercion. Huang and Cao argued that, as of 2008, Taiwan's Sexual Harassment Act of 2005 and Gender Equality in Employment Act were attempts to be recognized as a democracy but did not change the legal culture of the nation. As a culture based on collectivism, Western forms of government tend to take on symbolic meaning. In the first study of sexual harassment within the police force in Taiwan, Huang and Cao (2008) found that 46 percent of women police experienced hostile work environment sexual harassment, while 15 percent experienced quid pro quo sexual harassment. They found that perceived sexism was the driving force of hostile work environment sexual harassment, while prejudice, hostile attitudes, social pressure, sexual discrimination, and the boys club were driving forces for quid pro quo sexual harassment. However, the collectivist values of Eastern Asian culture, which is a non-litigation culture, often do not result in women seeing themselves as victims or even considering that sexual harassment has occurred. Huang and Cao concluded that Taiwan's power and labor differences among men and women reflect a gendered organization within the police.

The South African Police Service (SAPS) introduced the Sexual Harassment Policy in 1998 (Ulicki 2011). However, Ulicki argued that the policy does not attempt to change the systemic causes of gender inequality that results in sexual harassment and only reinforces the cultural tolerance of this behavior within policing. Ulicki interviewed over 60 policewomen and found that 18 percent experienced sexual harassment and 49 percent knew policewomen who were sexually harassed. Furthermore, two thirds of the women felt that sexual harassment was a problem in the SAPS. Women in the SAPS tend to be isolated and rarely report these crimes. While perpetrators included colleagues, most were supervisors. Fears of retaliation and barriers to promotion are driving forces for not reporting. Furthermore, while African women are the numerical majority, they are the power minority and are more likely to experience sexual harassment. One participant in Ulicki's study stated, "White women are off limits to Black men, but African women are fair game to all men" (2011, p. 103).

Sexual harassment research in most other countries is lacking. As Kringen and Novich (2020) discuss in their review of gender discrimination and sexual harassment around the world, much of the information can be found in the news and not the research. For example, in Afghanistan, a news report cited that 70 percent of women police were harassed, sexually harassed, and/

or raped by male colleagues (Rubin 2013). The information was obtained from an unpublished UN report that was shared only with Afghani officials. Rubin described that Afghani women police typically serve in low-level security positions, are often the sole breadwinners for their families, and are poorly paid. Additionally, the public tends to see female police as morally loose because they work in public with non-related males. Any admission of sexual coercion would result in pressure to quit or the murder of the women for a perceived dishonor. Using rape myths and victim-blaming tactics, Minister of the Interior Ghulam Mujtaba Patang claimed that the information was false; otherwise, the women would have reported such serious crimes. He also claimed that they are largely illiterate and looking for attention. He has stepped down from his position. Unfortunately, the UN report was never released and there is no empirical research investigating the extent of sexual harassment and assault in the Afghani police.

Policing Gender-Based Violence

Gender-based violence (GBV) is a global problem that was incorporated into police work as late as the 1980s in some countries. GBV affects females of all nations, ages, socioeconomic backgrounds, religions, races, and ethnicities. GBV includes physical, sexual, psychological/emotional, and financial abuse. It can take the form of physical violence, including femicide, sexual violence, genital mutilation, psychological/emotional abuse, financial abuse, stalking, and child marriages. GBV is perpetrated by acquaintances, family members, intimate partners, and strangers. Initially, intimate partner violence (IPV) was identified as family violence. However, with broadened understanding and defining of this crime, the name has changed. In India, for example, family violence includes harassment and dowry murders committed by the wife's in-laws, whereas IPV is violence committed by one's spouse. Additionally, family violence was initially identified as domestic violence, which excluded violence committed during or after dating relationships or after a marriage has ended. Today, while different countries use different names for this offense, the term gender-based violence is used internationally in order to capture the various forms of violence discussed prior.

Criminalizing and Tracking Gender-Based Violence

Through its Global Database on Violence against Women, UN Women (2016) has provided data on laws, policies, services, prevention, research, and statistics for over a hundred nations since 2009. The categories covered include violence against women and girls, child early and forced marriage, sexual violence, domestic violence/IPV, sexual harassment, trafficking, stalking, and other harmful practices. Among some of the laws collected by

2016, 103 nations have submitted IPV laws, 40 nations have provided laws prohibiting GBV and female mutilation, and 121 nations have submitted laws prohibiting sexual violence. The protections and limitations of these laws is beyond the scope of this book; however, we do know that in many cases of GBV, spouses are exempt from rape laws. China, Ghana, India, Indonesia, Jordan, Lesotho, Nigeria, Oman, Singapore, Sri Lanka, and Tanzania allow for spousal rape.

In this discussion, I will focus on policing strategies to address IPV. UN Women reported that in 2013, 35 percent of the world's females were victims of physical or sexual violence (UN Women 2019b). The World Health Organization (2020) found that in 2010, 30 percent of the world's ever-partnered females aged 15 to 69 had been victims of IPV. As 2010 has the most complete data, I present these data for the sub-regions around the world (see Table 6.4). The data show that the women of Africa and MENA experience the greatest IPV (42 percent). Specifically, women of Central Sub-Saharan Africa experience the most IPV (66 percent). This region includes countries such as Burundi, Chad, Cameroon, Congo, Equatorial Gabon, and Rwanda. West Sub-Saharan Africa and South Asia have the same amount of IPV (42 percent). East Asia and Western Europe report the least amount of IPV (16 and 19 percent, respectively). However, this is still a large proportion of women. While these data show a large amount of IPV victimization, research has revealed that these crimes are likely to go unreported, especially in nations that frown upon marital separation and have a low gender equality index.

According to Tavares and Wodon (2018), 24 percent of the nations around the world still have not nationally criminalized IPV. A quarter of the world's nations do not have a specific IPV law, a third do not include sexual violence as a form of IPV, half do not include economic violence as a form of IPV, and two-thirds do not protect unmarried intimate partners in their IPV laws. All of the East, South, and Pacific Asian countries have IPV laws. However, only a third of the countries of MENA have IPV laws and within Sub-Saharan Africa and North America, only half of the countries have IPV laws. Tavares and Wodon's research showed that as of 2017, 11.4 percent of the world's women were not protected by IPV laws. Within MENA, 74.2 percent of women were unprotected and Sub-Saharan Africa did not protect 34.9 percent of the women. East Central Asia did not protect 22.6 percent of the women. North America (10.4 percent) and Latin America and the Caribbean (1.6 percent) did a better job. However, since there are only two countries in North America, proportionally this is about the same 5 percent for each of the MENA countries. States, provinces, or territories within some countries may have IPV laws but without national criminalization, the overall culture does not come to define IPV as a serious crime and social problem in need of attention. Within countries that have laws but have high levels of IPV, this is largely a result of poor enforcement, often a combination of underreporting and lack of enforcement.

Table 6.4 Percent IPV Prevalence among Ever-Partnered Females (15–69) by Sub-Region, 2010

Region	*IPV (Percent Range)*
Asia Pacific, High-income	28.45 (20.64–36.27)
Asia, Central	22.89 (15.77–30.01)
Asia, East	16.30 (8.87–23.73)
Asia, South	41.73 (36.28–47.19)
Asia, Southeast	27.99 (23.73–32.25)
Asia Avg.	**27.47**
Australasia[1]	28.29 (22.66–33.92)
Oceania	35.27 (23.80–46.74)
Oceania Avg.	**31.78**
Europe, Central	27.85 (22.65–33.04)
Europe, Eastern	26.13 (20.64–31.63)
Europe, Western	19.30 (15.86–22.73)
Europe Avg.	**24.43**
Caribbean	27.09 (20.84–33.33)
Latin America, Andean	40.63 (34.81–45.45)
Latin America, Central	29.51 (24.63–34.39)
Latin America, Southern	23.68 (12.82–34.53)
Latin America, Tropical	27.43 (20.69–34.18)
North American, High-income	21.32 (16.24–26.39)
Americas Avg.	**28.28**
MENA[2]	35.38 (30.44–40.32)
Sub-Saharan Africa, Central	65.64 (53.57–77.71)
Sub-Saharan Africa, East	38.83 (34.58–43.08)
Sub-Saharan Africa, Southern	29.67 (24.27–35.07)
Sub-Saharan Africa, West	41.75 (32.90–50.60)
Africa Avg.	**42.25**
WORLD	**30.01 (27.80–32.21)**

Source: World Health Organization. 2020. *Global Health Observatory*. www.who.int/data/gho/data/themes/theme-details/GHO/violence-against-women (accessed June 9, 2020).

[1] Australia and Oceania are separated.
[2] MENA was placed in Africa for the purposes of this table.

For example, Malawi has an IPV law yet 24.3 percent of all ever-partnered females between the ages of 15 to 46 are victims of physical and/or sexual violence by a current or former intimate partner (World Health Organization 2020). It should be stressed that many countries have not criminalized IPV. As a result, the following discussion on IPV pertains to those countries that have.

Police Attitudes Toward Intimate Partner Violence

Historically, police organizations refused to acknowledge that IPV was a crime under the assumptions that women are the property of their spouses, the family is a private institution, and women are required to obey their husbands. Research shows that officers who support traditional gender roles are less likely to arrest in cases of marital violence and more likely to blame the victim (Saunders and Size 1986). In the U.S., this has manifested in dual arrests in which the victim is arrested along with the perpetrator (Garcia and McManimon 2011). As nations began to define this violence as criminal and as behavior falling under the purview of the police, different tactics were adopted. For nations that embraced the integration of women police into general policing, fighting IPV became a matter of enforcing laws and sometimes developing domestic violence units within police departments. For nations that embraced specialist roles for women police, WPSs were often developed. Regardless of the police strategy, IPV law enforcement is not effective if the police do not believe that it is their job to stop offenders.

The perceptions that police hold toward policing IPV are a reflection of the larger society. UNICEF (2019) found that between 2012 and 2018, 37 percent of male adolescents between the ages of 15 and 19 in much of the world believed that husbands are justified in hitting or beating their wives for at least one circumstance (i.e., burning the food, arguing with husband, going out without telling him, neglecting the children, and/or refusing to have sex with him). Thirty eight percent of females of the same age bracket felt the same. Data, however, were not available for the Americas, East and Pacific Asia, and Western Europe. In all regions for which data were gathered, girls were more likely to support this belief.

Student Attitudes Toward IPV: China and the U.S.

Some research has focused on student attitudes. Sun, Su, and Wu (2011) found that U.S. college students were less likely to support male dominance than were Chinese students. U.S. students also had less tolerance for violence, were more likely to view IPV as a crime, and were more likely to believe that gender equality has not yet been achieved. All of these cultural differences were statistically significant. When examining police intervention, U.S. students were also significantly more likely to support proactive police responses and less likely to support traditional, nonintervention police responses. This tends to explain why only about 40 percent of female victims of violence in the world seek help and only 10 percent report their victimizations to the police (United Nations 2015).

Police Attitudes in China

As these attitudes transcend policing, we can see some research findings in line with the beliefs of students. Examining police attitudes toward IPV is important because police have great discretion in the actions they take. Tam and Tang (2005) found that Chinese police, as compared to social workers, are more likely to hold conservative gender attitudes and restrictive definitions of psychological abuse. Furthermore, male police are more conservative than female police. Their findings revealed that police are more likely than social workers are to endorse IPV, such as husbands being justified with their violence and not arresting abusive husbands. However, the belief that husbands have a right to discipline their wives was statistically significant for gender and man's entitlement to sex was statistically significant for the police profession. The researchers argue that, in part, the occupation of policing has more influence on perceptions than gender.

Zhao et al. (2018) provided IPV vignettes to 520 Chinese male and female police. In the first vignette, the abusive husband claims that his injured wife deserved his violence. In the second vignette, the injured wife continues to argue with her husband in front of the police. Zhao et al. found that while officers were more likely to inform the victims of their rights, they also stated that they would mediate as opposed to arrest her abuser. The next likely actions they reported were to warn the abuser of a possible arrest and to convey understanding to the victim. Only 4.47 out of 10 officers would arrest, while 4.14 out of 10 reported that they would discourage the victim from seeking an arrest. The most unfortunate finding was that some officers reported that they would arrest the female victim.

Huang and Cao (2008) argued that the collectivist culture of many Eastern Asian societies stresses the cohesiveness and collective functioning of the group over the individual and does not embrace individualistic conflict resolution. Coupled with traditional gender roles that require females to be good, obedient, and loyal daughters, wives, and mothers, mediation is the preferred course of action in many Asian cultures. If we then look to Western cultures, today we see a more egalitarian view of gender and IPV. Sun, Su, and Wu (2011) found that U.S. students hold a strong belief that IPV is a crime. However, while they hold a strong belief in proactive police responses to IPV, many hold a relatively strong belief in traditional police responses (11.53 out of 20). U.S. students also hold low, but present, levels of male dominance and tolerance for violence.

Police Views on IPV in the SAPS

Sinclair (2017) argued that gender must be analyzed in relation to the interconnections between subjective and unconscious levels of power that occur at different levels of society. The hegemonic masculine police culture in South Africa devalues and under-protects women. Sinclair found that many SAPS officers believe that victims were deceptive and manipulative and as a result, do not consider IPV a serious crime. They believe that victims' financial and familial dependency increases the victims' unwillingness to follow through, thus wasting police time. Female SAPS officers believe that violence is evitable thus internalizing the normalization of IPV. Furthermore, officers of SAPS believe that women police are naturally better at handling IPV cases, as well as cases dealing with children.

While women police hold stereotypical myths of IPV, some male officers still believe that women are the property of men. The hyper-sexualized male is viewed as being justified in rape, by some, if his wife denies sex and he does not have another woman, especially in rural areas. South Africa values the Christian family values imposed on them by colonialization. However, many silently embrace the "vat and sit" ("take and stay") relationships with other women that became a norm during the apartheid labor system that did not allow African families to live together in cities. However, the police often blame individual morality for these relationships and blame women for being financially manipulative. Pressure is placed on the man to support two families, his legal family and the "vat and sit" family, which is believed to result in IPV. What was included in Sinclair's study that was missing in other perception studies of IPV was the racialized nature of IPV. While the police tend to claim that people of all races are parties to IPV, there was repeat stress that "blacks living in the squatter area" are used to violence and more likely to report IPV to the police. Thus, police tend to normalize IPV in poor Black families. Additionally, the gendered nature of violence is so ingrained in South African culture, as in all cultures, that male victims of IPV are denied (Barkhuizen 2015). However, one can add that the lack of interest in handling IPV cases in general results in the same outcomes for these male victims as occurs for most female victims, i.e., warnings to victims and suggestions that victims seek counseling.

Police Attitudes Toward IPV in North America and Australia

In a review of the literature, Lockwood and Prohaska (2015) found that the some police still hold negative views toward IPV. Officers in the U.S. still hold patriarchal views, simplified views of IPV, blame victims, and define them as uncooperative. However, there is evidence of progressive thinking among other officers in understanding the complexities of IPV and of leaving abusive relationships. Officers holding to traditional ideals of policing have more negative views than those who support community-policing ideals. The latter are also likely to support police intervention in IPV cases. Mounties of the Royal Canadian Mounted Police were similar to police in the SAPS in that they view IPV in a gender-specific way. Mounties view IPV as less serious when the victim is in a same-sex IPV relationship. This supports research discussed in Garcia and McManimon (2011) that found that U.S. police are less likely to arrest the perpetrator in sex-same IPV crimes and often arrest the victim. Other research found that female officers are more likely to make an arrest when the victim desired it, while male officers do not consider the victim's wishes. Additionally, female officers are more likely to define women's violence as self-defense and men's violence as abusive. Earlier research has mixed findings on who should respond to IPV. Belknap (1996) found that officers believed that men should respond to IPV calls or have a male-female team respond. However, my own research found that female officers were often pressured to join the domestic violence unit that was typically called to respond to all IPV cases (Garcia 1995).

Police perception studies have been conducted in Australia and found similar biases toward handling IPV as in other nations. In a comparative survey, McPherdan, Gover, and Mazerolle (2017) found similarities between Australian and U.S. police. For example, Australian and U.S. police tend to believe that police are more likely to be injured during IPV calls than during other types of calls (76.3 and 78.9 percent, respectively) and that IPV calls take too much of the officers' time and effort (71.2 and 64.4 percent, respectively). However, officer injury during IPV is a commonly held myth that officers often cite as a justification not to respond to these calls for help. Both police forces are also likely to believe that most calls are simply arguments, that victims can easily leave the violent relationship but do not, that women are just as likely to be abusive, and that arrest seldom reduces future IPV. However, both Australian and U.S. officers strongly believe that IPV offenders must be arrested even if the victim does not want it, most IPV is a result of power and control over victims, and that IPV laws should protect same-sex partners. Officers from both countries also believe that same-sex IPV occurs for the same reasons as does heterosexual IPV.

Australian officers are significantly more likely than U.S. officers to believe that IPV is a private matter and not a police matter (23.2 percent and 9.1 percent, respectively) and are more likely to report that they would not make an arrest if the offender is cooperative (32.5 percent and 7.1 percent, respectively). These findings reveal that many Australian police and some U.S. police are not be willing to enforce the laws. Australian officers are more likely to believe that minorities are more likely be abusers but less likely to call the police. These differences are also statistically significant. When comparing the differences in attitudes across gender in Australia, male officers are more likely than female officers are to want more discretion handling IPV calls and to believe that these calls take too much time and effort. Apparently, increased discretion would result in less enforcement. On the other hand, female officers are more likely to believe that IPV is about power and control over the victim and that same-sex partners should receive protections. These findings are in line with Tam and Tang's (2005) findings of Chinese police and social workers; that is, profession seems to be more relevant than gender. Additionally, people with certain proclivities are likely to select policing as a profession.

Generalized Policing Strategies for Combating Intimate Partner Violence

As research has discovered, police who support traditional gender roles are less likely to arrest in IPV cases (Saunders and Size 1986). Regardless of the strategy, if the police do not believe that IPV is a crime or should be under the purview of the police, their discretion can influence the outcome. We saw earlier that many of the attitudes are similar for male and female police reflecting the larger culture as well as the police culture. However, female officers tend to support a more reactive approach to IPV in some countries than male officers do. Policing IPV in gender-integrated systems often does not mandate gender-specific divisions or units. Policing IPV in these countries typically involves police responding to calls for help, arresting the perpetrator when violence is evident, providing victims with information for needed services, and enforcing protection orders. During early U.S. intervention, police grudgingly enforced the law which makes it ineffective (Buzawa, Buzawa, and Stark 2017; Garcia and McManimon 2011). As we saw with national statistics presented in this chapter, this occurs in many nations.

Within the U.S., as with many other countries, police response may also involve creating domestic violence units (Garcia and McManimon 2011; Exum et al. 2014; Regoeczi and Hubbard 2018). Typically, both male and female police are assigned to these units, although many female officers feel pressured to join. In a study I conducted in the 1990s, I found that enforcing IPV laws was so distasteful that officers in one U.S. police department renamed the domestic violence unit the D.I.R.T. squad (i.e., Domestic Intervention Response Team) (for a discussion and more recent comparisons see Garcia and McManimon 2011). The research finds that the use of police domestic violence units results in greater police response, investigation, and services to victims, as well as prosecutions of offenders. Unfortunately, most IPV still goes unreported either because of cultural or personal constraints, victims turn to another group for help such as family or social service providers, or victims do not believe that the police can or will do anything to help them.

Until 2019, the U.K. did not have a comprehensive IPV law. Similar to the U.S., the U.K. has treated IPV as a crime since the 1980s (Hester 2013). Tactics included pro-arrest and pro-prosecution. Unlike the U.S., the U.K. does not have mandatory arrest and prosecution policies. Initially, arrests for IPV were filed as assaults, actual or grievous bodily harm, attempted murder, and other related crimes. Police relied on laws such as the Violence Against the Person Act of 1861, the Public Order Act of 1986, and the Protection from Harassment Act of 1997 (Hester 2013). Police were urged to identify the primary aggressor and to avoid dual arrests. Within the U.S., police have reported that it is difficult to determine who the primary aggressor is (McPhedran, Gover, and Mazerolle 2017), and dual arrests are common for victims of color and same-sex IPV relationships (Garcia and McManimon 2011). Hester (2013) found that police in England also have difficulty identifying the perpetrator. She also found that while police are more likely to arrest men, women are disproportionately arrested. This tended to occur because women are more likely to use weapons in their violence, which often occurred in self-defense or retaliation to men's violence. However, they are not likely to be arrested if they threaten to kill the man. In 2019, the U.K. passed the Domestic Abuse Bill (Home Office 2020). The law provided a clear definition of IPV and gave various protections for victims including the right to protection orders, mandated certain police action, and protected the victim from harassment in the court. Research is needed to determine the effectiveness of this new law.

In 2015, China legislated the Anti-Domestic Violence Law, which created comprehensive legal procedures. The law allowed victims to obtain protective orders and created a written warning system mandating intervention by police, among other critical groups. However, with the current cultural gender role norms and collectivist culture, policing has not changed much. A 2011 study revealed that before China's national law, victims of IPV had to rely on the Marriage Law of the People's Republic of China of 1980 (Sun, Su, and Wu 2011). The law's amendment in 2001 introduced the country's first use of the term domestic violence and required police to stop the violence at the request of the victim. The law did not require specific action such as an arrest and did not sanction police for failing to help. Chinese police in 2011 acted similarly to U.S. police of the 1980s in that they rarely intervened, believing that IPV was a private family matter. When they did respond, officers simply made reports. The more progressive police departments created complaint-receiving stations such as in Wuhan City or reporting hotlines such as in Shenyang City. However, research is needed to determine if police actions have changed because of the Anti-Domestic Violence Law of 2015.

South Africa's murder rate was six times the global average in 2013, and it had the highest rate of IPV female homicide in the world (Ryan, Esau, and Roman 2018). South Africa's Domestic Violence Act (DVA) of 1998 includes physical, emotional, sexual, and economic abuse, as well as harassment, stalking, property damage, and unlawful entry, among other controlling or abusive behavior (Sinclair 2017). The DVA protects legally married, cohabitating, dating, heterosexual, and same-sex couples, as well as blood relatives. The act also stipulates that police must ensure the safety of the victim, obtain shelter and medical treatment for victims, and provide victims with notice of available remedies. Furthermore, the DVA mandates charging officers with misconduct if they do not follow the law. However, police are not inclined to arrest perpetrators of IPV and tend to blame the victim (Sinclair 2017). Research shows that even though economic constraints keep women from reporting IPV, the culture in South Africa plays a large role in non-reporting (Govender 2015). However, of the women who reported IPV to the police, most instances qualify as crimes but are not investigated (70 percent). Abusers are more likely to be warned. Other cases do not lead to prosecution because either the victims withdraw their complaints or the case is closed as a false report. Most cases in which police follow through are mediated or referred to counseling. Additionally, victims are accused of wasting police time and many officers are unaware of the option of a protection order.

In 2006, the SAPS underwent a restructuring of its Family Violence, Child Protection and Sexual Offense (FCS) unit in order to improve services and organizational functioning (van Graan 2012). An evaluation of the new FCS structure revealed that the amount and quality of services declined as SAPS personnel were not well informed of the changes. FCS detectives now have to deal with so many internal problems that victims do not receive the needed services. FCS detectives are also required to work overtime without remuneration and are rejected by other SAPS officers. The FCS experiences a high amount of nepotism, assigned many officers with less experience and training in the area, and lacks resources. An official report concluded that the FCS services currently reflect a reversal in development and that the government and SAPS no longer prioritize victims of GBV (Frank et al. 2009). The report also noted that it is worth considering WPSs in the SAPS since many efforts around the world have resulted in a decrease in GBV. However, women police often support the same traditional gender roles that are found in the larger culture within their respective countries and that are supported by male police.

Specialist Policing Strategies for Combating Intimate Partner Violence

Regardless of the way gender is structured within a police force (i.e., integrated or specialist/segregated), research shows that police forces tend to treat policing IPV as women's work. As a result, even integrated police forces sometimes create all-women units or police stations to handle GBV as well as child victims. Countries that have created women's police stations (WPS) include Colombia, Ecuador, Nicaragua, Pakistan, Peru, Philippines, and Uruguay. However, India and Brazil lead with their work with WPSs as well as with the amount of research on their effectiveness. WPSs serve multiple purposes. UN Women (2011b) has argued that WPSs in Latin America (Brazil, Ecuador, Nicaragua, and Peru) are the most important entry point for females of GBV to obtain justice and services. The access and support provided by WPSs should also work to increase women's knowledge of their rights. On a larger scale, WPSs make GBV visible and redefine it as a social problem.

UN Women, however, acknowledges that more needs to be done to improve the services and outcomes of WPSs for victims of GBV. The UN Women (2011b) study found that an all-female unit does not always improve services, such as in Brazil and Ecuador. Santos (2005) found that many women in Sao Paulo's WPSs resented being relegated to WPSs feeling as if the post hindered their career trajectory. Additionally, while WPSs were created to help fight GBV, most of the women police in Brazil held the same traditional gender views as male police and did not help most of the women (Santos 2005; Hautzinger 2007). Hautzinger (2020) found that WPSs in Brazil have undergone three stages: initial implementation (1985–1996), prioritized but under-criminalization of GBV (1996–2006), and overall success (2006–present). Hautzinger argues that the overall success stage has seen improved legislation, improved victims' services, and increasing leadership of women police.

Frank et al. (2009) reviewed WPSs and identified several well-functioning WPSs around the world. India's all-women WPSs are the most well-known. Kerala, India opened the first modern WPS in 1973 (Amaral, Bhalotra, and Prakash 2019). Tamil Nadu opened its first WPS in 1992 (Natarajan 2008). By 2013, India had 479 WPSs with 41 percent located in Tamil Nadu. Today, India has over 500 WPSs (Hautzinger 2020). Women officers within India's WPSs receive special training in GBV and case processing (Frank et al. 2009). The goal is to have a safe, male-free environment for handling GBV, especially dowry deaths which has a prevalence of 39 percent (see Bhalotra, Chakravarty, and Gulesci 2020). Natarajan's (2014) research shows that most women police believe that women are more capable of handling GBV and many prefer the specialist role for women police. A study of India's WPSs found female deaths and IPV were unchanged with the implementation of WPSs (Amaral, Bhalotra, and Prakash 2019). However, there was a 22 percent increase in the reporting of crimes, and arrests in female kidnappings increased 15 percent. The cultural influences toward GBV, especially in the areas of IPV and dowry deaths, are as yet untouched by the WPS police strategy.

Frank et al. (2009) also identified Nepal's Central Women and Children Service Centre within its police force. There are 25 Centres located around the country. Female officers and detectives receive specialized training, investigate crimes, and deliver services. Nepal reported that public awareness has increased, as has IPV reporting. Argentina implemented all-women Mobile Domestic Violence Units in 2006. These Units operate 24-hours and have resulted in a substantial amount of IPV complaint filings. In Liberia, a new Women and Children Protection Section was created in 2007 in collaboration with the UN Mission in Liberia. The section started as an integrated police section but soon only women were recruited. Soon after their implementation, like many of the WPSs around the world, the sections lacked resources and adequate remuneration. While UN Women (2011b) argues that WPSs make the social problem of GBV more visible to the nation, many nations have seen a marginalization of GBV. In Brazil, WPSs are often under resourced and women police are under paid (Santos 2005). Additionally, facilities are often dilapidated. So marginalized was GBV with *comisarias de la mujer* in Nicaragua that most WPSs were closed down (Neumann 2018). Only after major protesting has Nicaragua started reopening these facilities (Canal 4 2020).

Conclusion

Gendered organizations tend to devalue women and issues that are associated with women and femininity. The entry of women into male-dominated gendered organizations often leads to backlash that manifests in sexual harassment and marginalizing crimes against women. We have seen that no matter the culture's gender role norms, traditional or modern, women still struggle for equal treatment and equal protection in the workforce and in the larger society. Sexual harassment of women in the police force is a global problem. While nations have passed legislation protecting women against this crime in the workplace, their joining a hegemonic masculine organization has been unforgiven. The police organization is supposed to be one of service and protection. The police with its masculinist culture should want to protect women and children in all situations. However, history has shown us that hegemonic masculinity draws the line when women step out of their gender role expectations and into men's roles.

On the other hand, women policing GBV should be accepted as women doing women's work. Yet, we see continued resistance through the underfunding and marginalization of these units and the women (and men) who work them. Identifying IPV units or WPSs as D.I.R.T. squads (Garcia 1995) or the "kitchen of the police" (Hautzinger 2007, p. 224) exemplifies the level of disdain held for this work and those assigned. Policing GBV and crimes against and by children has come to be defined as community policing (Garcia 2005). Community policing is identified as women's work and is therefore rejected and marginalized by mainstream policing. In the same way, we can see that sexual harassment of women in the police force falls in the same category, especially when many countries have not criminalized this offense. Without a change in the police culture, these problems persist. Recruiting people who will support this culture will only reproduce this culture and perpetuate a gendered organization and the organizational violence. Furthermore, isolating women in all-women stations or units and penalizing women police for working against the gendered structure of policing perpetuates this inequality and further forces women to participate in their own oppression.

Chapter 7

Revisiting the Police Organization

Future Directions

Throughout this book, I have examined women's work in the face of traditional and modern gender ideologies, legislative restrictions and equality, and police culture in the gendered organization of policing. The review of women in policing around the world covered in Chapters 3 and 4 uncovered six patterns. First, in all countries around the world no matter the century or decade, we saw women enter on the premise that women are naturally qualified to work with women and children. Earlier entry focused on prostitution while later entry focused on gender-based violence, particularly intimate partner violence. Second, women entered first as civilians, working as support staff, often unpaid, or as social service providers. When women entered as policewomen, they did not have the full police powers that men had. If women had arrest powers, they were often limited to the arrest of women and children. Third, women were relegated to women's work often in the form of women's units or women's police stations. Fourth, no matter the time of entry, women's entry has been rejected by the police culture. Resistance takes the form of negative attitudes, verbal abuse and harassment, and sexual harassment and assault.

Gendered policing guides the treatment of women and women's work in policing and presents a fifth pattern. Gendered policing has been demonstrated in the gendered substructure and subtext used for recruitment, training, and deployment in every country in the world. Countries have moved from creating legal barriers to entry to altering barriers to allow women to engage only in women's work. Once women gained official entry as policewomen or women police, organizational barriers obstructed their success in the application and training stages. A sixth pattern reveals that these same gendered substructures and subtexts hinder women's movement into leadership roles. Chapter 5 demonstrated that these gendered processes and practices are clearly in place throughout the world.

Chapters 5 and 6 further demonstrated the final efforts of the police organization to drive women out of this male-dominated organization. In a seventh pattern in every country, gender-based violence, including violence against women police, has been marginalized. Throughout the world, women police have had to work extra hard to prove that they are just as capable of policing as men are. Women have also had to develop a thick skin in order to deal with the isolation, marginalization, gender discrimination, and the sexual harassment. Furthermore, the crimes against women within the police organization and in the larger society have been minimized first through legal denial and then refusal to enforce the laws. Relegating cases of gender-based violence to women and then marginalizing this work rejects women. In each country, women have been told to fit in instead of requiring the police organization to change. These barriers have placed undue stress on women that is particular to their gender. In this chapter, I examine the stress that women experience because of their rejection and marginalization. Then, I examine mentoring efforts taken on by many police forces and women police networks. A brief discussion of the United Nations' efforts to increase women's presence in global peacekeeping is included. The chapter ends with a few suggestions for improving conditions for women police.

Gendered Stress

Much of the research on police stress has focused on police stress in general not accounting for gender. Police stress includes inherent work stressors, organizational stressors, and personal stressors that are gender-specific. Dowler and Arai (2008) defined inherent stressors as those stressors that occur during routine police work, such as boredom, use of force and discretion, and continued exposure to negative events. Organizational stressors are the policies and practices within the organization such as excessive paperwork, bureaucracy, shift work, insufficient training and resources, and poor work relations with supervisors and colleagues. Personal stressors involve events in one's life that can impact work, such as role conflict.

Dowler and Arai (2008) found different stressors for men and women on the U.S. police force. Early research found that men were more likely than were women to experience greater emotional exhaustion and job dissatisfaction, while women were more likely than were men to experience stress from danger, the threat of violence, and exposure to tragedy (see Dowler and Arai 2008 for a discussion). A recent study of Swedish police found that female and male police had similar levels of emotional stress (Backeteman-Erlanson, Padyab, and Brulin 2013). However, female police were less likely than male police to depersonalize the job. Morash and Haarr (1995) found that in the U.S., sexual harassment was linked to work-related stress. Dowler and Arai (2008) found that men and women police perceive the organization differently. Women experience more gender-related jokes and being held to a higher standard, whereas men do not perceive this reality but do believe that women police are treated more leniently by supervisors. If these perceptions held by male officers were reality then the all of the research and current patterns worldwide would be false. Dowler and Arai found that women police experience more symptoms of stress, although work-related stressors are the same for men and women. Dowler and Arai suggest that the police culture may insulate men from this stress resulting in fewer symptoms. This can also be seen with the finding that male officers who report that women are held to a higher standard experience less stress. The researchers suggest that men may feel more at ease knowing that they are evaluated less harshly. The higher standards for women tend to reproduce hegemonic masculinity, which should comfort those who support this ideology. Women police experience greater organizational stress directly related to gendered subtext.

On the other hand, Hassell, Archbold, and Stichman (2011) did not find, in a department with female representation (20 percent) above the national average in a U.S. (12 percent), statistical differences in workplace problems between women and men. Additionally, there was no significant gender difference with stress and job satisfaction. The researchers suggested that the higher representation of women within the department might have worked to change the department's culture to accept women on the force. It is apparent that women are policing differently if they are depersonalizing less (Backeteman-Erlanson, Padyab, and Brulin 2013).

Research has found that women police in India receive disapproval from coworkers and family for choosing men's work (Nandini, Karunanidhi, and Chitra 2015). Their emotional and physical capabilities are questioned, requiring that women continuously prove themselves. However, the more time on the job the less stress they experience. Some research finds that women experience role conflict in relation to policing and family and occupational stress. Onkari and Itagi (2018) examined stress among women police in India and found that work hours increased stress among women. Among their sample, 25 percent of the women police worked 9 to 16 hours a day while 20 percent worked 17 or more hours per day. Additionally, the further they worked from home the more stress they experienced. However, women with larger families experienced less stress. Dowler and Arai's (2008) study of U.S. women police found that social support from family and friends did not buffer their stress. Tundwal and Behmani (2016) found that Indian women police experience high levels of organizational stressors including role stagnation, role overload, role erosion, self-role distance, and inter-role distance (Figure 7.1).

Sajjad and Rehman (2014) examined depression, anxiety, and stress among Pakistani police. They found that male officers experience moderate stress while female officers experience severe stress. While their research did not attempt to identify the sources of stress, they stated that women in Pakistan have fewer rights and experience inequality in policing such as violence and harassment. Because Pakistani women police do not work in the public, the researchers speculate that their stress is a result of organizational stressors. Acquadro et al. (2014) found that in Italy, female police are more likely than

Figure 7.1 Israeli Police Officers, 2019.

Source: Photo used with permission from the Israel Police Heritage Center.

are male police to experience family stressors. They are also more likely to experience emotional and physical symptoms of stress. Both men and women report that their organizational stressors include lack of expertise, superficiality, and inflexibility of rules. Yet, women police are more likely to experience stress from criticism and an undermining of their work. They are more likely to experience unfair treatment and prejudice. However, women are more likely to self-blame if they could not help the public while men are more likely to blame the public. At the same time, women are more likely than are men to use emotional support, venting, and religion to cope with their stress. These findings support the fact that historically and globally women tend to internalize the responsibility of helper. However, the prejudice and discrimination coupled with a lack of organizational support tends to increase their stress. It is apparent that for most of the research, organizational and family stressors tend to affect women differently. Additionally, lack of support tends to increase this stress and affect job satisfaction (Aremu and Adeyoju 2003).

Social Capital, Mentorship, and Women's Networks

The stress that women police experience is, in part, gender specific. Unlike male police, women experience structural discrimination, prejudice, and sexual harassment and/or assault from male coworkers and supervisors and greater family constraints. Additionally, women are less likely to have social capital within the police organization. Organizational social capital refers to the interpersonal relationships and networks within the organization that allow for trust, mutual-support relationships, and networks that provide access to resources (for a discussion see Yamaguchi 2013). Yamaguchi found that among Japanese and U.S. workers, a lack of relational/cognitive social capital weakens team autonomy and job satisfaction. Relational and cognitive social capital are the intangible elements of our human networks and include interpretations (relational) and feelings (cognitive) of our networks that allow for resource exchange. They include the value systems and norms of the organization and work relationships and manifest in trust, friendships, and informal mentoring among other things.

While Yamaguchi examined workers in general and did not examine the effects of gender, we can apply this to women police. Women police lack social capital in a gendered organization that rejects women and uses hegemonic masculinity as a measuring rod for recruitment, training, deployment, and promotion. This results in a lack of structural social capital, which is tangible and can be seen in the actual networks and rules and policies of the organization (Figure 7.2). The lack of social capital can also be seen in

Figure 7.2 Israeli YASAM (SWAT) Operative, 2019.

Source: Photo used with permission from the Israel Police Heritage Center.

the discrimination and sexual harassment of women police and police work that is defined as women's work. We also see it in the lack of mentoring that women receive. For example, we see it in Canada when pregnant police are denied special training (Langan, Sanders, and Gouweloos 2019), when Turkish pregnant police must forfeit their position (Gültekin, Leichtman, and Garrison 2010), and when Indian women police are made to feel isolated (Bano and Talib 2014).

Mentorship

Social capital can be increased through mentoring within policing. Mentoring increases job performance, professional growth, and job satisfaction and can increase promotional opportunities. Aremu and Adeyoju (2003) found that among Nigerian Police, female police who are equally mentored are more satisfied with their jobs than are male police. Within the U.K., the College of Policing has implemented formal and informal mentoring opportunities for women (Sebire 2020), and the Organization for Security and Co-operation in Europe (OSCE) stresses the importance of mentoring women (2017). The OSCE provides mentoring training materials for women working in the male-dominated police organization. The UN Police's (UNPOL's) mentoring program for post-conflict nations stresses gender equality (2017). Within the manual for monitoring and mentoring post-conflict police forces, UNPOL stresses that police forces must commit to women's rights and gender equality. Police organizations should adapt to changing social dynamics such as integrating women into the police force who have served in combat during the conflict. The UN's police gender initiative has worked to bring women into UNPOL thus providing mentoring as well as training women UNPOL to become mentors (see Box 7.1).

Morabito and O'Connor Shelley (2018) examined how women police in the U.S. access the formal and informal opportunities within policing. They applied constrained agency theory in order to explain how women in the police organization overcome obstacles. They contend that change can only happen when women take advantage of slippage or the intersection of women's agency (self-advocacy) and authority (often White men) where opportunities for change present themselves. They found that opportunities for slippage present themselves throughout a woman's life and career, from the encouraging media images of women police to the female colleagues that serve as support or mentors. Many female police gain social capital (not the term used by Morabito and O'Connor Shelley) when they encounter female colleagues and trainers at the academy. These networks provide social support and help with academy training. They also symbolize hope that women can move up in the organization. Women also report that support

Box 7.1 Women in the UNPOL: Training, Mentoring, and Leadership

In 2009, the United Nations launched an initiative, known as the Global Effort, to deploy more women police within the UNPOL (UN Police n.d.). In 2009, there were 900 female officers serving with the UNPOL, and women's numbers increased to 1,300 in 2016. The Global Effort urged police-contributing countries (PCCs) to create policy that set a percentage for female police that would be on par with their national ratio. The UN also encouraged PCCs to ensure gender equality in their recruitment requirements and procedures for international deployment. In 2015, Security Council Resolution 2242 reaffirmed this goal. Resolution 2242 called for the increased support of WPSs, collaboration with civil society, and increased funding for gender-responsive training, analysis, and programs.

Another initiative created the all-female selection assistance and assessment team (SAAT) in order to train women officers before deployment. India, Bangladesh, and Rwanda deployed all-female formed police units (FPUs). In 2015, the UN also worked with national police to improve mainstreaming gender-sensitive police and created a Gender Toolkit. In efforts to increase awareness and advocacy, the UN engages in outreach with PCCs and female police associations. In January of 2020, there were 1,323 (15 percent) female police officers and 3,961 (5.3 percent) female military officers working with the UNPOL (UN Peacekeeping 2020). The UN has set a target goal of 20 percent female police officers by 2028.

Sources: UN Police. n.d. *UN Police gender initiatives*. https://police.un.org/en/un-police-gender-initiatives (accessed June 13, 2020); UN Peacekeeping. 2020. Gender. https://peacekeeping.un.org/en/gender (accessed June 13, 2020).

from family, female leaders or role models, mentors, and previous connections positively influence their promotion. Jones (2017) found that mentoring helps women police cognitively, in skills development, self-efficacy, and social networks. Without mentors, many women police do not apply for promotion, especially when male authority often restricts their upward mobility. However, senior male mentorship may also serve to help women progress within the organization, unless these men presume that gender will get women their promotion (Archbold and Schulz 2008).

Women's Police Associations

Just as women's rights associations were influential in gaining women's suffrage, women's police associations have been influential mentors around the world. The International Association of Women Police (IAWP) was founded in Los Angeles, California in the U.S. in 1915 for the purposes of strengthening, uniting, and mentoring women police (International Association of Women Police 2012). The IAWP has 26 regions that cover every continent and members from 60 countries. Within the U.S., there are over 30 state, regional, and national associations for women in policing. The European Network of Policewomen (ENP) was founded in 1989 with the goal of increasing women's mobility within European law enforcement (European Network of Policewomen 2020). The ENP stresses networking and professional development. Many of the organizations organize conferences and training in order to encourage networking and mentoring. Newsletters and published reports are also commonly disseminated. Today, most of the women's police associations use social media, such as Facebook, in order to keep their members connected (Figure 7.3).

Future Directions

It is apparent that the gendered substructure and subtext of police organizations throughout the world work to keep women out of policing and to keep those who have entered in marginalized positions. The result has been a global underrepresentation of women in policing as well as a global underrepresentation of women in police leadership roles. Additionally, globally

Figure 7.3 Israeli Patrol Officer, 2019.

Source: Photo used with permission from the Israel Police Heritage Center.

women police are subjected to discrimination and sexual harassment on the job resulting in a gendered form of stress. Through mentoring and networking, both formally and informally, some women police have been able to gather a level of social capital that is actively kept from them within the police organization. Women's agency has resulted in national and international efforts to increase their representation and their equal access to resources and power positions. However, more is needed to improve conditions for women police.

I do not advocate that the integration of women into generalized policing is the best way to gain equality. If this were the case then women police in Finland, Norway, the Netherlands and Sweden, countries with the highest global freedom scores (Freedom House 2019) would not have the same problems as police departments in the rest of the world. While the representation of women police in the Netherlands (32 percent) has surpassed the tip-over point, research shows that over 60 percent of Dutch women police experience sexual harassment on the job (de Hass et al. 2010). The U.S. has a greatly integrated police force, but women only represent 12 percent and experience a substantial amount of sexual harassment and discrimination (Garcia 2017). Furthermore, if the specialist model is the best method then India that is lauded for its WPSs would have more than 7.3 percent female representation and they would be treated with equity (Bano and Talib 2014; Common Cause 2019). The solutions for integrated and specialist nations must come in changed and enforced policy and mentorship. The gendered nature and culture of policing is a reflection of the larger culture. As a result, we cannot simply say that changing the culture is the answer.

In order to change the culture of policing, you must change the policies and procedures at the management level, the selection process, and the socialization methods, which start with training (Kingshott 2012). However, first you must change policies at the national level. Because cultural change is a slow process, the change must begin with the creation of national policies that mandate gender representation and equity in the workforce. Acknowledging women's reality in relation to family and childcare and providing accommodations such as flexible work schedules or part-time work is a step toward equity. In most countries, women's familial role is central. As a result, it is imperative that these nations give women the resources to function in the workforce while holding to their maternal role. In countries that do not stress motherhood as strongly, the reality is that these duties most often fall to women. We must then recognize this fact and act accordingly. Sexual harassment must be criminalized at the national level also allowing for civil remedies and criminal penalties. This would first punish the offenders and set an example to others but it would also provide for remediation for women who have been denied promotion, demoted, or fired for rejecting the harassment or for whistleblowing.

At the management level, police policies must be reviewed for equality and equity. This starts with the function of the police force. Police must remember that their function is to serve and protect, not control and oppress. Most countries are not war torn so do not require a war-on-crime mentality. However, as the UN stresses, post-conflict nations must work toward gender equity and community policing in order to heal the nation (UN Police 2017). There should be a distinction between the military and the police. The war-on-crime mentality tends to increase militarization of policing which ushers in greater forms of hegemonic masculinity, and this is the root of the problem for women. However, changing the role of the police is also a very difficult process that would require changing recruitment as well. Police policies and procedures for recruitment must be reviewed and changed to ensure the recruitment of individuals who are not criminal, prejudiced, or power hungry. Recruits should be people with good communication skills with a strong desire to help but with the physical capability to perform the job. Recruits should be a representation of the people they serve in order to maximize the possibility that they will know how to work with these people and to minimize the development of a "we–them" mentality. Recruitment should enact minimum quotas for women and other minority groups with strict enforcement to ensure equity. When applicants for these groups are low then special recruitment campaigns should be implemented.

Physical requirements during recruitment and training must be reexamined. As was discussed in Chapter 5, most physical requirements and training do not reflect the reality of policing. If this were the case then all police would be required to undergo physical testing throughout their careers and would be fired if they could not pass. Instead, there is an entry test that is forgotten in most police forces once the officer is deployed. The physical requirements and academy training must be changed to stress what police actually do on a daily basis. Therefore, while physical agility must be a component, community policing and legal training must be a larger component. This will ensure that police know the law and have the communication and problem-solving skills to help their communities instead of ignoring them or further victimizing them.

Specific to women police, special training for women and removed barriers for deployment must be implemented in order to put them on par with men in the police force who have already gained such training and experience because of their sex. Women are currently behind the curve in policing because policies and practices, both formal and informal (i.e., subtext), have kept them down. Removing barriers for deployment and providing special training would enable equity for women and allow them to qualify for deployment in units of their choice. Policies and procedures must not assume that women, by their very sex, are better at handling cases involving women and children. If women police want to work these cases, it should be a choice without mandates and without barriers. However, laws must be put into place at the national and state levels that criminalize gender-based violence and these laws must be actively enforced without prejudice. Police forces must recognize that gender-based violence is criminal and under the purview of the law. Women and children must know that the police will protect them. Furthermore, special external and neutral commissions with enforcement powers must be put into place that will serve as the watchdog of the police to ensure that they are doing their job. Over time, this may help to ensure equal protection of women and children under the law.

Within the police force, we must also see formal policies, which complement national policies and that protect pregnant women from being penalized. Part-time or flexible work schedules must be considered for pregnant women. This could also be a time for increased training instead of setting pregnant women aside for desk duty. Policies must also ensure that women's promotion track is not affected because of maternity leave. While the goal is to put women on equal ground to men, we cannot deny the fact that women's pregnancy, a fact that reproduces members of society, makes certain schedules and duties of policing more difficult. This does not make them useless to the profession. This only temporarily alters the way they can police but can allow women to contribute in other ways that are not devalued and stigmatized. Saving desk duty for pregnant women, for example, tends to stigmatize the duty and thus stigmatizes women and pregnancy.

At the same time, police policies regarding sexual harassment and discrimination of all forms must be revised for clarity and strict implementation. External and neutral commissions with enforcement power must be created in order to ensure proper and strict implementation of these policies. Police are supposed to uphold the law. As a result, they must be held to the law. We should not see crimes within the police force. Since so much sexual harassment and discrimination occurs within policing, it is obvious that the police organization cannot be relied on to oversee enforcement of these laws and policies.

Finally, formal and informal mentoring must be implemented within the police force. The gendered nature of policing starts women with less social capital than men. Mentoring programs can work to build that capital. This will work to decrease the gendered stress we find in policing and to encourage victims of discrimination and sexual harassment to report their victimizations. Mentoring can also help guide women through the promotion process from preparation to application. With the changed policies and procedures, over time we should see a change in police socialization, recruitment, training, and deployment. This will allow mentoring to be more effective when women apply for promotion. We must ensure that police agencies enforce gender equality and gender equity policies. I have given my utopian laundry list that I do not imagine will happen in most nations, or at least that will not happen in a timely manner. However, ensuring gender equality and equity is not a quick fix and no one solution will make this happen. The gendered organization must be taken down on many fronts. As time passes, we may see an increased value in women and greater gender equity.

References

Acker, J. 1992. Gender institutions: From sex roles to gendered institutions. *Contemporary Sociology,* 21:565–569.

Acker, J. 2012. Gendered organizations and intersectionality: Problems and possibilities. *Equality, Diversity and Inclusion: An International Journal,* 31(3):214–224.

Acquadro, M., D., A. Varetto, M. Zedda, and M. Franscini. 2014. Stress among Italian male and female patrol police officers: A quali-quantitative survey. *Policing,* 37(4):875–890. http://dx.doi.org.proxy.libraries.rutgers.edu/10.1108/PIJPSM-05-2014-0056

Aderinto, S. 2012. Of gender, race, and class: The politics of prostitution in Lago, Nigeria, 1923–1954. *A Journal of Women Studies,* 33(3):71–92.

Afroze, R. S. 2017. Modernization and policing in South Asia: The case of Bangladesh with particular reference to women in policing. In *Crime, criminal justice, and the evolving science of criminology in South Asia: India, Pakistan, and Bangladesh,* ed. S. M. Shahidullah, 247–272. London: Palgrave Macmillan.

Akinjobi-Babatunde, T. 2015. Women police in the Nigerian security sector. *African Security Review,* 24(4):438–444.

Aleem, S. 1991. *Women in Indian police.* New Delhi: Sterling Publishers.

Alemika, E. E. O. 1988. Policing and perceptions of police in Niageria. *Police Studies: The International Review of Police Development,* 11(4):161–176.

Alhashmi, T. 2018. Cracking the glass ceiling: Gulf women in the police. In *Cracking the glass ceiling.* https://agsiw.org/cracking-glass-ceiling-gulf-women-police/ (accessed May 13, 2020).

Amaral, S., S. Bhalotra, and N. Prakash. 2019. *Gender, crime and punishment: Evidence from women police stations in India.* Boston University, Department of Economics, The Institute for Economic Development Working Papers Series, dp-309. http://barrett.dyson.cornell.edu/NEUDC/paper_32.pdf (accessed May 21, 2020).

American Bar Association. 2019. *A current glance at women in law, April 2019.* Chicago: American Bar Association. www.americanbar.org/content/dam/aba/administrative/women/current_glance_2019.pdf (accessed June 14, 2020).

Amnesty International. 2020. *Uzbekistan 2019.* www.amnesty.org/en/countries/europe-and-central-asia/uzbekistan/report-uzbekistan/ (accessed May 19, 2020).

Archbold, C. A., and D. M. Schulz. 2008. Making rank: The lingering effects of tokenism on female police officers' promotion aspirations. *Police Quarterly,* 11(1):50–73.

Archer, K. M. 1965. *Official year book of the Commonwealth of Australia, No. 51–1965.* Canberra, Australia: Commonwealth Bureau of Census and Statistics.

Aremu, A. O., and C. A. Adeyoju. 2003. Job commitment, job satisfaction and gender as predictors of mentoring in the Nigeria police. *Policing: An International Journal of Police Strategies and Management*, 26(3):377–385.

Ashkenazi, A. 2019. No longer a closed male club: The female revolution of the Israeli Police. *Walla News*, March 8. https://news.walla.co.il/item/3223201 (accessed May 22, 2020).

Augustsson, S. R, E. Bersas, E. M. Thomas, M. Sahlberg, J. Augustsson, and U. Svantesson. 2009. Gender differences and reliability of selected physical performance tests in young women and men. *Advances in Physiotherapy* 11:64–70.

Augustyn, A. 2020. New France. *Encyclopedia Britannica*. www.britannica.com/place/New-France (accessed May 26, 2020).

Austin, T. L., and D. Hummer. 1999. What do college students think of policewomen? An attitudinal assessment of future law enforcement personnel. *Women and Criminal Justice*, 10(4):1–24.

Australian Federal Police. 2019. *Annual report, 2018–19*. www.afp.gov.au/sites/default/files/PDF/Reports/AnnualReport2018-19.pdf (accessed May 22, 2020).

Australian Human Rights Commission. 2004. *Sexual harassment (a code in practice)—compliant procedures*. https://humanrights.gov.au/our-work/sexual-harassment-code-practice-complaint-procedures (accessed June 8, 2020).

Backeteman-Erlanson, S., Padyab, M., and C. Brulin. 2013. Prevalence of burnout and associations with psychosocial work environment, physical strain, and stress of conscience among Swedish female and male police personnel. *Police Practice and Research*, 14(6):491–505.

Badran, M. 2001. *Feminists, Islam, and nation: Gender and the making of modern Egypt*. Princeton: Princeton University Press.

Banda, C. 1971. *A history of the Malawi police force*. Marlow: C. Zomba.

Bano, B., and P. Talib. 2014. Sex and rank differences in Indian police: An empirical analysis. *Indian Journal of Industrial Relations*, 49(4):618–634.

Barkhuizen, M. 2015. Police reaction to the male victim of domestic violence in South Africa: Case study analysis. *Police Practice and Research: Global Issues in Contemporary Policing*, 16(4):291–302. https://doi.org/10.1080/15614263.2015.1038025

Barlow, D. E., and M. Hickman Barlow. 2000. *Police in a multicultural society: An American story*. Prospect Heights: Waveland Press, Inc.

Basinska, B. A. 2015. Women in police logistics facilities. *Problems in Management, Finance and Marketing*, 41(10):223–235. [Polish]

BBC. 2015. *Saudi Arabia's women vote in election for first time*, December 12. www.bbc.com/news/world-middle-east-35075702 (accessed May 20, 2016).

BBC Monitoring Asia Pacific. 2004. *Fiji police chief wants more women in force*, March 8, p. 1. http://search.proquest.com/docview/460714227/ (accessed May 20, 2020).

BBC News. 2012. *Timeline: Canada*. http://news.bbc.co.uk/2/hi/americas/country_profiles/1203358.stm (accessed May 26, 2020).

Beck, A., V. Barko, and A. Tatarenko. 2003. Women militia officers in Ukraine: Exploring their experiences in a post-soviet policing organisation. *Policing*, 26(4):548–565.

Becker, H. K., and D. L. Becker. 1986. *Handbook of the world's police*. Metuchen, NJ: The Scarecrow Press, Inc.

Beckley, A. 2007. United Kingdom. In *World encyclopedia of police forces and correctional systems*, vol. 2, 2nd ed., ed. G. T. Kurian, 937–951. Detroit, MI: Gale.

Belknap, J. 1996. Policewomen, policemen, or both? Recruitment and training implications for responses to woman battering. *Journal of Contemporary Criminal Justice,* 12(3):215–234.

Belknap, J. 2015. *The invisible women: Gender, crime, and justice,* 4th ed. Belmont, CA: Cengage.

Bell, D. J. 1982. Policewomen: Myths and realities. *Journal of Police Science and Administration,* 10:112–120.

Ben Saga, A. 2019. Video: Morocco's DGSN celebrates policewomen on women's day. *Morrocco World News*. www.moroccoworldnews.com/2019/03/267591/moroccos-policewomen-womens-day/ (accessed May 13, 2020).

Bhalotra, S., A. Chakravarty, and S. Gulesci. 2020. The price of gold: Dowry and death in India. *Journal of Development Economics*, 143. https://doi.org/10.1016/j.jdeveco.2019.102413

Birzer, M. L., and D. E. Craig. 1996. Gender differences in police physical ability test performance. *American Journal of Police,* 15(2):93–108.

Blackstone, W. 1765–9. *Commentaries on the laws of England in four books*. https://books.google.com/books?id=IrJRKAaEZPsC&pg=PA366&dq=william+blackstone+commentaries+on+the+laws+of+england&hl=en&sa=X&ved=0CFoQ6AEwCWoVChMIsa3M0_6HxgIVwX6SCh0QqwCF#v=onepage&q=legal%20existence&f=false (accessed June 11, 2015).

Bley, H. 1971. *South-West Africa under German rule 1894–1914*. London: Heinemann (German original 1968).

Blignaut, C. 2013. Doing gender is unavoidable: Women's participation in the core activities of the Ossewa-Brandwag, 1938–1943. *Historia,* 58:1–18.

Boraas, S., and W. M. Rodgers III. 2003. How does gender play a role in the earnings gap? An update. *Monthly Labor Review,* 9–15. www.bls.gov/opub/mlr/2003/03/art2full.pdf (accessed October 13, 2015).

Bradley v. State, 1 Miss. 156 (1824).

Bradwell v. Illinois, 83. U.S. (16 Wall.) 13 (1873).

Bragina, Y., and S. Jones. 2017. Inside the Russian police force answering thousands of calls for help from battered women. *The World*. www.pri.org/stories/2017-03-08/inside-russian-police-force-answering-thousands-calls-help-battered-women (accessed May 18, 2020).

Brewer, J. D. 1991. Hercules, Hippolyte and the Amazons—or policewomen in the RUC. *British Journal of Sociology*, 42:231–247.

Brown, J. M. 1997. European policewomen: A comparative research perspective. *International Journal of the Sociology of Law,* 25(1):1–19.

Brown, J. M. 1998. Comparing charges: The experience of discrimination and harassment among women police officers serving in Australia, the British Isles and the United States of America. *International Journal of Police Science and Management,* 1:227–240.

Brown, J. M. 2000. Discriminatory experiences of women police. A comparison of officers serving in England and Wales, Scotland, Northern Ireland and the Republic of Ireland. *International Journal of the Sociology of Law*, 28:91–111.

Brown, J. M., and F. Heidensohn. 2000. *Gender and policing: Comparative perspectives*. New York: St. Martin's Press, LLC.

Brown, J. M., and M. Silvestri. 2020. Women police in the United Kingdom: Transforming leadership. In *Women policing across the globe: Shared challenges and successes in the integration of women police worldwide*, eds. C. Rabe-Hemp and V. Garcia, 85–110. Lanham, MD: Rowman & Littlefield.

Brown, M. C. 1984. The plight of female police: A survey of NW patrolmen. *The Police Chief* 61:50–53.

Brown, T. C., J. M. Baldwin, R. Dierenfeldt, and S. McCain. 2020. Playing the game: A qualitative exploration of the female experience in a hypermasculine policing environment. *Police Quarterly*, 23(2):143–173.

Brysk, A. 2018. *The struggle for freedom from fear: Contesting violence against women at the frontiers of globalization*. New York: Oxford University Press.

Bury, R. G. 1967/1968. *Plato in twelve volumes, Vols. 10 & 11*. Cambridge, MA: Harvard University Press.

Buzawa, E. S., C. G. Buzawa, and E. D. Stark. 2017. *Responding to domestic violence: The integration of criminal justice and human services*, 5th ed. Thousand Oaks, CA: Sage Publications, Inc.

Calgary Police Service. 2018. *Calgary police service history*. www.calgary.ca/cps/Pages/Calgary-Police-Service-history.aspx (accessed May 26, 2020).

Canal 4. 2020. *Policia Nacional reinauguran las comisarias de la mujer y la ninez en Boaco*. www.youtube.com/watch?v=UsO-RL-1O98 (accessed May 24, 2020).

Caparini, M., and K. M. Osland. 2016. *MINUSTAH's specialized police team to combat sexual violence in Hait*. Norwegian Institute of International Affairs. https://css.ethz.ch/content/dam/ethz/special-interest/gess/cis/center-for-securities-studies/resources/docs/NUPI-MINUSTAs%20Specialized%20Police%20Team%20to%20Combat%20Sexual%20Violence%20in%20Haiti-1.pdf (accessed May 24, 2020).

Carrington, K., N. Guala, M. V. Puyol, and M. Sozzo. 2020. How women's police stations empower women, widen access to justice and prevent gender violence. *International Journal for Crime, Justice and Social Democracy*, 9(1):42–67.

Castelhano, J., M. Lacomblez, M. Santos, and C. Valverde. 2012. Police training course for agents-entry into the profession and also into the disnction between men and women. *Work*, 41:4637–4641.

Central Intelligence Agency. 2020. *The world factbook*. www.cia.gov/library/publications/the-world-factbook/geos/tz.html#field-anchor-people-and-society-religions (accessed May 11, 2020).

Chan, A. H., and L. K. Ho. 2017. *Women in the Hong Kong police force: Organizational culture, gender and colonial policing*. London: Palgrave Macmillan.

Chan, J., S. Doran, and C. Marel. 2010. Doing and undoing gender in policing. *Theoretical Criminology*, 14(4):425–446.

Chiang, L. N., and Y. Liu. 2011. Feminist geography in Taiwan and Hong Kong. *Gender, Place and Culture: A Journal of Feminist Geography*, 18:557–569.

Ching, J., and J. Ching. 2001. *Individual rights and civil responsibility: Women's rights*. New York: The Rosen Publishing Group.

Christie, J. 1986. History and development of the Gulf Cooperation Council: A brief overview. *American-Arab Affairs*, 18:1–11. file:///D:/Research/Routledge/Women_Police/Sources/GCC_History.pdf (accessed May 13, 2020).

Chu, D. 2013. Gender integration in policing: A comparison of male and female police officers perceptions in Taiwan. *International Journal of Comparative and Applied Criminal Justice*, 37(2):143–157.

Chu, D. 2017. Officers' views on women in policing: A comparison of male and female police officers in the United Arab Emirates and Taiwan. *Policing: An International Journal*, 41(6):734–748.

Chu, D. 2020. Gender progression in policing in Dubai and Taipei: A tale of two cities. In *Women policing across the globe: Shared challenges and successes in the integration of women police worldwide*, eds. C. Rabe-Hemp and V. Garcia, 129–140. Lanham, MD: Rowman & Littlefield.

Chu, D., M. A. Cretacci, and C. Jin. 2019. Comparison of Chinese male and female police cadets' perceived occupational self-efficacy. *Policing and Society*. https://doi.org/10.1080/10439463.2019.1632845

Chu, D., and I. Y. Sun. 2006. Female police officers' job-related attitudes: A comparative study of Taiwan and the United States. *Women & Criminal Justice*, 18(1/2):107–130.

Chu, D., and C. Tsao. 2013. Attitudes toward women in policing: An empirical inquiry into the gender views of police cadets in Taiwan. *Policing: An International Journal of Police Strategies and Management*, 37(2):324–339.

Clancy, C. 2009.50 years later: Women in policing. *An Garda Siochana Management Journal*, 22–28. www.garda.ie/en/About-Us/Publications/Communique/Communique-Dec-09-.pdf (accessed May 27, 2020).

Cole, B. 1998. Post-colonial system. In *Policing across the world: Issues for the twenty-first century*, ed. R. I. Mawby, 88–108. New York: Garland Publishing.

Common Cause. 2019. *Status of policing in India report 2019: Police adequacy and working conditions*. www.commoncause.in/uploadimage/page/Status_of_Policing_in_India_Report_2019_by_Common_Cause_and_CSDS.pdf (accessed May 20, 2020).

Congressional Executive Commission on China. 2016. *Labor law of the people's republic of China*. www.cecc.gov/resources/legal-provisions/labor-law-of-the-peoples-republic-of-china (accessed June 2, 2020).

Congressional Research Service. 2020. *Women in congress: Statistics and brief overview*. https://fas.org/sgp/crs/misc/R43244.pdf (accessed June 14, 2020).

de Hass, Stans, G. Timmerman, M. Hoing, M. Zaagsman, and I. Vanwesenbeeck. 2010. The impact of sexual harassment policing in the Dutch police force. *Employee Responsibilities and Rights Journal*, 22:311–323.

Delhi Police. 2019. *Direct recruitment for the post of head constable (ministerial) in Delhi Police examination, 2019*. https://gradeup.co/delhi-police-head-constable-eligibility-qualifi cation-i (accessed June 2, 2020).

Dene, E. 1992. A comparison of the history of entry of women into policing in France and England and Wales. *Police Journal*, 65:236–242.

Denney, L. 2019. *Gender and security toolkit: Policing and gender*. Geneva Centre for Security Sector Governance. www.osce.org/odihr/442519?download=true (accessed May 18, 2020).

Department of Veteran Affairs. 2017. *Women veterans report: The past, present and future of women veterans*. www.va.gov/vetdata/docs/SpecialReports/Women_Veterans_2015_Final.pdf (accessed February 9, 2018).

Ding, R. 2020. Chinese women police. Personal Communication. May 24, 2020.

Direnberger, L. 2016. Representation of armed women in Soviet and Post-Soviet Tajikistan: Describing and restricting women's agency. *Journal of Power Institutions in Post-Soviet Societies*, 17. https://journals.openedition.org/pipss/4249#ftn49 (accessed May 19, 2020).

Donadio, M. 2019. Women, security forces and peacekeeping in the MENA region. *RESDAL*. www.resdal.org/assets/resdal-policy_brief_mena-final.pdf (accessed May 13, 2020).

Dothard v. Rawlinson, 15 FEP 11 (1977).

Dowler, K., and B. Arai. 2008. Stress, gender and policing: The impact of perceived gender discrimination on symptoms of stress. *International Journal of Police Science and Management*, 19(2):123–135.

Dubois, L. 2012. *Haiti: The aftershocks of history*. New York: Metropolitan Books.

Duffy, D. M. 2000. Social identity and its influence on women's roles in East-Central Europe. *International Feminist Journal of Politics*, 2:214–243.

Dzinesa, G. A. 2015. *Peacekeeping contributor profile: Zimbabwe*. www.providingforpeacekeeping.org/2015/03/23/contributor-profile-zimbabwe/ (accessed May 12, 2020).

Ellis, A., J. Cutura, N. Dione, I. Gillson, C. Manuel, and J. Thongori, J. 2007. *Gender and economic growth in Kenya: Unleashing the power of women*. Washington, DC: The World Bank. file:///F:/Research/Taylor&Francis/Women_Police/Sources/Gender+and+Economic+Growth+in+Kenya.pdf (accessed October 13, 2015).

Ellison, G., and N. W. Pino. 2012. *Globalization, police reform and development: Doing it the western way?* New York: Palgrave Macmillan.

Ellwanger, S. J. 2015. Learning police ethics. In *Justice, crime and ethics*, 8th ed., eds. M. C. Braswell, B. R. McCarthy, B. R., and B. J. McCarthy, 47–72. Waltham: Anderson Publishing.

El-Mahdi, R. 2010. Does political Islam impede gender-based mobilization? The case of Egypt. *Totalitarian Movements and Political Religions*, 11:379–396.

Ephesians 5. 1968. *The new American Bible*. New York: Catholic Book Publishing.

European Network of Policewomen. 2020. *Quality through equality*. www.enp.eu/about/ (accessed June 13, 2020).

Exum, M. L., J. L. Hartman, P. C. Friday, and V. B. Lord. 2014. Policing domestic violence in the post-SARP era: The impact of a domestic violence police unit. *Crime and Delinquency*, 60(7):999–1032.

Fabian, K. 2006. Bridges across the public-private divide: The welfare-related activism of Hungarian women after 1989. In *Women's movements: Networks and debates in post-communist countries in the 19th and 20th centuries*, eds. E. Saurer, M. Lanzinger, and E. Frysak, 47–64. Germany: Bohlau Verlag GmbH & Cie, Koln.

Farsedakis, J. 2006. Greece. In *World encyclopedia of police forces and correctional systems*, vol. 1, 2nd ed., ed. G. T. Kurian, 436–448. Detroit, MI: Gale.

Finkel, C. 2005. *Osman's dream: The history of the Ottoman empire*. New York: Basic Books.

Fleming, S. 2020. Women policing in Australia: Indigenous women in blue. In *Women policing across the globe: Shared challenges and success in the integration of women police worldwide*, eds. C. Rabe-Hemp and V. Garcia, 111–128. Lanham, MD: Rowman & Littlefield.

Foster, K. L. R. 2009. *The frequency and type of force employed by male and female police officers: An examination into the law enforcement culture* (Order No. 3399324). Available from ProQuest Central; ProQuest Dissertations & Theses Global. (305174811). http://search.proquest.com/docview/305174811?accountid=12793 (accessed June 15, 2016).

Frank, C., S. Waterhouse, R. Griggs, and R. Rontsch. 2009. *Raising the bar: A review of the restructuring of the SAPS Family Violence, Child Protection and Sexual Offenses Units*. RPACAN. http://pmg-assets.s3-website-eu-west-1.amazonaws.com/docs/090909fcsreport.pdf (accessed June 11, 2020).

Freedom House. 2015. *Freedom in the world, 2015*. https://freedomhouse.org/report/freedom-world/freedom-world-2015#.VXskafm6fIU (accessed November 15, 2015).

Freedom House. 2019. *Freedom in the world, 2019.* https://freedomhouse.org/sites/default/files/Feb2019_FH_FITW_2019_Report_ForWeb-compressed.pdf (accessed May 23, 2020).

Gajic, S. S. E. Dhembo, M. Zvizdic, A. Stanic, F. Raifi, E. Anchevska, G. Odanovic, and M. Bjelos. 2013. *Women, peace and security in western Balkans: Independent review of translation of UNSCR 1325 into policy in Albania, Bosnia and Herzegovina, Kosovo, Macedonia, and Serbia.* www.bezbednost.org/upload/document/assessment_report_%5bweb%5d.pdf (accessed May 18, 2020).

Galligan, Y., S. Clavero, and M. Calloni. 2007. *Gender politics and democracy in post-socialist Europe.* Farmington Hills: Barbara Budrich Publishers.

Garcia, V. 1995. *The D.I.R.T. squad and the diaper dicks: Deviance within the police department.* Presented at the Annual Meeting of the American Sociological Association, Washington, DC.

Garcia, V. 2003. 'Difference' in the police department: Women, policing and 'doing gender'. *Journal of Contemporary Criminal Justice,* 19:330–344.

Garcia, V. 2005. Constructing the 'other' within police culture: An analysis of a deviant unit within the police organization. *Police Practice and Research,* 6(1):65–80.

Garcia, V. 2017. Assessing the current status of women in policing: The presence of the past. In *Change and reform in law enforcement: Old and new efforts from across the globe,* eds. S. W. Phillips and D. K. Das, 173–190. Boca Raton: CRC Press.

Garcia, V. 2020. Women police and societal change: Future directions. In *Women policing across the globe: shared challenges and successes in the integration of women police worldwide,* eds. C. Rabe-Hemp and V. Garcia, 193–199. Lanham, MD: Rowman & Littlefield.

Garcia, V., and P. McManimon. 2011. *Gendered justice: Intimate partner violence and the criminal justice system.* Lanham, MD: Rowman & Littlefield.

Garcia, V., and E. J. Schweikert. 2010. Cultural images—media images: "Doing culture" and victim blaming of female crime victims. In *Female victims of crime: Reality reconsidered,* eds. V. Garcia and J. E. Clifford, 3–19. Upper Saddle River: Pearson Education, Inc.

Geraghty, K. T. 2008. Taming the paper tiger: A comparative approach to reforming Japanese gender equality laws. *Cornell International Law Journal,* 41:503–543.

Geva, S. 2019. Case closed: Women in the Israel police, 1948–1958. *Israel Studies,* 24(1):100–125.

Gibbs, J. C., J. Ruiz, and S. A. Klapper-Lehman. 2015. Sugar and spice . . . and a badge and a gun: A cross-national descriptive comparison of women's involvement in policing. *International Journal of Police Science & Management,* 17(3):155–163.

Gillis, W., and A. Hasham. 2020. *Are women's police stations a solution to gender-based violence in Canada?* www.thestar.com/news/gta/2020/05/19/are-womens-police-stations-a-solution-to-domestic-violence-in-canada.html (accessed May 26, 2020).

Gokulsing, D., and V. Tandrayen-Ragoobur. 2014. Gender, education and labour market: Evidence from Mauritius. *The International Journal of Sociology and Social Policy,* 34(9):609–633. http://draweb.njcu.edu:2053/10.1108/IJSSP-01-2013-0001

Govender, D. 2015. Is domestic violence being policed in South Africa? *African Journal of Criminology and Victimology,* 28(2):32–46.

Government of Canada. 2018. *The women of the municipal police services of Lebanon are there to stay.* www.international.gc.ca/world-monde/stories-histoires/2018/lebanon_police-liban.aspx?lang=eng (accessed May 13, 2020).

Government of Mauritius. 2019a. *Scheme of service specified under regulation 16 of the disciplined forces service commission regulations: Women police constable.* http://civilservice.govmu.org/English/Documents/Scheme%20of%20Service/Scheme%20of%20Service%20-%20All%20Folders/Police%20Depart/Woman%20Police%20Constable.pdf (accessed May 10, 2020).

Government of Mauritius. 2019b. *Scheme of service specified under regulation 16 of the disciplined forces service commission regulations: Police constable.* http://civilservice.govmu.org/English/Documents/Scheme%20of%20Service/Scheme%20of%20Service%20-%20All%20Folders/Police%20Depart/Police%20Constable.pdf (accessed May 10, 2020).

Grey, J. 2008. *A military history of Australia*, 3rd ed. New York: Cambridge University Press.

Gruber, J. E., and P. Morgan. 2005. *In the company of men: Male dominance and sexual harassment.* York: Maple.

Gültekin, K., E. C. Leichtman, and C. G. Garrison. 2010. Gender issues and the women of the Turkish National Police. *Police Practice and Research,* 11(5):423–436.

Haarr, R. N. 2005. Factors affecting the decision of police recruits to "drop out" of police work. *Police Quarterly*, 8(4):431–453.

Haarr, R. N., and M. Morash. 2013. The effect of rank on police women coping with discrimination and harassment. *Police Quarterly*, 16(4):395–419.

Haberfeld, M. R. 2020. Former Israeli nation police officer. Personal Communication. May 22, 2020.

Haiti Libre. 2013. Only 8% of police officers are women. *Haiti Libre, Haiti Security*, July 4. www.haitilibre.com/en/news-8282-haiti-security-only-8-of-police-officers-are-women.html (accessed May 24, 2020).

Haiti Libre. 2018. Towards more women in PNH. *Haiti Libre, Haiti Security*, June 8. www.haitilibre.com/en/news-25170-haiti-security-towards-more-women-in-the-pnh.html (accessed May 24, 2020).

Hakeem, F. 2008. Emergence of modern Indian policing: from Mansabdari to constabulary. In *Comparative policing: The struggle for democratization*, eds. M. R. Haberfeld and I. Cerrah, 169–182. Thousand Oaks, CA: Sage Publications, Inc.

Hassell, K. D., C. A. Archbold, and A. J. Stichman. 2011. Comparing the workplace experiences of male and female police officers: Examining workplace problems, stress, job satisfaction and consideration of career change. *International Journal of Police Science and Management,* 13(1):37–53.

Hautzinger, S. J. 2007. *Violence in the city of women: Police and batterers in Bahia, Brazil.* Berkeley, CA: University of California Press.

Hautzinger, S. J. 2020. Responding to crime victims and community needs: Nongendered versus specialized women's units. In *Women policing across the globe: shared challenges and successes in the integration of women police worldwide*, eds. C. Rabe-Hemp and V. Garcia, 143–162. Lanham, MD: Rowman & Littlefield.

Heidensohn, F. 1992. *Women in control? The role of women in law enforcement.* New York: Oxford University Press.

Hellenic Police. 2011. *Women in the Hellenic police force.* www.astynomia.gr/index.php?option=ozo_content&perform=view&id=66&Itemid=57&lang=EN (accessed May 27, 2020).

Herbert, S. 2001. 'Hard charger' or 'station queen'? Policing and the masculinist state. *Gender, Place and Culture,* 8:55–71.

Hester, M. 2013. Who does what to whom? Gender and domestic violence perpetrators in English police records. *European Journal of Criminology*, 10(5):623–637.

Higgs, P., and C. Bettess. 1987. *To walk a fair beat: A history of the South Australian women police, 1915–1987*. Lockleys, S. Australia: Past and Present Policewomen's Association.

Holmes, J. 2018. *Belfast's first female police officer, 1914 to 1943*. NiDirect Government Services. www.nidirect.gov.uk/articles/belfasts-first-female-police-officers1914-1943 (accessed May 27, 2020).

Home Office. 2019. *Police workforce, England and Wales, 31 March 2019*, 2nd ed. https://assets.publishing.service.gov.uk/government/uploads/system/uploads/attachment_data/file/831726/police-workforce-mar19-hosb1119.pdf (accessed May 27, 2020).

Home Office. 2020. *Domestic abuse bill 2020: Overarching factsheet*. www.gov.uk/government/publications/domestic-abuse-bill-2020-factsheets/domestic-abuse-bill-2020-overarching-factsheet (accessed June 10, 2020).

Horne, P. 1980. *Women in law enforcement*, 2nd ed. Springfield, IL: Thomas.

Huang, L., and L. Cao. 2008. Exploring sexual harassment in a police department in Taiwan. *Policing: An International Journal of Police Strategies & Management*, 31(2):324–340. https://doi.org/10.1108/13639510810878758

Hunt, J. 1984. The development of rapport through the negotiation of gender in field work among police. *Human Organization*, 43(4):283–296.

Hutzel, E. L. 1933. *The policewoman's handbook*. New York: Columbia University Press.

Immigration and Refugee Board of Canada. 2002a. *Uruguay: Recourse available to women who have been sexually assaulted by their supervisor or manager while working in a military or quasi-military setting (2001-February 2002)*, March 5, 2002. www.refworld.org/docid/3df4bec08.html (accessed May 23, 2020).

Immigration and Refugee Board of Canada. 2002b. *Uruguay: The location of the Women's Police Stations (Comisarías de Defensa de la Mujer y la Familia) and protection, including restraining orders, available to female victims of domestic or sexual violence, specifically those cases where a police officer is the aggressor (October 9, 2002)*. www.refworld.org/docid/3f7d4e320.html (accessed May 24, 2020).

International Association of Women Police. 2012. *Mission statement*. https://iawp.wildapricot.org/ (accessed June 13, 2020).

International Association of Women Police. 2018. *Canadian history of women in policing*. http://iawp.cpsevents.ca/2018/05/31/canadian-history-of-women-in-policing/ (accessed May 26, 2020).

International Labour Organization. 2013. *Public sector employment*. http://laborsta.ilo.org/ (accessed August 3, 2015).

International Labour Organization. 2017. *C183 — Maternity protection convention, 2000 (No. 183)*. www.ilo.org/dyn/normlex/en/f?p=NORMLEXPUB:12100:0::NO::P12100_ILO_CODE:C183 (accessed June 5, 2020).

International Labour Organization. 2019. *Understanding the gender pay gap*. www.ilo.org/wcmsp5/groups/public/-europe/-ro-geneva/-ilo-ankara/documents/publication/wcms_707580.pdf (accessed May 5, 2020).

Jackson, R. A., and M. A. Newman. 2004. Sexual harassment in the federal workplace: Influences on sexual harassment by gender. *Public Administration Review*, 64:705–717.

Jones, J. 2017. How can mentoring support women in a male-dominated workplace? A case study of the UK police force. *Palgrave Communications*, 3(1):1–11. http://dx.doi.org.proxy.libraries.rutgers.edu/10.1057/palcomms.2016.103

Karazi-Presler, T., O. Sasson-Levy, and E. Lomsky-Feder. 2018. Gender, emotions management, and power in organizations: The case of Israeli women junior military officers. *Sex Roles*, 78(7–8):573–586. https://doi.org/10.1007/s11199-017-0810-7

Karim, S., M. J. Gilligan, R. Blair, and K. Beardsley. 2018. International gender balancing reforms in postconflict countres: Lab-in-the-field evidence from the Liberian National Police. *International Studies Quarterly*, 62:618–631.

Kasenally, R. 2018. Political leadership in Mauritius: The trappings of the poster child syndrome. In *The Mauritian paradox : Fifty years of development, diversity and democracy*, eds. R. Ramtohul and T. H. Eriksen, 43–63. Reduit: University of Mauritius Press.

Keitner, C. I. 2002. Victim or vamp? Images of violent women in the criminal justice system. *Columbia Journal of Gender and the Law,* 11:38–72.

Kim, B., and J. Gerber. 2019. Attitudes toward gender integration in policing: A study of police cadets in China. *International Journal of Law, Crime and Justice*, 57:91–102.

Kingshott, B. F. 2012. Revisiting gender issues: Continuing police reform. *Criminal Justice Studies: A Critical Journal of Crime, Law and Society*, 26(3):366–392.

Kramer, L. 2005. *The sociology of gender: A brief introduction.* Los Angeles: Roxbury Publishing Company.

Kringen, A., and M. Novich. 2020. Sexual harassment and discrimination: Comparative case studies. In *Women policing across the globe: Shared challenges and successes in the integration of women police worldwide*, eds. C. Rabe-Hemp and V. Garcia, 163–174. Lanham, MD: Rowman & Littlefield.

Kurian, G. T. 2006. Australia. In *World encyclopedia of police forces and correctional systems. Vol. 1: Overviews and countries A-L, Gale*, 2nd ed., ed. G. T. Kurian, 164–172. Gale *eBooks*. https://link.gale.com/apps/doc/CX3448200043/GVRL?u=new67449&sid=GVRL&xid=d2929c31 (accessed May 29, 2020).

Langan, D., C. B. Sanders, and J. Gouweloos. 2019. Policing women's bodies: Pregnancy, embodiment, and gender relations in Canadian police work. *Feminist Criminology*, 14(4):466–487.

Lehrer, S. 1987. *Origins of protective labor legislation for women, 1905–1925.* Albany: State University of New York Press.

Lehtinen, M. W. 1976. Sexism in police departments. *Trial,* 12:52–55.

Levine, P. 1994. "Walking the streets in a way no decent woman should:" Women police in World War I. *Journal of Modern History*, 66:34–78.

Lewis, G. B. 2013. The impact of veterans' preference on the composition and quality of the federal civil service. *Journal of Public Administration Research and Theory*, 23(2):247–265.

Lockwood, D., and A. Prohaska. 2015. Police officer gender and attitudes toward intimate partner violence: How policy can eliminate stereotypes. *International Journal of Criminal Justice Sciences,* 10(1):77–90.

Lokuji, A. S., A. S. Abatneh, and C. K. Wani. 2009. *Police reform in Southern Sudan.* Ontario: The North-South Institute. www.nsi-ins.ca/content/download/SSR%20 Sudan.pdf (accessed May 12, 2020).

Lonsway, K. A. 2003. Tearing down the wall: Problems with consistency, validity, and adverse impact of physical agility testing in police selection. *Police Quarterly*, 6(3):237–277.

Lonsway, K. A., R. Paynich, and J. N. Hall. 2013. Sexual harassment in law enforcement: Incidence, impact, and perception. *Police Quarterly*, 16(2):177–210.

Lonsway, K. A., M. Wood, and K. Spillar. 2002. Officer gender and excessive force. *Law and Order,* 50:60–66.

Loseke, D. R. 1999. *Thinking about social problems: An introduction to constructionist perspectives.* New York: Aldine de Gruyter.

Lowe, C. 2009. Algeria's women police defy danger and stereotypes. *Reuters.* www.reuters.com/article/us-algeria-police-women/algerias-women-police-defy-danger-and-stereotypes-idUSTRE5754S420090806 (accessed May 13, 2020).

Luscombe, S. 2012. *Entering and exiting the Empire.* www.britishempire.co.uk/timeline/colonies.htm (accessed August 17, 2015).

Ma, Y. 2008. The Chinese police. In *Comparative policing: The struggle for democratization,* eds. M. R. Haberfeld and I. Cerrah, 13–60. Thousand Oaks, CA: Sage Publications, Inc.

Maher, P. T. 1984. Police physical agility tests: Can they ever be valid? *Public Personnel Management Journal,* 13:173–183.

Mallicoat, S., and C. E. Ireland. 2014. *Women and crime: The essentials.* Los Angeles: Sage Publications, Inc.

Martin, S. E. 1980. *Breaking and entering: Policewomen on patrol.* Berkeley, CA: University of California Press.

Martin, S. E., and N. C. Jurik. 2007. *Doing justice, doing gender: Women in legal and criminal justice occupations,* 2nd ed. Thousand Oaks, CA: Sage Publications, Inc.

Matamoros, R. M. 2016. *Law 779 was severed in three seconds. That promotes impunity and more violence against women.* Envio: Informacion sobre Nicaragua y Centroamerica, 409. www.envio.org.ni/articulo/5164 (accessed June 15, 2020).

Matsui, M. 1990. Evolution of the feminist movement in Japan. *NWSA Journal,* 2:435–449.

Mawby, R. I. 1999. Variations on a theme: The development of professional police in the British Isles and North America. In *Policing across the world: Issues for the twenty-first century,* ed. R. I. Mawby, 28–58. New York: Routledge.

McKenzie, I. 1993. Equal Opportunities in policing: A comparative examination of anti-discrimination policy and practice in British policing. *International Journal of the Sociology of Law,* 21:159–174.

McKernan, B. 2018. Lebanese mayor orders female police officers to wear shorts. *Independent,* July 11, 2018. www.independent.co.uk/news/world/middle-east/lebanon-women-police-officers-shorts-sexism-brummana-a8442641.html (accessed May 13, 2020).

McPhedran, S., A. R. Gover, and P. Mazerolle. 2017. A cross-national comparison of police attitudes about domestic violence: A focus on gender. *Policing: An International Journal,* 40(2):214–227.

Messerschmidt, J. W. 2016. *Masculinities in the making: From the local to the global.* Lanham, MD: Rowman & Littlefield.

Ministry of Finance and Economic Development. 2019. *Digest of Crime, Justice and Security Statistics—2018,* vol. 11. http://statsmauritius.govmu.org/English/StatsbySubj/Documents/Digest/Crime_Justice_Security/Digest_CJS_Yr18.pdf (accessed May 10, 2020).

Momsen, J. H. 1991. *Women and development in the third world.* New York: Routledge.

Montevideo Police Department. 2020. *History.* www.montevideopolice.com/History.html (accessed May 23, 2020).

Morabito, M. S., and T. O'Connor Shelley. 2018. Constrained agency theory and leadership: A new perspective to understand how female police officers overcome the structural and social impediments to promotion. *Feminist Criminology*, 13(3):287–308.

Morash, M. 2006. *Understanding gender, crime, and justice*. Thousand Oaks, CA: Sage Publications, Inc.

Morash, M., and R. N. Haarr. 1995. Gender, workplace problems, and stress in policing. *Justice Quarterly*, 12(1):113–140.

Morin, R., K. Parker, R. Stepler, and A. Mercer. 2017. *Behind the badge: Amid protests and calls for reform, how police view their jobs, key issues and recent fatal encounters between blacks and police*. file:///D:/Research/Routledge/Women_Police/Sources/US_Pew%20Police-Report_FINAL_web.pdf (accessed June 4, 2020).

Morocco World News. 2014. Morocco: Female police officers join motorcycle unit. *Morocco World News*. www.moroccoworldnews.com/2014/11/143892/morocco-female-police-officers-join-motorcycle-unit/ (accessed May 13, 2020).

Morrison, C. J. 2004. Towards gender equality in South African policing. In *Policing in Central and Eastern Europe: Dilemmas of contemporary criminal justice*, eds. G. Mesko, M. Pagon, and B. Dobovsek. Slovenia: University of Maribor. www.ncjrs.gov/pdffiles1/nij/Mesko/207992.pdf (accessed May 11, 2020).

Morrison, C. J., and H. Conradie. 2006. Job satisfaction of female police officers in the South African Police Service. *African Journal of Criminology and Victimology*, 19(2):88–104.

Nandini, S., T. Karunanidhi, and T. Chitra. 2015. Job attitude in relation to perceived occupational stress, interrole-conflict and psychological well-being of women police. *Indian Journal of Positive Psychology*, 6(1):19–25.

Natarajan, M. 2008. *Women police in a changing society: Back door to equality*. Aldershot, UK: Ashgate.

Natarajan, M. 2014. Police culture and the integration of women officers in India. *International Journal of Police Science & Management*, 16:124–139.

National Bureau of Statistics. 2019. *Statistical report on women and men in Nigeria*. file:///D:/Research/Routledge/Women_Police/Sources/Statistics/Final_2018%20Statistical%20Report%20on%20Women%20and%20Men%20in%20Nigeria_Publication_SG%20OFFICE_29052019.pdf (accessed May 12, 2020).

National Center for Women and Policing. 2002. *Equality denied: The status of women in policing, 2001*. www.womenandpolicing.org/PDF/2002_Status_Report.pdf (accessed March 10, 2005).

National Center for Women and Policing. 2013. *History of women in policing*. http://womenandpolicing.com/history/historytext.htm (accessed May 26, 2020).

National Institute of Justice. 2019. *Women in policing: Breaking barriers and blazing a path*, July 2019. Washington, DC: U.S. Department of Justice. www.ncjrs.gov/pdffiles1/nij/252963.pdf (accessed May 27, 2020).

Nelson, S. 1996. Constructing and negotiating gender in women's police stations in Brazil. *Latin American Perspectives*, 23(1):131–148.

Neumann, P. J. 2018. Transnational governance, local politics, and gender violence law in Nicaragua. *Latin American Politics and Society*, 60(2):61–82.

New York Times. 1857–1922. Call for policewomen to protect the boys. *New York Times*, March 7, 1906.

Nigeria Police Act. 1967. *Chapter P19*. www.icla.up.ac.za/images/un/use-of-force/africa/Nigeria/Police%20Act%20Nigeria%201967.pdf (accessed May 12, 2020).

Nigeria Police Act. 2018. www.lawyersalertng.org/resources/NIGERIA%20POLICE%20BILL%202018%20.pdf (accessed May 12, 2020).

Offen, K. 2000. *European feminism 1700–1950: A political history*. Stanford: Stanford University Press.

Onkari, D., and S. Itagi. 2018. Occupational stress of women police. *Indian Journal of Health and Wellbeing*, 9(1):38–42. http://search.proquest.com/docview/1992818542/

Organization for Economic Co-Operation and Development. 2019. *Government at a glance-2019 edition*. https://stats.oecd.org/Index.aspx?QueryId=96152 (accessed May 5, 2020).

Organization for Security and Co-operation in Europe. 2017. *Police mentoring for women*. https://polis.osce.org/police-mentoring-women (accessed June 13, 2020).

Pancar, S. 2020. Turkey's first female traffic police officer shares career memories. *Anadolu Agency*, May 6, 2020. www.aa.com.tr/en/life/first-woman-to-lead-istanbuls-traffic-shares-memories/1830977 (accessed May 27, 2020).

Patterson, G. T. 2002. Predicting the effects of military service experience on stressful occupational events in police officers. *Policing*, 25(3):602–618.

Paul, D. Y. 1985. *Women in Buddhism: Images of the feminine in the Mahayana tradition*, 2nd ed. Berkeley, CA: University of California Press.

Paxton, P., and M. Hughes. 2007. *Women, politics, and power: A global perspective*. Los Angeles: Pine Forge Press.

Petruccelli, D. 2015. Pimps, prostitutes and policewomen: The Polish women police and the international campaign against the traffic in women and children between the world wars. *Contemporary European History*, 24(3):333–350.

Pew Research Center. 2020. *Pew-Templeton global religious futures project*. www.globalreligiousfutures.org/countries/uruguay#/?affiliations_religion_id=0&affiliations_year=2020&region_name=All%20Countries&restrictions_year=2016 (accessed May 23, 2020).

Pierson, R. R., and N. Chaudhuri. 1998. *Nation, empire, colony: Historicizing gender and race*. Bloomington, IN: Indiana University Press.

Police Service of Northern Ireland. 2020a. *A history of policing in Ireland*. www.psni.police.uk/inside-psni/our-history/a-history-of-policing-in-ireland/ (accessed May 27, 2020).

Police Service of Northern Ireland. 2020b. *Workforce composition statistics*. www.psni.police.uk/inside-psni/Statistics/workforce-composition-statistics/ (accessed May 27, 2020).

Prenzler, T., and G. Sinclair. 2013. The status of women police officers: An international review. *International Journal of Law, Crime and Justice*, 41(2):115–131.

Prokos, A., and I. Padavic. 2002. 'There oughtta be a law against bitches': Masculinity lessons in police academy training. *Gender, Work and Organization*, 9(4):439–459. https://doi.org/10.1111/1468-0432.00168.

Providing for Peacekeeping. n.d. *IPI peacekeeping database*. www.providingforpeacekeeping.org/contributions/ (accessed May 12, 2020).

Queensland Police Service. 2017. *Annual statistical review 2016–17*. www.police.qld.gov.au/sites/default/files/2019-01/AnnualStatisticalReview_2016-17.pdf (accessed May 22, 2020).

Rabe-Hemp, C. 2009. POLICEwomen or policeWOMEN? Doing gender and police work. *Feminist Criminology*, 4(2):114–129.

Ramtohul, R. 2018. Transcending intersectional identities: The women's movement in postcolonial Mauritius. In *The Mauritian paradox : Fifty years of development, diversity and democracy*, eds. R. Ramtohul and T. H. Eriksen, 135–154. Reduit: University of Mauritius Press.

Regamey, A., and B. M. Schechter. 2016. Introduction. *Journal of Power Institutions in Post-Soviet Societies*, 17. https://journals.openedition.org/pipss/4256 (accessed May 19, 2020).

Regoeczi, W. C., and D. J. Hubbard. 2018. The impact of specialized domestic violence units on case processing. *American Journal of Criminal Justice*, 43:570–590.

Reingle Gonzalez, J., S. Bishopp, K. Jetelina, E. Paddock, K. Gabriel, and M. Cannell. 2019. Does military veteran status and deployment history impact officer involved shootings? A case-control study. *Journal of Public Health*, 41(3):e245–e252. https://doi.org/10.1093/pubmed/fdy151

Republic of China. 2009. *Sexual harassment prevention act*. https://law.moj.gov.tw/Eng/LawClass/LawAll.aspx?PCode=D0050074 (accessed June 8, 2020).

Resetnikova, A., and D. M. Schulz. 2004. Women in policing. In *Encyclopedia of law Enforcement*, eds. L. E. Sullivan, M. S. Rosen, D. M. Schulz, and M. R. Haberfeld, 1386–1387. Thousand Oaks, CA: Sage Publications, Inc.

Rief, R. M., and S. S. Clinkinbeard. 2020. Exploring gendered environments in policing: Workplace incivilities and fit perceptions in men and women officers. *Police Quarterly*, 0(0):1–24. https://doi.org/10.1177/1098611120917942

Rosenblum, K. E., and T. M. C. Travis. 1996. *The meaning of difference: American constructions of race, sex and gender, social class, and sexual orientation*. New York: McGraw-Hill.

Roth, F. P. 2007. Mauritius. In *World encyclopedia of police forces and correctional systems*, vol. 2, 2nd ed., ed. G. T. Kurian, 638–642. Detroit, MI: Gale.

Roudik, P. 2008. Policing the Russian federation. In *Comparative policing: The struggle for democratization*, eds. M. R. Haberfeld and I. Cerrah, 139–168. Thousand Oaks, CA: Sage Publications, Inc.

Rubin, A. J. 2013. Afghan policewomen say sexual harassment is rife: [foreign desk]. *New York Times*, September 17, 2013. https://draweb.njcu.edu/login?url=https://draweb.njcu.edu:2126/docview/1432932791?accountid=12793 (accessed June 8, 2020).

Ryan, J., M. Esau, and N. Roman. 2018. Legislative response to family violence in South Africa: A family centered perspective. *Aggression and violent Behavior*, 42:1–8. http://search.proquest.com/docview/2124116424/

Sahgal, P. 2007. Gender discrimination: Beliefs and experiences: A comparative perspective of women and men in the Delhi police. *Journal of International Women's Studies*, 9(1):135–152.

Sajjad, W. H. R., and A. Rehman. 2014. Depression anxiety and stress among female and male police officers. *Pakistan Journal of Clinical Psychology*, 13(1). http://search.proquest.com/docview/1561634282/

Santos, C. M. 2005. *Women's police stations: Gender, violence, and justice in Sao Paulo, Brazil*. New York: Palgrave Macmillan.

Saunders, D. G., and P. B. Size. 1986. Attitudes about woman abuse among police officers, victims, and victim advocates. *Journal of Interpersonal Violence*, 1(1):25–42.

Schmidt, B. R. 2016. *Women on the force*. www.canadashistory.ca/explore/women/women-on-the-force (accessed May 26, 2020).

Schulz, D. M. 1995. *From social worker to crimefighter: Women in United States municipal policing*. Westport: Praeger.

Schulz, D. M. 2004. A precinct of their own: The New York city women's precinct, 1921–1923. *New York History*, 85(1):39–64.

Schulze, C. 2020. Pregnancy and motherhood: Maternity leave policies and policing. In *Women policing across the globe: Shared challenges and successes in the integration of women police worldwide*, eds. C. Rabe-Hemp and V. Garcia, 175–192. Lanham, MD: Rowman & Littlefield.

Sebire, J. 2020. Why gender equality in policing is important for achieving United Nations sustainable development goals 5 and 16. *International Journal for Crime, Justice and Social Democracy*, 9(1):80–85.

Shadmi, E. 1993. Female police officers in Israel: Patterns of integration and discrimination. *Feminist Issues*, 13(2):23–45. https://draweb.njcu.edu:2055/10.1007/BF02685733

Shen, A. 2020. Women policing in China: Separate but equal? In *Women policing across the globe: shared challenges and successes in the integration of women police worldwide*, eds. C. Rabe-Hemp and V. Garcia, 67–84. Lanham, MD: Rowman & Littlefield.

Sherman, L. J. 1973. A psychological view of women in policing. *Journal of Police Science and Administration*, 1:385–394.

Sherman, L. J. 1977. Policewomen around the world. *International Review of Criminal Policy*, 33:25–33.

Silvestri, M. 2003. *Women in charge: Policing, gender and leadership*. Devon, UK: Willan Publishing.

Sinclair, I. M. 2017. Gendered discourse in the South African Police Service talk and text of domestic violence. *Families, Relationships and Societies*, 6(2):257–272. https://doi.org/10.1332/204674317X14931348746736

Spasic, D. V. 2011. Police culture and gender identity. *Western Balkans Security Observer*, 19:25–35.

State v. Oliver, 1879.70 N.C. 60, 61–62.

Statistica. 2020. *Gender distribution of full-time law enforcement employees in the United States in 2018*. www.statista.com/statistics/195324/gender-distribution-of-full-time-law-enforcement-employees-in-the-us/ (accessed May 27, 2020).

Steinþórsdóttir, F., and G. Pétursdóttir. 2018. Preserving masculine dominance in the police force with gendered bullying and sexual harassment. *Policing: A Journal of Policy and Practice*, 12(2):165–176. https://doi.org/10.1093/police/pax009

Steyn, J. 2015. 'Darker shades of blue:' A ten year gender comparison of police culture attitudes in South African Police Service. *African Journal of Public Affairs*, 8(3):166–189.

Strobl, S. 2008. The women's police directorate in Bahrain: An ethnographic exploration of gender segregation and the likelihood of future integration. *International Criminal Justice Review*, 18(1):39–58.

Strobl, S. 2010. Progressive or neo-traditional? Policewomen in Gulf Cooperation Council (GCC) countries. *Feminist Formations*, 22:51–74.

Strobl, S. 2016. "The dream recently came true": Globalization and media discourse about Kuwaiti policewomen. *NIDABA: An Interdisciplinary Journal of Middle East Studies*, 1(1):6–18.

Strobl, S. 2020. Women and policing in Kuwait: Deferring gender inclusion. In *Women policing across the globe: Shared challenges and successes in the integration of women police worldwide*, eds. C. Rabe-Hemp and V. Garcia, 49–66. Lanham, MD: Rowman & Littlefield.

Sun, I. Y., M. Su, and Y. Wu. 2011. Attitudes toward police response to domestic violence: A comparison of Chines and American college students. *Journal of Interpersonal Violence*, 26(16):3289–3315.

Swanson, G. W. 1972. The Ottoman police. *Journal of Contemporary History*, 7(1): 243–260.

Tam, S., and C. Tang. 2005. Comparing wife abuse perceptions between Chinese police officers and social workers. *Journal of Family Violence*, 20(1):29–38. https://doi.org/10.1007/s10896-005-1507-1

Tavares, P., and Q. Wodon, Q. 2018. *Ending violence against women and girls: Global and regional trends in women's legal protection against domestic violence and sexual harassment.* Washington, DC: The World Bank. http://pubdocs.worldbank.org/en/679221517425064052/EndingViolenceAgainstWomenandGirls-GBVLaws-Feb2018.pdf (accessed June 9, 2020).

The Economist. 2015. *Democracy index 2014: Democracy and its discontents.* New York: The Economist Intelligence Unit Limited. www.eiu.com/public/topical_report.aspx?campaignid=Democracy0115 (accessed May 13, 2020).

The Economist. 2018. The long legs of the law: Why a mayor in Lebanon has dressed policewomen in hot pants. *The Economist.* www.economist.com/middle-east-and-africa/2018/07/12/why-a-mayor-in-lebanon-has-dressed-policewomen-in-hot-pants (accessed May 13, 2020).

The Economist. 2020. *Democracy index 2019. A year of democratic setbacks and popular protest.* New York: The Economist Intelligence Unit Limited.

The Mauritius Police Force. 2019. Police e-news. *MPF*, 8(1). http://police.govmu.org/English/Publication/e-news/Documents/Police%20%20Vol%208%20%20No%201%20-%202019.pdf (accessed May 10, 2020).

U.S. Equal Employment Opportunity Commission. 2000. *Title VII of the civil rights act of 1964.* www.eeoc.gov/statutes/title-vii-civil-rights-act-1964 (accessed June 16, 2020).

Thomas, M. C. 2013. *Women in Lebanon: Living with Christianity, Islam, and multiculturalism.* New York: Palgrave Macmillan.

Tu, S., and P. Liao. 2006. Gender differences in gender-role attitudes: A comparative analysis of Taiwan and Coastal China. *Journal of Comparative Family Studies*, 37(4):619–640. https://doi-org.proxy.libraries.rutgers.edu/10.3138/jcfs.37.4.619

Tundwal, S., and R. Behmani. 2016. Relationship between organisational role stress and life satisfaction among female police personnel. *Indian Journal of Health and Wellbeing*, 7(2):225–228. http://search.proquest.com/docview/1788198673/

Ulicki, T. 2011. "Just the way things are:" Gender equity and sexual harassment in the South African Police Service. *Transformation: Critical Perspectives on Southern Africa*, 76(1):95–119. https://doi.org/10.1353/trn.2011.0031

UNICEF. 2019. *Attitudes and social norms on violence.* https://data.unicef.org/topic/child-protection/violence/attitudes-and-social-norms-on-violence/ (accessed June 10, 2020).

United Kingdom. 2020. *Equality act 2010.* www.legislation.gov.uk/ukpga/2010/15/contents (accessed June 8, 2020).

United Nations. n.d.a. *Landmark resolution on women, peace, and security*. www.un.org/womenwatch/osagi/wps/ (accessed June 2, 2016).

United Nations. n.d.b. *Taskforce on women, peace, and security*. www.un.org/women watch/ianwge/activities/tfwpsecurity.htm (accessed June 2, 2016).

United Nations. 2012. Table 1. Labour force participation rate. In *Key indicators of the labour market (KILM)*. New York: International Labour Office. http://unstats.un.org/unsd/demographic/products/indwm/default.htm (accessed November 15, 2015).

United Nations. 2014. *Human development report 2014*. New York: United Nations. http://issuu.com/undp/docs/hdr14-report-en/1?e=3183072/9245907 (accessed November 15, 2015

United Nations. 2015. *The world's women 2015: Trends and statistics*. New York: United Nations. https://unstats.un.org/unsd/gender/downloads/WorldsWomen2015_report.pdf (accessed May 5, 2020).

United Nations. 2020a. *Integration of the human rights of women and the gender perspective: Violence against women*. https://evaw-global-database.unwomen.org/-/media/files/un%20women/vaw/country%20report/america/haiti/haiti%20srvaw.pdf?vs=2834 (accessed June 8, 2020).

United Nations. 2020b. *U.N. is committed to addressing its peacekeepers' sexual abuse of women in Haiti, Opinion*. https://conduct.unmissions.org/un-committed-addressing-its-peacekeepers%E2%80%99-sexual-abuse-women-haiti-opinion (accessed June 8, 2020).

United Nations Office of Drugs and Crime. 2015. *Police personnel*. https://dataunodc.un.org/data/crime/Police%20personnel (accessed May 5, 2020).

United Nations Office of Drugs and Crime. 2017. *Prosecution personnel*. https://datau nodc.un.org/data/crime/Prosecution%20personnel (accessed May 5, 2020).

United Nations Office of Drugs and Crime. 2020. *Administration of justice*. www.unodc.org/unodc/en/data-and-analysis/statistics/crime.html (accessed May 11, 2020).

United Nations Peacekeeping. 2018. *UN police*. https://peacekeeping.un.org/en/un-police (accessed May 12, 2020).

United States Bureau of Labor Statistics. 2019. *Highlights of women's earning in 2018*. www.bls.gov/opub/reports/womens-earnings/2018/pdf/home.pdf (accessed June 14, 2020).

United States Bureau of Labor Statistics. 2020. *Usual weekly earnings of wage and salary workers news release*. https://www.bls.gov/news.release/archives/wkyeng_04152020.htm (accessed June 14, 2020).

United States Commission on Civil Rights. 2000a. *Revisiting who Is guarding the guardians? A report on police practices and civil rights in America*. www.ncjrs.gov/pdffiles1/bja/249021.pdf (accessed June 4, 2020).

United State Commission on Civil Rights. 2000b. *Police practices and civil rights in New York City*. file:///D:/Research/Routledge/Women_Police/Sources/US_Comm-Civil-Rights.pdf (accessed June 4, 2020).

UN News Centre. 2016. *Hailed as 'role models,' all-female Indian police unit departs UN mission in Liberia*, February 12, 2016. www.un.org/News/ (accessed June 2, 2016).

UN Peacekeeping. 2020. *Gender*. https://peacekeeping.un.org/en/gender (accessed June 13, 2020).

UN Police. n.d. *UN Police gender initiatives*. https://police.un.org/en/un-police-gender-initiatives (accessed June 13, 2020).

UN Police. 2017. *Police monitoring, mentoring and advising in peace operations*. United Nations Pease Operations. https://police.un.org/sites/default/files/sgf-manual-mma_2017.pdf (accessed June 13, 2020).

UN Women. 2011a. *Democracy and gender equality*. www.unwomen.org/en/news/stories/2011/5/democracy-and-gender-equality (accessed May 11, 2020).

UN Women. 2011b. *Women's police stations in Latin America case study: An entry point for stopping violence and gaining access to justice (Brazil, Peru, Ecuador and Nicaragua)*. www.endvawnow.org/uploads/browser/files/security_wps_case_study.pdf (accessed May 23, 2020.

UN Women. 2016. *Global database on violence against women*. https://evaw-global-database.unwomen.org/en/countries#S (accessed June 8, 2020).

UN Women. 2019a. *Gender equality: It's time*. https://eca.unwomen.org/en/digital-library/publications/2019/04/ukraine-its-time-gender-equality-brochure (accessed May 18, 2020).

UN Women. 2019b. *Facts and figures: Ending violence against women*. www.unwomen.org/en/what-we-do/ending-violence-against-women/facts-and-figures#notes (accessed June 9, 2020).

UN Women. 2020. *Gender equality: Women's rights in review 25 years after Beijing*. www.unwomen.org/en/digital-library/publications/2020/03/womens-rights-in-review (accessed May 23, 2020).

UN Women Africa. n.d. *Tanzania*. https://africa.unwomen.org/en/where-we-are/eastern-and-southern-africa/tanzania (accessed May 11, 2020).

U.S. Equal Employment Opportunity Commission. 1997. *Facts about sexual harassment*. www.eeoc.gov/publications/facts-about-sexual-harassment (accessed June 8, 2020).

Van der Lippe, T., A. Graumans, and S. Sevenhuijsen. 2004. Gender policies and the position of women in the police force in European countries. *Journal of European Social Policy*, 14(4):391–405.

van Graan, J. 2012. An impact evaluation of the restructuring of the South African police services family violence, child protection and sexual offences units: The case of the West Rand FCS unit. *African Journal of Criminology and Victimology*, 25(1):97–113.

Verfurth, E. M. 2011. Post-conflict society: Excellent work for women. *Development and Cooperation*. www.dandc.eu/en/article/advantages-having-many-women-nicaraguas-police-force (accessed May 24, 2020).

Verguiero, L. F. T. 2008. *Brazilian security structure*. https://fas.org/irp/world/brazil/fabrverg.pdf (accessed May 24, 2020).

Vrajolli, M. 2011. Gender representation in the Kosovo security sector. *Western Balkans Security Observer*, 6(19):58–67.

Walsh, D. M. 2012. Does the quality of democracy matter for women's rights? Just debate and democratic transition in Chile and South Africa. *Comparative Political Studies*, 45(1):1323–1350.

Weaver, K. M. 2007. Women's rights and Shari'a law: A workable reality? An examination of possible international human rights approaches through the continuing reform of Pakistani Hudood Ordinance. *Duke Journal of Comparative & International Law*, 17:483–510.

West, C., and S. Fenstermaker. 1993. Power, inequality, and the accomplishment of gender: An ethnomethodological view. In *Theory on gender/feminism on theory*, ed. P. England, 151–174. New York: Aldine.

West, C., and D. H. Zimmerman. 1987. Doing gender. *Gender & Society*, 1:125–155.

Wilkinson, V., and I. D. Froyland. 1996. Women in policing. *Australian Institute of Criminology: Trends and Issues in Crime and Criminal Justice*, 58:1–6.

Wilmore, J. H., and J. A. Davis. 1979. Validation of a physical abilities field test for the selection of state traffic officers. *Journal of Occupational Medicine*, 21:33–40.

Women Police Officers Network. 2012. *Guidelines for gender sensitive policing: With an emphasis on recruitment, selection and professional development of women in police services.* https://issuu.com/undp_in_europe_cis/docs/womenppolice (accessed May 18, 2020).

Women Police Officers Network. 2015. *Women in police services in South East Europe.* United Nations Development Programme Istanbul Regional Hub. www.seesac.org/f/docs/Gender-and-Security/Women-in-Police-Services-in-South-East-Europe-.pdf (accessed June 11, 2020).

Women Suffrage and Beyond. 2015. *Women suffrage and beyond: Confronting the democratic deficit.* http://womensuffrage.org (accessed June 1, 2015).

Woollacott, A. 2015. *Settler society in the Australian colonies: Self-government and imperial culture.* Oxford, UK: Oxford University Press.

World Bank Group. 2016. *Paving the way for women's economic inclusion in the Gulf Cooperation Council (GCC).* http://documents.worldbank.org/curated/en/530451467995640868/pdf/105816-v1-WP-ADD-SERIES-GCC-engagement-note-PUBLIC.pdf (accessed May 13, 2020).

World Bank Group. 2019. *Labor force participation rate, female (% of female population ages 15–64) (modeled ILO estimate).* https://data.worldbank.org/indicator/SL.TLF.ACTI.FE.ZS (accessed May 5, 2020).

World Bank Group. 2020a. *Gender statistics.* https://databank.worldbank.org/source/gender-statistics# (accessed May 5, 2020).

World Bank Group. 2020b. *Women, business and the law.* https://wbl.worldbank.org/en/data/exploretopics/wbl_sj (accessed May 30, 2020).

World Health Organization. 2020. *Global health observatory.* www.who.int/data/gho/data/themes/theme-details/GHO/violence-against-women (accessed June 9, 2020).

Yamaguchi, I. 2013. A Japan—US cross-cultural study of relationships among team autonomy, organizational social capital, job satisfaction, and organizational commitment. *International Journal of Intercultural Relations*, 37(1):58–71.

Yeniseyev, M. 2016. Uzbek women join police. *Caravanserai*, Women's Rights, June 16. https://central.asia-news.com/en_GB/articles/cnmi_ca/features/2016/06/16/feature-02 (accessed May 19, 2020).

Young, K. K. 1987. Introduction. In *Women in world religions*, ed. A. Sharma, 1–36. Albany: State University of New York Press.

Zhao, R., H. Zhang, Y. Jiang, and X. Yao. 2018. The tendency to make arrests in domestic violence: Perceptions from police officers in China. *International Journal of Offender Therapy and Comparative Criminology*, 62(16):4923–4941.

Zollmann, J. 2020. Becoming a good farmer—Becoming a good farm worker: On colonial educational policies in Germany and German South-West Africa, circa 1890 to 1918. In *Education and development in colonial and postcolonial Africa: Policies, paradigms, and entanglements, 1890s-1980s*, eds. D. Matasci, M. B. Jeronimo, and H. G. Dores, 109–142. Cham: Palgrave Macmillan.

Index

Page numbers in *italics* indicate a figure and page numbers in **bold** indicate a table on the corresponding page. Page numbers followed by 'b' indicate a box.

Acquadro, M. 146–147
Act 108, 1996 Constitution 59
Adeyoju, C. A. 149
Africa 20, 24, 30b, 38–39, 43–44, 57, **133**; *see also* MENA; Sub-Saharan Africa
Afroze, R. S. 55
aggression and violence 36
agriculture and service sectors 19
Albania State Police (ASP) 71, 102
Aleem, S. 52
all-female selection assistance and assessment team (SAAT) 150b
all-female Women Support and Investigation Division 54
all-women Mobile Domestic Violence Units, in Argentina 142
all women police stations 52, 101, 112, 140; *see also* Women's Police Stations (WPS)
Al Mina, Lebanon 66
Amnesty International 73
Anti-Domestic Violence Law of 2015 (China) 139
Arab feminism 15–16
Arab Gulf States Institute 67
Arai, B. 145–146
Archbold, C. A. 146
Aremu, A. O. 149
arrest powers 1, 31, 41, 84, 89, 144
Asia 12, 14, 20, 24, 42–43, 49–56, 86, **97**, **122**, **133**; Afghanistan 30b, **49**, 130; Asia-Pacific 30b; Bangladesh 12, **49**, 53–55, 98, **100**, 102, 108, 123, **125**, 126, 150; Bhutan **49**; Burma 30b; Cambodia **49**; China **19**, 24, 29, 30b, 43, 48, 49, **49–50**, 55–56, 70, 71, 98, **100**, 101, 102, 107–110, 113, 120, **125**, 130, 132, 134–135, 139; East Asia 20, 132; Hawaii 30b; Hong Kong 16, **19**, 24, 29, 30b, 49, **49**, 55; India 5, **19**, 30b, 39, 43, 48, 49, **49**, 51–53, 70, 84, 98, **100**, 101, 104, 107, 112, 120, **125**, 131, 132, 140, 141, 146, 150, 152; Indonesia 30b, 43, **49**, 132; Israel 43, 62, 63–65, **63**, 98, **100**, 103, 117–119, **125**; Japan 17, 23, 43, **49**, 55, 148; Laos **49**; Malaysia 30b, 43, **49**; Mongolia 12, **49**; Myanmar **49**, **50**; Nepal 9, 18, **19**, 20, 34, **49**, 141–142; North Korea 10, **49**; Pakistan **19**, 30b, 43, **49**, 52, 54, 140, 146; Papua New Guinea **49**; Philippines 20, 21, 23, 30b, 34, 43, 49, 140; Singapore 30b, **49**, **50**, 132; South East Asia 20, 132; South Korea 43, **49**; Sri Lanka 14, 30b, 43, **49**, 132; Taiwan 17, **49**, 101, 102, 120, 126, 130; Thailand 49, **49**, 130; Timor-Leste 19–20, 22, **49**, **50**, 102; Vietnam 38, **49**; *see also* Oceania
Asia-Pacific 30b
assault, sexual *see* sexual harassment/ assault
Augustsson, S. R 105
Australasia 2, 12, 16, 49, **133**; *see also* Asia; Australia; Oceania
Australia **11**, 12, 20, 30b, 34, 38, 42, 49, **49**, 50–51, **50**, 98, **100**, **125**, 126, 130, 136–138; *see also* Oceania
Australian Federal Police (AFP) 50, 51

authoritarian regimes, women police in 28–29; China **49**, 55–56; GCC **63**, 66–68; Nicaragua **76**, 80–81; Russia/Tajikistan/Uzbekistan **68**, 72–73; Sub-Saharan region **56**, 62

backlash 16, 64, 142
Bahia, Brazil 79, 116
Bahrain, Islamic revivalism in 31–32
Baldwin, L. 84
bangharda 41
Bar Tzvi, S. *111*
Basinska, B. A. 70
Behmani, R. 146
Beijing 55
Belknap, J. 137
Bell, V. 82
Berlin Conference (1884–1885) 38
Bill of Rights 59
Birzer, M. L. 105–106
Blackstone, W. 29, 31
Blandengues Corps 76
Boniface, G. 83
Border Police 50
boys, play activities of 4
Bradburn, L. 83
Bradley v. State 1824 34
Brazil 98, **99**, **124**; flawed democracy **76**, 78–79; gender pay gap 9; law 126; specialist model for women 84; WPS 101, 116, 120, 140–141, 142
British South Africa Company 39
Brown, J. 57, 63, 94, 126, 127, 129
bullying and sexual harassment 128; *see also* sexual harassment/assault
Busson, B. 83

Calgary Police Service 82
Cambridge School Certificate 59
Campbell, K. 83
Cao, L. 130, 135
Capital Police Department (Nanking) 55
carcereiras 78
Castelhano, J. 104–105
Central and Eastern Europe 11, 14, **133**
Central Intelligence Agency 73
Central Police College, in Nanking 56
Central Women and Children Service Centre (Nepal) 141
Chekiang Police College 55
Chiang, L. N. 16
Chu, D. 56, 73, 120
City Police Force, Greece 90
Civic Guard (*An Garda Siochana*, Ireland) 41, 88, 89, 127
Civil Code of 1804, Napoleon's 58
civilian police forces 38, 78
civil liberties 10–12, 14, 20, 25, 49, 75
Civil Police 78
civil remedies, for sexual harassment 123
Civil Rights Act of 1964, Title VII (U.S.) 15, 126
cognitive social capital 148
Cole, B. 38–39
colonialism 37, 39
colonial policing 78
comisarias de la mujer 80
Commentaries on the Laws of England (Blackstone) 29
Commission on Civil Rights (U.S.) 103, 110, 123
Commission on Human Rights (UN) 123
Commonwealth Police Force 50
Commonwealth Year Book (1965) 51
community policing 120, 142, 153
Constabulary of Ireland 88
Contagious Diseases Act 87
Convention on the Elimination of all Forms of Discrimination against Women 60
Coracan policewomen 45
Craig, D. E. 105–106
Cretacci, M. A. 56
Crime Control Act (1973, U.S.) 85
crime fighting 36, 52, 53, 55, 72, 87, 106
criminal penalties 123
Croft, H. 87
cultural change 152
cultural norms, in patriarchal society 6
culture: collectivist 135; police 34–37; political ideologies of power 32; religious ideologies 33

Davis, J. A. 36
Debayle, A. S. 80
decision-making 22, 51, 53
de Hass, S. 127
delegada 78
Delhi Police 104
democracy 49, 76, 130; *see also* flawed democracy, women police in; full democracy, women police in
democracy index 11, 12, 48, 49, **49**, **56**, **63**, **68**, **76**, **85**; authoritarian regime 55–56, 62, 66–68, 72–73, 80–81; flawed democracy 51–53, 57–60,

63–65, 69–70, 78–79, 83–85, 89–90; full democracy 50–51, 57–60, 76–78, 81–83, 86–89; hybrid regime 53–55, 60–62, 65–66, 70–72, 79–80, 90–91
democracy regimes: in Asia and Oceania **49**, 50–56; in Eastern Europe 68–73, **68**; in Latin America and Caribbean 75–81, **76**; in MENA 62–68, **63**; in North America 81–85; in Sub-Saharan Africa 56–62, **56**; in Western Europe 85–91, **85**
deployment 74, 91, 107, 144, 153
Deputy Commissioner for Women Affairs, INP 65, 119b
devshirme system 37
Dhaka Metropolitan Police Act (1976) 54–55
difference 4; emphasizing within society 8; gender and 5–8; *see also* other
Ding, R. 109
D.I.R.T. squad (Domestic Intervention Response Team) 138, 142
discrimination 14, 16; Bill of Rights and 59; eliminating in workforce 88; gender 59, 61, 72, 121; in hiring/recruitment 41, 91; institutional 103, 104; in policing 70, 108; prejudice and 147; prohibition of 17; in promotion 108, 110; sex 14, 107, 108; sexism and 65; sexual harassment and 117–119b, **122**, **124**, **125**, 152; social capital and 148; in workforce 25
division of labor 17, 18
doing gender 4, 28, 31, 115–121
doing policing 115–121
Domestic Abuse Bill (U.K.) 139
domestic violence 131, 139
Domestic Violence Act (DVA) of 1998 (South Africa) 139
double marginality 130
double tokenism 51
Dowler, K. 145–146
Dravidian ethnic group 51
dual arrests 139
Dubai 25, 67–68, 101, 120

earnings gap 34
Eastern Europe 12, 49, 68–73, 86, **97**, 98, **122**, **133**; Albania **11**, 16, **68**, **69**, 70–71, **100**, 102, **125**; Armenia 12, 23–24, **68**; Azerbaijan 12, 23, **68**; Belarus **11**, **19**, **68**; Bosnia and Hercegovina 22, **68**, **69**; Bulgaria 10, 16, 37, **68**, **69**; Croatia 10, **68**, **69**; Czechoslovakia 16, 42; Estonia **11**, 16, **68**, 69, **69**; Georgia **11**, 12, **68**; Hungary 16, 37, **68**, 69, **69**, **100**, **125**; Kazakhstan 12, **68**, **69**; Kyrgyz Republic **11**, 12, 22, 23, **68**; Latvia **11**, 16, **19**, 21, 23, **68**, 69, **69**; Lithuania 16, 18, **19**, **68**, 69, **69**; Moldova 10, **68**; Montenegro **68**, **69**, 123; North Macedonia **68**, **69**; Poland **11**, 16, 41, **68**, 69–70, **69**, 93, 98, **99**, 108, **124**; Romania 16, 23, 37, **68**, **69**; Russia **11**, 23, 29, **68**, 69, **69**, 71, 72–73, **100**, **125**, 126; Serbia 22, 23, **68**, 69, **69**; Slovakia **11**, **68**, **69**; Slovenia 23, **68**, 69, **69**; Tajikistan 12, 23, **68**, 72–73, **100**, 106, **125**, 126; Turkmenistan 12, **68**; Ukraine **11**, **68**, 71–72, 98, **100**, **125**; Uzbekistan **68**, 73, **100**, **125**, 126; Yugoslavia 16; *see also* Central and Eastern Europe
East India Company 39
Economist, The 12, 49, 56, 59, 60, 62, 65, 75, 76, 81, 85
Ellwanger, S. J. 37
emancipation 16
emotional stress 145
employment opportunities for women 15
Equal Employment Opportunity Act of 1972 (EEOA) 15
Equal Employment Opportunity Law (EEOL) 17
equality 9, 17, 32, 33, 41, 150b
Equality Act of 2010 (U.K.) 126
equal pay 98, **99–100**
equity, gender 33, 74, 85, 152–153, 155
escriva 78
essentialism 4
ethnicity 5, 83
Europe 30b
European Network of Policewomen (ENP) 151
European Union (EU) 71
evaluations 2, 44, 129
Export Processing Zone 58

Facebook 151
family: ideologies 29–31; violence 131
Family Violence, Child Protection and Sexual Offense (FCS) unit 140
Fell-Shik, Z. 63
female(s): cadets 56, 93, 108, 111, 120; first "safety worker" 39; homicide 139;

labor force 9; Mounties 83; prosecutors, representation of 23–24; sexual exploitation of 123; victims of physical/sexual violence 132
Female Metropolitan Police 45
Female Police Unit (FPU, India) 5b, 32, 150b
femininity 3, 8
feminist movement 13–15, 18, 84, **97**; first wave 9, 14, 16; second wave 13–14, 41; third wave 15–16
Fiji Police Force 53–54
Fikriye Yavuz 90
flawed democracy, women police in: Greece **85**, 89–90; India **49**, 51–53; Israel 63–65, **63**, *64*; Mauritius/South Africa **56**, 57–60; Poland **68**, 69–70; Sao Paulo **76**, 78–79; U.S. 83–85; *see also* democracy
Fleming, S. 130
Fortune, R. 82
Foster, K. L. R. 36
Frank, C. 141
Freedom House 10–13, 20
French West African police 38
full democracy, women police in: Australia **49**, 50–51; Canada 81–83; Mauritius/South Africa **56**, 57–60; U.K./Ireland **85**, 86–89; Uruguay 76–78, **76**; *see also* democracy

Garcia, V. 1, 3, 4, 28, 31, 32, 36, 84, 85, 94, 95, 98, 107, 110, 116, 128, 129, 134, 136–139, 142, 152
Garda Siochana, An 41, 88, 89, 127
Garrison, C. G. 90–91, 103
Garven, P. 28b
gendarmerie 37, 90
gender: criminal justice and 101; defined 3; and difference 4, 5–8; discrimination 59, 61, 72, 121; doing gender 4, 31; embodying 4; equity 33, 74, 85, 152–153, 155; femininity 3, 8, 14–17; inequalities 95; institutionalization of 19; intersex 3, 4; leadership/policing 21–24; pay gap 9, 20–21, 58; in policing 24; and religious ideologies 9; roles 3, 4; segregation 67; and sexual harassment 128; as social constructs 4; sociology of 3–4, 94; stratification 8–9; and work 17–20; *see also* ideologies
Gender Balance Council (UAE) 101
gender-based violence (GBV): criminalizing and tracking 131–133; domestic violence 131, 139; legislation of 131–133; marital rape 132, 136; sexual violence 132; special training on 79, 107; stalking 131; trafficking 131; *see also* intimate partner violence; sexual harassment/assault
gendered organizations 1, 142; barriers to promotion 108–113; gendered substructures 94, 95, 106, 107, 113, 144, 151; gendered subtext 94, 95, 102, 106, 107, 113, 144, 151; pay gap and gender 9, 20–21, 58; policing as 37; recruitment of women into policing 95–106; training 106–108; workforce 17–20
gendered policing 115–143, 144
gendered stress 145–147
gendered substructure and subtext, of police organizations 94, 95, 102, 106, 107, 113, 144, 151
gender equality 33, 41, 47, 149, 150b, 155; index 101, 132; legislation 71, 94, 101, 102
Gender Equality Department (Taiwan) 101
Gender Equality in Employment Act (2000, Taiwan) 17, 130
Gender Policy for the Nigeria Police Force, A (NPF report) 61
gender-restricted roles, of women police in India **49**, 51–53
Gender Toolkit 150b
general policing duties 45, 84, 93–94
Geraghty, K. T. 17
Gerber, J. 120
Geva, S. 63–65
Gibbs, J. C. 71
girls, play activities of 4
Global Database on Violence against Women (UN Women) 131
Global Effort 150b
Gokulsing, D. 58
Goldzier, J. 28b
Gouweloos, J. 112
Gover, A. R. 137
government: communism 49, 55, 71; forms of 27–28; multiparty democracy 71; parliamentary republic 50, 51, 53, 54, 57, 59, 63, 65, 66, 69, 70, 89; presidential republic 57, 60, 65, 73, 77, 78, 80, 90; semi-presidential federation 71, 72, 79; women in local 22–23

Government of Ireland Act (1920) 88
Granera, A. 80
Graumans, A. 102, 112
Great Britain 30b, 31, 76, 81
Great Depression 40, 84
Greater Bombay, India 52
guardianship law 67
Gulf Cooperation Council (GCC), women police in 25b, 66–68, 98, 101
Gültekin, K. 90–91, 103
guns, use of 35

Haarr, R. N. 108, 129, 145
Haberfeld, M. 116, 117–119b, *117*, *118*, *127*
Hall, J. N. 128
Han Chinese 55
hard charger 26
Harris, L. 82
Hassell, K. D. 146
Hausa, ethnic group in Nigeria 60
Hautzinger, S. J. 78–79, 116, 141
heads of state, women 22
hegemonic ideologies 6, 8, 26, 58
hegemonic masculinity 26, 36, 94–95, 108, 115, 142, 146, 148, 153
Heidensohn, F. 87, 93–94, 126
Hellenic Police 89–90, 102, 107
Herbert, S. 26, 34–36, 94
Hester, M. 139
hostile work environment sexual harassment 130
Huang, L. 130, 135
Hughes, M. 9, 14, 25
Hunt, J. 36
hybrid regimes, women police in: Albania/Ukraine **68**, 70–72; Algeria/Lebanon/Morocco **63**, 65–66; Fiji and Bangladesh **49**, 53–55; National Police of Haiti (PNH) **76**, 79–80; Nigeria Police Force **56**, 60–62; Turkish National Police (TNP) **85**, 90–91

Icelandic police force, sexual harassment in 128
ideologies: family 29–31; hegemonic 6, 8, 26, 58; men and gender 33–34; political 31–32; religious 32–33; work 32
Igbo, ethnic group in Nigeria 60
imperial armies 38
incivilities 116
income, higher levels of 8
independence 16; Albania 70–71; Algeria 65; Australia 50; Bangladesh 54; Brazil 78; China 55; Fiji 53; Haiti 79; India 51; Israel 63; Kuwait 67; Lebanon 65; Mauritius 57; Morocco 66; Nicaragua 80; Nigeria 60; Poland 69; Tajikistan 73; Turkey 90; Ukraine 71; Uruguay 76–77; Uzbekistan 73
Indo-Aryan ethnic group 51
Indo-Fijian ethnic group 53
industry sector jobs 20
inherent work stressors 145
institutional discrimination 103, 104
institutionalization of gender 19
institutionalized masculinity 34–37
integration phase 41, 47–48, 65, 85, 88, 93–94
Interagency Taskforce on Women, Peace and Security 5b
Interior Security Forces (ISF), Lebanon 66
International Association of Policewomen 84
International Association of Women Police (IAWP) 150–151
International Council of Women in 1888 10
International Labour Organization (ILO) 18, 111
International Woman Suffrage Alliance, in 1904 10
intersectionality 16, 129
intersex 3, 4
intimate partner violence (IPV): arrests 135, 136–137, 138–140; dual arrests 134, 139; economic violence 132; family violence 131; generalized police strategies for 138–140; legislation of 132, 134, 139; police attitudes of 133–138; prevalence among ever-partnered females **133**; same-sex partners 136, 137, 139; specialist police strategies for 140–142; statistics of 134, 135, 137; student attitudes of 134; victims of 132; and WPS 76
Iran 9
Irish Free State 88
Iron Curtain, fall of 16
Islamic (*shari'a*) law 33, 37, 38, 65, 66, 67
Israel Border Police *96*
Israel Defense Forces (IDF) 63–64
Israeli policewoman *44*, *147*
Israeli YASAM (SWAT) operative *105*, *148*

Israel National Police (INP) 63–65, 116, 118b
Itagi, S. 146
iTaukei ethnic group 53

Jackson, A. 82
Jin, C. 56
job satisfaction: promotion and 112, 149; relational/cognitive social capital and 148; retention and 54; stress and 146, 147
Johnson, J. 77
Jones, J. 150
Judicial Police *see* Civil Police
judiciary, women in 23

Kanpur, India 52
Kenyan Bill of Rights 31
Kerala, India 52
"khaki fever" 89
Kim, B. 120
Kosovo Police 107, 108
Kramer, L. 8
Kringen, A. 130

labor force, women in 9, 16, 19–20, **19**
labor laws, in workplace: discrimination and sexual harassment **122**, **124**, **125**; women's movement **97**, **99**, **100**
Labour Standards Law (1947, Japan) 17
Lagos Ladies League 61
Lagos Women's Party 61
Langan, D. 112
latency and depression 84, 88
Latin America and the Caribbean 20, 22, 75–81, **97**, **122**, 132, **133**; Antigua and Barbuda 12; Argentina 45, 76, **76**, 106, 142; Bahamas 12, 30b; Barbados 12, **19**, **77**, 121, 126; Belize 22, 30b; Bermuda 21–22, 30b, 34; Bolivia 12, 75, **76**; British Columbia 30b, 45; British Guiana 30b; Chile 12, 38, 75–76, **76**, **77**, 126; Colombian 45, 119; Costa Rica 21, 24, 75, 76, **77**; Cuba 12, 75, **76**; Dominica 12; Dominican Republic **76**; Ecuador 12, 75, **76**, 140, 141; El Salvador 12, 21, 75, **76**, **77**; Grenada 12, **77**; Guatemala 75, **76**; Guyana 23, 24, 30b, 76, **76**, **77**, 86; Haiti 12, 75, **76**, 79–80, 98, **99**, 107, 123, **124**; Honduras 23, 75, **76**, **77**; Jamaica 23, 45, **76**; Mexico 24, 39, 76, **76**, **77**, 126; Nicaragua 12, 75, 76, **76**, 80–81, 98, **99**, 103, 108, **124**, 140, 141, 142; Panama 24, 30b, **76**; Paraguay 12, 21, 34, **76**, **77**; Peru **76**, **77**, 123, 140, 141; Saint Kitts and Nevis 12, 23; Saint Lucia 12, 21; Saint Pierre and Miquelon 30b; Saint Vincent 12; Suriname 12, 30b, **76**; Trinidad and Tobago 24, 76, **76**, **77**, 86; Uruguay 12, 24, 45, 70, 76–78, **76**, 98, **99**, 106, **124**, 140; Venezuela 12, 45, 75, **76**
Law 3488/2006: Framework on Equal Treatment of Men and Women (Brazil) 126
leadership 21–24
legal system: Christian law 63; Civil law 39, 55, 65, 66, 71, 77, 79, 80, 89, 90; English common law 51, 53, 60, 63, 83; French law 65, 66; Islamic (*shari'a*) law 33, 37, 38, 65, 66, 67; tribal law 67
Legion of Women Volunteers (*Ochotnicza Legia Kobiet*, OLK) 70
legislative prohibitions, against sexual harassment 121–126
Leichtman, E. C. 90–91, 103
Levine, P. 70, 87
Liao, P. 56
Liberia National Police (LNP) 102
Liu, Y. 16
local government, women in 22–23
Lockwood, D. 136
Lonsway, K. A. 36, 106, 128

Macao (China) 24, 29, 49, **50**
Madhya Pradesh, India 52
Maher, P. T. 36
male: coworkers 129; police 120; protectionism 43; supremacy 103; *see also* masculinity; men
manufacturing gender pay gap 21
marginalization 142, 145
marital violence 134
Marriage Law of the People's Republic of China of 1980 139
Martin, S. E. 40
masculinity 3, 8; cult of 95; expressions of 34; hegemonic 26, 36, 94–95, 108, 115, 142, 146, 148, 153; institutionalized 34–37
maternity leave policy and policing 111–112, 154
Maternity Protection Convention of 2000 111

matrons 1, 40, 43, 82, 84, 87
Mawby, R. I. 82, 83
Mazerolle, P. 137
McManimon, P. 136
McPhedran, S. 137
men: career aspirations of 4; and gender ideologies 33–34; in patriarchal society 6–7
Men for Change 60
mentoring 60, 148, 149–150, 152, 154
Messerschmidt, J. W. 36
Metropolitan Police Act (1829, U.K.) 87
Middle East and Northern Africa (MENA) 12–14, 33, 56, 62–68, 96, **97**, 98, **122**, 132, **133**; Bahrain **11**, 12, 20, 25b, 28, 30, 32, 34, 48, **63**, 66, 67–68, **100**, 121, **125**, 126; Egypt 14, 15, 30b, 37, 56, 62, **63**; Gulf Cooperation Council 25b, 66–68, 98, 101; Iran 9, 20, 30b, 34, 43, **63**; Iraq 22, **63**; Israel 43, 62, 63–65, **63**, 98, **100**, 103, 117–119, **125**; Jordan 12, 37, 43, **63**, 132; Kuwait **11**, 25, **63**, 66–68, **100**, 107, 123, **125**, 126; Lebanon 37, 62, **63**, 65–66, **100**, 101, **125**, 126; Libya 22, 56, **63**; Morocco 56, 62, **63**, 65–66; Oman **11**, 12, 19, 22, 25, **63**, 66, 67, **100**, **125**, 132; Palestine 15, 20, 37, **63**; Qatar **11**, 12, 19, 22, 25, 29, **63**, 66, 67, 68, **100**, 123, **125**, 126; Saudi Arabia 7, **11**, 12, 13b, 22, 25b, **63**, 66, 67–68, **100**, 101, 121, **125**, 126; Sudan 30b, 56, 62, **63**, 123; Syria 10, 37, **63**; Tunisia 33, 56, 62, **63**, 121, 126; United Arab Emirates (UAE) 12, 25, 48, **63**, 66, 67, **100**, 101, 106, 121, **125**, 126; Yemen 19, 20, 22, 30b, **63**; *see also* Africa; Asia
military 28, 35, 37–39, 52, 65, 71, 78, 79, 89, 95, 103, 153
Miller, M. 82
Ministry of Finance and Economic Development for Mauritius 58
Ministry of Internal Affairs of Russia 72
Momsen, J. H. 18
Montevideo Police Department 77–78
Montevideo, Uruguay 45, 77–78
Morabito, M. S. 113, 120, 149
Morality Bureau, Toronto 82
moral reformers stage 87
Morash, M. 129, 145
Morin, R., K. 110
Mounted Police 50
Natarajan, M. 45, 53, 73, 120, 141
National Center for Women and Policing 36
National Institute of Women and Family (*Instituto Nacional de la Mujer y Familia*), in Uruguay 77–78
National Police Board of Sweden 42
National Police Department of Denmark 41
National Police of Haiti (PNH), women in **76**, 79–80
nations: to grant women's suffrage 10–12, **11**; women in labor force **19**
Native Police 50
nature of policing 25, 26–29, 87, 114, 115, 120, 152, 154
networks 147–150
Neumann, P. J. 80
New South Wales Police Force 50
New York Police Department (NYPD) 103, 110, 123
Nigeria Police Academy 62
Nigeria Police Act of 2018 61, 106
Nigeria Police Force (NPF) 60–62, 102, 106
night-watchman system 82, 83, 87
norms 6
North America 81–85, **97**, 98, **122**, 132, 136; Canada 11–12, 24, 30b, 38, 44, 76, **77**, 81–83, 93, 98, **99**, 107, 112, **124**, 149; United States 7, 9, 11–12, 14–15, 28b, 31, 34, 39, 40, 83–85, 101, 103, 104, 110, 116, 119, 123, 126, 134, 136–137
Northern Ireland 88
Northern Territory Police Force 50
Novich, M. 130

occupation 21, 28b, 34, 37, 43, 101, 116, 135
occupational stress 146
Oceania 12, 16, 20, 42, 49–56, **97**, **122**, **133**; Australia 12, 20, 30b, 34, 38, 42, 49, **49**, **50**, 51, 98, **100**, **125**, 126, 130, 136–138; Fiji 30b, **49**, 53–55, **100**, 102, 125; New Zealand 10, **11**, 12, 30b, 42, 43, 49, **49**; Samoa **11**, 12; Tonga 12; Tuvalu 12; *see also* Asia
O'Connor Shelley, T. 113, 120, 149
Onkari, D. 146
Opium Wars 55
organizational social capital 148
organizational stressors 145

organizational violence 126–131; *see also* sexual harassment/assault
Organization for Security and Co-operation in Europe (OSCE) 149
Osman I 37
other 6, 8
Ottoman Empire, and colonial influence on policing 37–39
overall success stage 141
Owens, M. 84

Padavic, I. 93, 108
Paleolog, S. 70
paramilitary police forces 38, 50
partition 52, 69, 70, 88
patriarchal societies 6–8, 129
Paxton, P. 9, 14, 25
pay gap, gender and 9, 20–21, 58
Paynich, R. 128
peacekeepers 55, 62
personal stressors 145
Petruccelli, D. 69–70
Pétursdóttir, G. 128
Pew Research Center 89
physical agility testing 104, 106, 153
physical endurance entrance tests 104
physical violence 131
P.I.L.L. squad 112
police: attitudes toward IPV 133–138; culture 34–37; stress 145–147
Police Authority for Northern Ireland 89
police-contributing countries (PCCs) 150b
Police Reform Programme, Bangladesh 54
Police Service of Northern Ireland 89
policewomen 2; in Africa 43–44; in Americas 44–45; in Asia and Oceania 42–43; in Bahrain 121; in Canada 82; in early 1900s 28b; in Europe 41–42; hiring 39–40; in India 5b, 32, **49**, 51–53, 104, 112, 141, 146, 150b, 152; movement 69; SAP 59; in Toronto 44–45; training *40*; in U.K. 87; *see also* sexual harassment/assault; women police
Police Women Forum (Bangladesh) 54
policing: barriers to promotion 108–113; civilian models of 38; danger and violence in 34–35; early history of women in 39–45; gender-based violence 131–133; gendered 115–143; generalized strategies for combating IPV 138–140; inequality in 146; leadership and 21–24; as masculinist organization 94; masculinity of 34–37; maternity leave policy and 111–112, 154; nature of 25, 26–29, 87, 114, 115, 120, 152, 154; Ottoman Empire and colonial influence on 37–39; recruitment of women into 95–106; specialist strategies for combating IPV 140–142; token status in 47, 114, 115, 126; training *40*, 106–108; women and 24, 25b, 26–46, *27*, 28b; *see also* gendered organizations; sexual harassment/assault; women police
Polish Women Police in Warsaw 70
political ideologies 31–32
political rights and civil liberties 10, 20
polzeihostess 42
Portuguese Public Security Police 105, 107, 119
power 6–9, 22–25, 31, 91, 144, 154
pregnancy and motherhood 111–112, 149, 154
prejudice 71, 130, 147
Prenzler, T. 54, 61
primary aggressor 139
Prohaska, A. 136
Prokos, A. 93, 108
promotion: barriers to 108–113, 130; and retirement 43
prosecutors 23–24
prostitution, focus on 61, 91, 106, 144
Protection from Harassment Act of 1997 139
protective laws 18, 32, 34
public childcare facilities 113
Public Order Act of 1986 139
public sphere, of society 21, 33
pushups 105

Queensland Police Service 51

Rabe-Hemp, C. 119
race 3, 14–16, 31, 60, 129, 136; and sexual harassment, in South Africa 129–130; *see also* ethnicity
Rajasthan, India 52
Ramtohul, R. 57, 58
reaction training 107
recruitment: efforts 102–106; legislative labor restrictions 95–101, **97**; police policies and procedures for 153; of women into policing 95–106
Rehman, A. 146

relational/cognitive social capital and 148
religions 27; Buddhism 32–33; Christianity 53, 57, 58, 59, 60, 71, 77, 78, 79, 81, 83, 90; Confucianism 33; Hinduism 33, 51, 53, 54, 58; Islamism 31–32, 33, 51, 54, 57, 58, 60, 67; Judaism 33, 83; Muslim 33, 65, 66, 70, 73, 74, 86, 90
religious ideologies 32–33
Republic of Ireland 88
Republic of Turkey 90–91
Resetnikova, A. 102
resistance 21, 27, 91, 115–121, 144
Resolution 1325, UNs' 5b
retaliation 128–129, 130, 139
right to vote/work, feminism and 10–17, **11**, 13b, 31
Roudik, P. 72
Royal Canadian Mounted Police (RCMP) 82–83, 136
Royal Commissions 87
Royal Irish Constabulary (RIC) 52, 88, 89
Royal Niger Company 39
Royal Ulster Constabulary (RUC) 88–89, 127
Rubin, A. J. 131
Russell, V. 82
ryousai kenbo 17

Saad Abdullah Police Academy 68
Sahgal, P. 120
Sajjad, W. H. R. 146
same-sex IPV relationships 136, 137, 139
Sanders, C. B. 112
Sandista guerillas 80
Santos, C. M. 78, 141
Schulz, D. M. 40, 41, 102
Schulze, C. 111
Security Council Resolution 2242 150b
segregation 63, 67
self-blame 147
self-efficacy 56, 108, 113, 116, 120
Sevenhuijsen, S. 102, 112
sex: defined 3; discrimination 14, 107, 108; *see also* gender
Sex Discrimination Act: in Australia 126; in U.K. 88
Sexual Harassment Act of 2005 (Taiwan) 130
sexual harassment/assault: and bullying 128; defined 121; and discrimination, on job 117–119b, **122**, **124**, **125**, 152; as form of organizational violence 126–131; labor laws in workforce **122**, **124–125**; legislative prohibitions against 121–126; from male coworkers 148; neutralization of 129; as physical sexual coercion 130; in police force 121–131; and sexual teasing 129; statistics 126; training of 123, 129; and work-related stress 145
Sexual Harassment Policy in 1998 130
Sexual Harassment Prevention Act (Taiwan) 126
sexual impurity 33
sexual teasing 129
Shadmi, E. 63, 64–65
Shanghai 55
shari'a law *see* Islamic (*shari'a*) law
Shen, A. 56, 73
Sherman, L. 41
Silverberg, C. 83
Silvestri, M. 57, 94, 106
Sinclair, G. 54, 61
Sinclair, I. M. 135, 136
Smith, E. 87
social: constructionism 37; norms 8; stratification 8; structure 8, 9, 17; support 16, 146, 149
social capital 148–149; cognitive 148; organizational 148; relational 148; structural 148
society 3–9
sociology of gender 3–4, 94
South African Police Service (SAPS) 59–60, 130, 140; police views on IPV in 135–136
South Australia Police Force 50
Southern Ireland 88
Spasic, D. V. 72
specialist policing strategies, for combating IPV 140–142
specialists and pioneers stage 87
specialist training, for women 106–107
Spillar, K. 36
spinster 34
spousal rape 132
State Military Police (Brazil) 78
State v. Oliver 1879 34
station queen 26
Status of Policing in India Report 2019 53
Steinþórsdóttir, F. 128
Steyn, J. 59
Stichman, A. J. 146
stress 145–147; occupational 146; personal 145; work 145

Strobl, S. 25b, 30, 45, 73, 121
structural social capital 148
student attitudes toward IPV 134
Sub-Saharan Africa 13, 14, 18, 20, 22, 56–62, **122**, 132, **133**; Angola **19**, **56**; Benin **19**, **56**; Botswana 19, **56**; British Kaffraria/Cape Colony 30b; Burkina Faso **56**; Burundi 18, **19**, **56**, 62, 132; Cabo Verde **56**; Cameroon 13, **56**, 62, 132; Central African Republic 10, **11**, **56**; Chad 10, 38, **56**, 62, 132; Comoros 56, **56**; Congo (Brazzaville) 5, 10, **56**, 132; Côte d'Ivoire **56**; Democratic Republic of Congo 10, **56**; Djibouti 13, 56, **56**, 121, 126; Equatorial Guinea **56**; Eritrea **56**; eSwatini **56**; Ethiopia 38, **56**; Gabon **56**, 123, 132; Gambia 30b, **56**; Ghana 30b, 44, **56**, 132; Goree 30b; Guinea **19**, 30b, **49**, **56**, 62; Guinea-Bissau **56**; Kenya 7, **11**, 31, 44, **56**, 57, **57**; Lesotho **56**, 132; Liberia 5b, 13, **56**, 102, 142; Madagascar 19, **19**, 20, **56**, 57, **57**; Malawi **56**, 133; Mali **56**; Mauritania **56**; Mauritius **56**, 57–59, **100**, 104, 108, **125**; Mozambique 18, **19**, **56**; Namibia **11**, 13, 30b, 38, **56**; Niger 13, 56, **56**, 62; Nigeria 23, 30b, 38, **56**, 60–62, 98, **100**, 106, 123, **125**, 132, 149; Rwanda 18, 19, **19**, 22, 24, 56, **56**, 62, 132, 150b; Senegal 13, 30b, 38, 56, **56**; Seychelles 13, 30b; Sierra Leone **19**, 30b, **56**; South Africa **11**, 13, 22, 29, 43, 59–60, 98, **100**, **125**, 129–130, 135–136, 139–140; Tanzania 19, **19**, **56**, 57, **57**, 132; Togo 13, **19**, 23, **56**, 62; Uganda **56**; Zambia 30b, 44, 56, **56**; Zimbabwe **19**, 30b, **56**, 62
suffrage, women's 9–14, *10*, **11**, 13b
Su, M. 134, 135
Sun, I. Y. 134, 135

Tamil Nadu Police 53, 107
Tam, S. 134, 137
Tandrayen-Ragoobur, V. 58
Tang, C. 134, 137
Tasmania Police Force 51
Tavares, P. 132
Tel-Aviv 63, 65
temptresses 32
Third World nations 18, 19–20, 42
tip-over stage, for women in policing 57, 60
Title VII, Civil Rights Act of 1964 (U.S.) 15, 126
traditional gender role ideologies 27; family ideologies 29–31; men and gender ideologies 33–34; political ideologies 31–32; religious ideologies 32–33; work ideologies 32
traffic duty 44, 52, 55, 64, 65, 96
training *40*, 45, 52, 55, 61, 67–68, 71, 79, 82, 106–108, 123
Travancore, India 52
Treaty of Paris (1763) 81
Tsao, C. 120
Tundwal, S. 146
Turkish National Police (TNP), women in **85**, 90–91
Tu, S. 56

Ulicki, T. 129–130
UNICEF 134
United Kingdom: College of Policing 149; female labor force 9; feminist movement 9; gender wage gap 9; weaker patterns of patriarchy 7; women policing in 39, **85**, 86–89; women's wages 9
United Nations 22; Commission on Human Rights 123; Indian Female Police Unit 5b; Mission for Justice Support in Haiti (UN MINUJUSTH) 80; Peacekeepers 123; Resolution 1325 5b; UN Police's (UNPOL's) mentoring program 149, 150b; UN Women 131, 132, 141, 142
United Nations Office of Drugs and Crime (UNODC) 23–24, 49, **50**, 51, 57, 66, 69, 76
United States: bona fide occupational qualifications 101; Bureau of Labor Statistics 21, 34; colonial rights of unmarried women 31; Commission on Civil Rights 103, 110, 123; feminism and right to work 14–15; feminist movement 9; gender wage gap 9; hiring of policewomen 40; physical agility testing 104; police attitudes toward IPV 136–137; police organizations 104; policewomen in early 1900s 28b; promotion 110; right to vote 11–12; student attitudes toward IPV 134; Title VII of the Civil Rights Act of 1964 15, 126; weaker patterns of patriarchy 7; women police 39, 83–85, 116, 120

Van der Lippe, T. 102, 112
Vargas, G. 78
Victoria, Queen 30b
Victorian Era: cult of domesticity 29; gender and work during 18; ideologies of womanhood 32; traditional gender roles of 29, 30b; *volksmoeder* 29
violence: aggression and 36; gender-based 131–133; harassment and 146; perception of 35; within policing 35; against women 14, 31, 62, 72, 123; *see also* intimate partner violence (IPV)
Violence Against the Person Act of 1861 139
volksmoeder 29

Walsh, D. M. 76
War of Independence (Israel) 63
war-on-crime mentality 153
Wells, A. S. 84
Western Europe 11, 22, 49, 85–91, **85–86**, **97**, 98, **122**, 132, **133**, 134; Andorra 10; Austria **11**, 42, 69, 85, **85**, **86**, 102, 113; Belgium **11**, 20, 85, **85**, **86**, 102; Cyprus 23, 24, **85**, 86, **86**; Denmark **11**, 12, 20, 41, **85**, **86**; Finland 10, **11**, 20, **85**, **86**, 102, 152; France 10, 21, 55, 65, 66, 79, 81, **85**, **86**, 123, 126; Germany **11**, 16, 38, 39, 41, 42, 55, 70, 71, 81, **85**, **86**, 89, 93; Gibraltar 30b; Greece 23, 30b, 37, **85**, 86, **86**, 89–90, 98, **99**, 102, 107, **124**; Heligoland 30b; Iceland 10, **11**, 22, 23, 24, 42, **85**, **86**, 127, 128; Ireland **11**, 21, 30b, 41, **85**, 86–89, **99**, **124**, 127; Italy 10, 41, 71, 85, **85**, **86**, 89, 146; Liechtenstein 10, 23; Luxembourg **11**, 23, **85**, **86**; Malta 21, 30b, 42, 85, **85**, **86**; Netherlands, the **11**, 41, **85**, 86, **86**, 102, 103, 112, 127, 152; Norway 10, **11**, 20, 21, **85**, 102, 152; Portugal **19**, 30b, 67, 76, 85, **85**, **86**, 104, 116, 119; Spain 23, 42, 76, 80, 85, **85**, **86**, 102, 112; Sweden 9, 10, **11**, 21, 23, 41, 42, **85**, 86, **86**, 102, 112, 152; Switzerland 10, 42, **85**; Turkey 37, 42, 62, 85, **85**, 90–91, 98, **99**, 102, 103, 104, 106, 108, 112, 113, **124**; United Kingdom 7, 9, 39, **85**, 86–89, 149
Wilmore, J. H. 36
Wodon, Q. 132
Woman Police Constable, Mauritius 59
women: in agriculture and service sectors 19; barriers to promotion 108–113; career aspirations of 4; crimes against 145; denying equality 14; early history, in police work 39–45; earnings gap 34; emancipation 16; employment opportunities 15, 57; equal rights in employment 101; of FPU 5b, 32, 150b; in gendered police organization 93–114; heads of state 22; integration of officers 45–46; joining police force in early 1900s (U.S.) 28b; in judiciary 23; in labor force 9, 16, 19–20, **19**; labor rights to 33; in law enforcement 4, 31, 51, 74, 96, 118b; legislative labor restrictions for 95–101, **97**, **99–100**; in local government 22–23; mentoring opportunities for 149; moving into equality and power 9; as other 6; as peacekeepers 62; physical agility testing 104; and policing 24, 25b, 26–46, *27*, 28b; prohibition of discrimination in workforce 17, 70; prosecutors 23–24; protecting from gender-based violence 5b; racial and ethnic minority 129; recruitment into policing 95–106; rights and work 9–17, 31; as self-proclaimed moral reformers 84; as specialists and pioneers 84; stress among 146; suffrage 9–14, *10*, **11**, 13b; token status 47, 114, 115, 126; training *40*, 106–108; in UNPOL 150b; violence against 14, 31, 62, 72, 123; wages 9; womanhood and role in home 29, 30; at work 4, 6, 7, *7*; working as legislators 21; *see also* discrimination; female(s); policewomen; sexual harassment/assault
Women and Children Protection Section (2007, Liberia) 142
Women, Business and the Law 2020 report 121
women police 2, 41; in Algeria 65; in Argentina 106; in Asia and Oceania 49–56, **50**; in Australia 130; in China 109–110b; discrimination 108; in Eastern Europe 68–73, **69**; in Eastern Hemisphere 49–74; handling GBV 141; in India 5b, 32, **49**, 51–53, 104, 112, 141, 146, 150b, 152; in Latin America and Caribbean 75–81, **77**; in Lebanon 65–66; in Mauritius 57–59, 108; in MENA 62–68, **63**; in Morocco 66; in the Netherlands 152; in North America

81–85; in Portugal 119; resistance to 115–121; in Sao Paulo **76**, 78–79; in Scotland 127; sexual harassment of 126–127; in Sub-Saharan Africa 56–62, **57**; supervisory positions for 108; in U.K. 39, **85**, 86–89; in U.S. 116, 119, 146, 149; in Western Europe 85–91, **86**; in Western Hemisphere 75–92; *see also* policewomen
Women Police Officers Network 71
Women's Battalion of the Central Reserve Police Force, India 52
Women's International League for Peace and Freedom 10
women's movement *see* feminist movement
Women's Network 60
women's police associations 150–151
Women's Police Branch (Nigeria) 61
Women's Police Directorate of Bahrain 30, 32
Women's Police Stations (WPS) 91, 116, 134, 140–141; in Brazil 78, 120, 141, 142; in India 141, 152; in Latin America 141; in Nicaragua 80, 142; in Sao Paulo 78, 141; in Uruguay 76–78, **76**, 106
Wood, M. 36
work: gender and 17–20; ideologies 32–33; as temptresses 32; women at 4, 6, 7, 7, 14–17
working conditions 16, 18, 21, 74, 115
World Bank 96
World Health Organization 132
Wu, Y. 134, 135

Yamaguchi, I. 148
Yoruba, ethnic group in Nigeria 60

Zhao, R. 135

CPSIA information can be obtained
at www.ICGtesting.com
Printed in the USA
BVHW032258270822
645705BV00012B/857